WARFARE IN NORTHERN EUROPE BEFORE THE ROMANS

WARFARE IN NORTHERN EUROPE BEFORE THE ROMANS

Evidence from Archaeology

Julie Wileman

ARCHAEOLOGY

PEN & SWORD

First published in Great Britain in 2014 by
PEN & SWORD ARCHAEOLOGY
an imprint of
Pen and Sword Books Ltd
47 Church Street
Barnsley
South Yorkshire S70 2AS

ISBN 978 1 78159 325 7

A CIP record for this book is available from the British Library

Printed and bound in England
by CPI Group (UK) Ltd, Croydon, CR0 4YY

Typeset in Times New Roman by
CHIC GRAPHICS

Pen & Sword Books Ltd incorporates the imprints of
Pen & Sword Archaeology, Atlas, Aviation, Battleground, Discovery,
Family History, History, Maritime, Military, Naval, Politics, Railways,
Select, Social History, Transport, True Crime, and Claymore Press,
Frontline Books, Leo Cooper, Praetorian Press, Remember When,
Seaforth Publishing and Wharncliffe.

For a complete list of Pen and Sword titles please contact
Pen and Sword Books Limited
47 Church Street, Barnsley, South Yorkshire, S70 2AS, England
E-mail: enquiries@pen-and-sword.co.uk
Website: www.pen-and-sword.co.uk

Contents

Acknowledgements

Thanks are due to the many people who have helped put this book together, notably Dave Potts (Southampton University), and Petra Hickman, Patricia Brown and Karen Hill for the careful proofreading and helpful suggestions. I am also grateful to Karen for her illustration of a chariot. I would also like to thank Neil Burridge for his generosity with photographs of his splendid Bronze Age replicas – I hope the Rioja was acceptable!

List of Figures

List of Plates

Chapter 1

Northern Europe before
the Romans

Were prehistoric people waging war upon each other? As human species spread into Northern Europe, making stone tools for their hunting and fishing, and using caves and rock shelters to protect themselves from the cold, did they also use those tools to kill other people? When the last Ice Age slowly began to retreat, small human groups began to move northwards, across bleak and cold tundra lands, full of bogs and lakes, following the herds of primeval cattle, elk and deer, musk ox and mammoths. Perhaps groups of no more than a dozen closely related people struggled for existence in this cruel climate; when one group were lucky enough to kill a large beast after days of careful stalking, bringing it down at the risk of their own injury from flailing hooves and horns, they could look forward to at least a week of food, as well as a harvest of skin, bones and tendons, to turn into clothing and tools. But what if another group chanced upon them, as they butchered their kill – a group that had been less fortunate? Did the hunters share the bounty, or did they turn their stone-tipped spears on the newcomers, to protect their own survival?

There is a great deal of information about the classical world of the Greeks and the Romans, especially about their armies and battles, armour and weapons. Most people have some idea what a Greek warrior or a Roman legionary looked like, and they have heard of the Trojan Wars, or the Punic Wars of the Romans against Hannibal and the Carthaginians. At best, though, for many, their idea of a warrior from Northern Europe at the same periods is simply an uncultured barbarian savage, dressed in animal skins as like as not, covered in tattoos perhaps, whose notion of war was simply to run screaming into attack, with no idea of tactics or strategy. This book is intended to counter such perceptions and show, with the evidence recovered from archaeology, that warriors of Northern Europe in the classical period could be as sophisticated and resourceful as those of the Mediterranean lands. But we will start much earlier, and try to trace the development of warfare in the north back to the Stone Ages and then down through the centuries.

1

Before Northern Europe felt the influence of the classical civilisations of the Mediterranean, there had been thousands of years of regional development and change that saw the rise of many very different societies, technologies and beliefs. But the peoples of the north did not develop writing – theirs was a purely oral tradition of history, legend and knowledge, passed down through the generations in stories and songs. While we know (or think we know) a great deal about the Romans, the Greeks, the Egyptians, and even before them, the civilisations of ancient Mesopotamia, through the clay tablets, inscriptions and ancient scrolls which have survived, we do not have any such resource for the regions that would become Britain, France, Germany and so on. For the Romans, such a lack of written information made the northern peoples 'barbaric', uncivilised and therefore ripe for conquest.

In fact, we know that this was not true – the northern peoples had developed a very complex set of beliefs, technologies and skills, equally as advanced as those of the Romans, and in some cases even more sophisticated. But how do we know this without any written proof? There are some writings we can call upon – those of the Greeks and the Romans themselves when they described the northern tribes, and those which come from preserved traditions outside Roman influence, such as the sagas and stories of the Irish – which help to illuminate at least some of the later part of what we call 'prehistory'. But before these few records were written, there are centuries without any such evidence. Therefore, what we know must depend on the researches carried out by archaeologists.

Modern archaeology is a far cry from the simple 'digging for treasure' approach of the original antiquarians of previous centuries. There is now a vast battery of scientific and survey techniques available to help investigate the smallest detail of past lives, and more developments are happening all the time.

Archaeological methods
We can record the landscape in minute detail, both on and below the ground, using ground-penetrating radar, lidar scans (which can view the surface of the ground in detail *through* veiling features such as trees and crops), magnetometry and resistivity equipment (geophysical ways to record changes in the magnetic or electrical profiles of the soil caused by the presence of walls, ditches, hearths etc), analysis of macro- and micro-fossils (plant remains, animal remains, organisms such as tiny snails that live in very specific environments and so on) and soil chemistry that records climate change, plant cover, and land use at specific periods of the past. We can recreate houses and tools experimentally and then test them against the physical evidence of their forms and uses. We can analyse the use of pots,

2

tools and weapons – it is possible to find out exactly where a pot was made, and what it last contained, through analysis of the components of the clay and other materials that went together to make the pot, and the invisible residues of foods and drinks it once held. We can tell what a flint blade was used for – whether it was employed for cutting bone or wood or grass – by the microscopic scars left on the surface of the stone during the action of cutting these different materials.

We can even find out a great deal about individual human beings: their sex and age (by studying their bones), where they originally grew up (by looking at the elemental traces found in their teeth which can be matched to specific regions), their ethnicity and family relationships (through their DNA and blood groupings), what sort of diet they enjoyed (from trace elements in their skeletons), what sort of illnesses or injuries they had suffered from (and sometimes even the medical treatments they employed to cure these), and in many cases, how they died.

We can study their use of the landscape to understand their farming methods and their gathering of raw materials such as stone and metal ores; we can learn about their beliefs from their art and their monuments, their temples and cemeteries. We can also look at ourselves – our own histories and settlements – to see how they have been shaped by those prehistoric ancestors, because much of the past is still around us in the present in the form of monuments, field boundaries, routes and even the plants and trees still growing. We can look at modern and recent so-called 'primitive' societies through anthropological and ethnographical studies to compare how these people live with the lifestyles of similar groups of people in the past.

Sometimes, what can be learned through archaeology seems almost like magic – a real time machine. But there are still great gaps in our understanding, places where science cannot go. Archaeology cannot reveal what people were thinking, how they reacted emotionally to situations and events, what they said to each other. We do not have their names or details of their careers, except in the physical evidence we can excavate. For example, a body buried with arrowheads may suggest that here was an archer – but was he a good archer? Or did he enjoy being an archer? (Another possibility, that we shall return to later, is that he was killed by archers who did not retrieve their arrows from his body!) So it is always the case that, at some point, we have to rely on interpretation and theory to understand the information archaeology gives us. Informed guesswork is necessary – and it is the job of the archaeologist to gather as much information as possible to give the guess a reasonable chance of accuracy.

As the peoples and developments of the many centuries before the coming of the Romans may not be familiar to many readers, a brief account follows, tracing the time periods, cultures and changes that occurred – this is necessarily very condensed, but may prove useful to set the scene for the descriptions of warfare evidence in this book.

The ages before the Romans – the Stone Ages

The earliest evidence for modern humans in Northern Europe comes from before the last Ice Age, some 43,000 years ago, in what is called the Upper Paleolithic (the most recent part of the Old Stone Age). Two forms of humans co-existed in Europe – Homo sapiens (us) and Homo neanderthalensis (Neanderthals). By about 35,000 years ago the last Neanderthals had disappeared, leaving our own species dominant. These people were like us in most respects, and lived in small groups that foraged and hunted across the countryside, following herds of game and the seasonal ripening of fruits and other plants. They knew how to make fire, and made tools and weapons of stone, wood and bone or antler *(Plate 1)*, but they did not make permanent buildings and they did not know how to make pottery. They had, nevertheless, great skills, creating beautifully shaped tools and making astonishingly beautiful figurines and paintings. We characterise them by the different methods they used to make stone tools, each period being named after a site where the tools were originally identified – Aurignacian to about 25,000 BP (Before Present), the Solutrean and Gravettian to about 19,000 BP, the Magdalenian to around 10,000 BP. The differences between the tools of each of these periods are small and relate to the techniques used, and are too detailed to go into here! Much of the evidence for these early peoples comes from further south in Europe because the north was very inhospitable for long stretches of the period. This was the time of the Devensian (or Weichselian) Ice Age. Ice sheets covered much of the region as far south as the Thames and North Germany, and France and central Europe were tundra regions *(Figure 1)*. Britain was still joined to Europe at this stage. Humans who visited the north did so only seasonally, or in warmer spells, but they did not live permanently here – the conditions were just too tough.

Somewhere around 15,000 BP, the ice began to retreat. Sea levels rose, and people moved back into the north. By about 11,500 BP a new set of technical skills emerged in a period we call the Mesolithic (Middle Stone Age). These people hunted in the returning forests, and fished the rivers and coastlines. For the first time, there are traces of buildings, used for short periods in a life that was still mostly nomadic, although probably within smaller and more defined territories. It is possible that the dog had been domesticated by this time to help with the hunting; most modern dogs can trace their descent to the European/Asian Arctic wolf. A new range of tools appeared. In particular, the Mesolithic people made microliths – tiny shaped

4

flint blades that could be hafted into saws, harpoons and other tools. This period also saw the development of bows and arrows. They made boats (based on finds such as a wooden paddle from the Mesolithic site of Star Carr in Yorkshire and canoes from Tybrind Vig in Denmark) using woodworking tools such as adzes. Cemeteries have been found – the one at Vedbaek in Denmark is particularly interesting, as it contains evidence for conflict – a man, woman and child buried in a single grave. The man had a bone projectile point in his neck. Another mass grave was found at Strøøby Egede, also in Denmark, containing eight adults and children. There is further evidence of conflict in the Mesolithic from Germany, and we will consider it later.

Figure 1. The white areas show the maximum extent of the ice in the last major European glaciation.

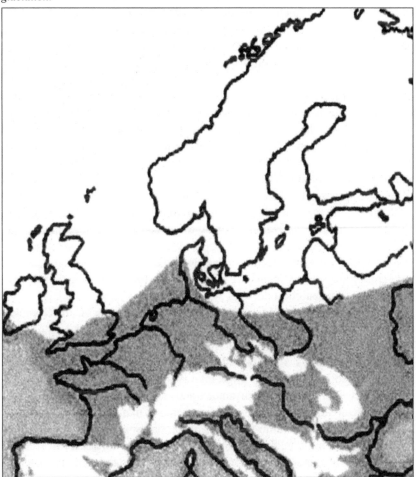

Mesolithic groups roamed over the North European plain, northern France and Denmark, and across Doggerland to Britain. Doggerland is the name given to the large land mass that now lies under the North Sea – fishing trawlers frequently bring up tools, weapons and bones in their nets. It was a wide plain crossed by rivers and studded with lakes and pools, a rich hunting and fishing ground. Then, around 6,500BC, everything changed. There are still arguments about how it actually happened, but at some point, as the ice continued to melt and sea levels rose, Doggerland was flooded and disappeared, cutting the British Isles off from mainland Europe. The people of Britain and those of continental Europe began to develop in isolation from each other. In Europe, new ideas were creeping across the continent from the Near East – the knowledge of farming spread, along with domesticated animals and crops. It is possible that there was conflict between the new farmers and the old hunters and gatherers as the very landscape changed – the forests were cut down, fields were made and ploughed, and more permanent houses and settlements began to appear. Eventually, these changes crossed the newly formed English Channel too. The Neolithic (New Stone) Age had begun.

The Neolithic began around 7,000BC in Greece, but the changes took time to reach the North, and it was not until between 5,000 and 4,000BC that they began to be felt in the region. The coming of farming meant several important things – people stopped moving around the landscape, becoming settled in place, and the more reliable food supply and less mobile lifestyle led to a sharp rise in population. This was followed by a sudden drop in the numbers of people, for reasons which are still unknown, but after a period of perhaps 1,500 years, the rise started again, and continued. Another area of debate is about how much of the Neolithic change was caused by actual movements of people bringing the new knowledge and technology with them, and how much was caused by a spread of ideas alone. DNA studies are being carried out across Europe to try to answer this, but at the time of writing there is still a great deal of research to do.

Elements for changes at the start of the Neolithic include the development of pottery making, which allowed people to make containers to store and cook food, the building of more permanent houses out of stone and timber, the use of new types of tools and weapons such as polished stone axes, mining technologies to obtain high-quality stone, further developments in archery, development of long-distance trade across Europe and to Britain by sea, and the creation of permanent monuments of many different types.

Massive communal tombs (or perhaps temples inhabited by the bones of ancestors) were built, such as Barnenez in Brittany, Newgrange in Ireland, West Kennet in England and Borger-Odoom, Netherlands. Many different types of these developed – passage graves *(Plate 2)*, chambered tombs, *allées couvertes*, round and rectangular cairns and more. Standing stones (menhirs) were erected, sometimes singly, and sometimes in alignments – many of which are spectacular, like those at Carnac in Brittany. Earthwork monuments were also built – circular areas enclosed by rings of interrupted banks and ditches, known as causewayed enclosures, which may have been meeting sites, or places to expose the dead before collection of the bones for burial. More complete banked enclosures are called henges, with just one or two entrances, and may or may not have standing stones within them – examples include the Ring of Brodgar in Orkney and Avebury in Wiltshire. Most henges seem to be a British phenomenon, although some sites in Germany are similar. Another British type of monument is the cursus – a parallel pair of banks up to 100m across and stretching for up to six miles across the countryside; we don't know what these were for – perhaps ceremonial processions? Examples include the Dorchester Cursus, the Stonehenge Cursus and the one underlying parts of Heathrow Airport. Mounds were built too – the largest being Silbury Hill near Avebury. The building of these massive monuments suggests that there must have been social organisation and cooperation of hundreds of people over long periods of time.

All across Europe villages sprang up, and many different regional cultures appeared – one of the largest in Northern Europe was the *Linearbandkeramik* (LBK) or Linear Pottery culture, named for the type of decoration on their ceramics. In the LBK region, for example along the River Rhine, defended villages were constructed, with palisades, and there is evidence for extreme violence in the skeletal remains found in some places. Violence is also clear in evidence from Britain, where archaeology has found settlements that were attacked and burned.

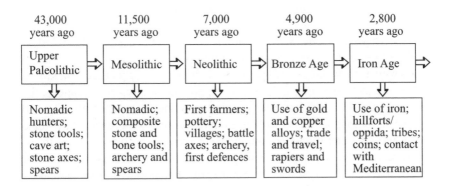

43,000 years ago	11,500 years ago	7,000 years ago	4,900 years ago	2,800 years ago
Upper Paleolithic	Mesolithic	Neolithic	Bronze Age	Iron Age
Nomadic hunters; stone tools; cave art; stone axes; spears	Nomadic; composite stone and bone tools; archery and spears	First farmers; pottery; villages; battle axes; archery, first defences	Use of gold and copper alloys; trade and travel; rapiers and swords	Use of iron; hillforts/ oppida; tribes; coins; contact with Mediterranean

The Metal Ages

None of the periods so far described had involved the use of metals (except as occasional decoration). The coming of metal technology in the North is part of a cultural change which archaeologists called the Beaker package. Once upon a time it was thought that the people who brought metal technology were a separate group, ethnically different from the local populations, but we now know this is not entirely true. Certainly some people travelled, sometimes for very long distances. The man found buried near Stonehenge and known as the 'Amesbury Archer' had grown up in the Alps. This was established by isotope analysis of the enamel of his teeth. As our adult teeth develop, they take up the local ratios of isotopic oxygen and other elements of the region where we live through the water we drink, and remain as a permanent indicator which is unaffected by movement from place to place later in life. These levels vary locally across Europe, and each region has its own signature that can be identified. Evidence for migration southwards has been found in strontium isotope analysis of the teeth of bodies from Bavaria in this period, and many other such studies are currently being started.

The Beaker package *(Figure 2)* included a new type of flint arrowhead (the 'barbed-and-tanged' form), stone archery bracers to protect the wrists of the bowman, the use of buttons to fasten clothing, and the knowledge of how to work copper and gold into ornaments and tools. These artefacts were accompanied by the Beaker pottery – well-made and decorated pots often shaped like upturned bells, and sometimes associated with the making and drinking of alcoholic beverages – millet beer, barley beer and mead have been identified in the microscopic residues inside these pots. These items appeared together from about 2,900BC, spreading rapidly along the Atlantic coasts of Europe and the British Isles, along the English Channel and round the edges of the North Sea, making their way down the rivers into France, Belgium, the Netherlands, Germany and Denmark, and also eventually into the western Mediterranean. The period is known as the Chalcolithic (Copper and Stone) Age, and lasted for up to a thousand years.

As well as their flat cast copper axes, their exquisitely worked flint knives and arrowheads, and their gold ornamentation on clothing and weapons, the people of the Chalcolithic also adopted new ideas about death. The old communal tomb monuments had gone out of use, and were replaced by single graves placed under round earth mounds, or barrows, with a variety of forms – bell barrows, disc barrows, pond barrows and others. This suggests that society had also changed – as the number of Chalcolithic barrow mounds is far fewer than the number of people who would have lived and died in the period, we can perhaps presume that only the most important people were honoured this way in death. In other words, there is social stratification and, probably, the emergence of chieftains – the beginnings of class systems, inequality among members of each community, and the politics of power.

The Chalcolithic era was followed by the Early Bronze Age from around 2700BC in the North. The difference is hard to establish in many areas for some time – the changes were small and gradual, and the speed of change varied from place to place. The main obvious new thing was that people learned that by alloying copper with another material – usually tin or arsenic – they could make a stronger metal, one that held an edge better and could be cast more easily: the alloy we call bronze. New cultures arose, using these copper alloys, such the Unetice culture in Central Europe with its rich burials, and in north Germany and Scandinavia, a society which buried its dead under mounds or settings of stones arranged in the form of a ship. Rock carvings of ships and warriors were made in their thousands in Scandinavia – the warriors depicted holding swords and axes. Later, bronze war horns, called *lurs*, are also found. The earliest true Bronze Age culture in Britain was called the Wessex culture, with items of gold, burial mounds and new forms of pottery, and showing clear evidence of cross-Channel contact with Brittany. In France, the Tumulus culture included elements of both the Unetice and Wessex forms.

Figure 2. The Beaker package.

The word 'culture' has appeared a great deal in the preceding paragraphs. What does it mean for archaeologists? It is a word that is often used rather loosely and without proper thought. In most cases, archaeologists consider that if a group of people in a particular area all tend to use very similar artefacts and styles, to make similar buildings and places, and to make their living in similar ways, then they represent a 'culture' that can be identified as different from other neighbouring groups and from other preceding or following periods. But that does not mean to say that all the people sharing these objects and styles were in fact united in any way; they may have had very different ideas from each other, different languages, different beliefs, different family arrangements. Today, many people across the world use similar pieces of equipment, drive similar cars, and build similar tower blocks, but that doesn't necessarily make someone from Brazil live or think the same as someone from Belgium. Looking at the evidence from the distant past, we can assume that people were living in groups that shared ideas and artefacts, but we must always remember that assumptions can be dangerous! The word 'culture' is convenient, but it is not set in stone.

The Bronze Age across Europe is notable for the increase in trade and movement that seems to have been happening – boats (like the Dover Boat discovered in 1991) crossed the seas and travelled down the rivers, horses were domesticated and ridden, and carts and wagons pulled by oxen crossed the plains and mountains. There are models of these vehicles as well as drawings that survive. Symbols such as waterbirds and sun-wheels suggest the importance that people placed on communications and travel. It was an era of great changes. In Britain, vast field systems were created, stretching in an ordered fashion over miles of countryside (the so-called 'Celtic' fields). Tools and weapons also developed and became more sophisticated – flat axes became palstaves, a form of axe with a stop-ridge to haft them more securely, and dirks became rapiers, which in turn developed into true swords. The first armour appeared – wooden and bronze shields, breastplates and helmets. Patterns of settlement varied across Europe – in some places large villages of rectangular houses were common, while in others there were just farms and hamlets; in Britain the preferred house form was circular.

Types of farming differed too, depending on the soils and topography – the shape and slope of the land. Much of Central Europe is covered with loess-type soils, good for arable farming, but there were also very large areas covered with forest at this time. In the Northern European regions, the soils are often poorer and more sandy, and here cattle raising was favoured. There are fewer metal or stone resources the further north one goes, while the hills of the central region have a variety of useful resources, especially iron ore. In each area, people made the best possible use of what was available, the populations grew, and most of the landscape became controlled and managed. The wilderness was disappearing rapidly.

As the Bronze Age wore on, further changes become evident. Sometime in the Later Bronze Age, perhaps around 1200BC or a little later, there was a major climate shift. In Britain, arable fields were abandoned as crops failed in the cold damp weather, and large ranch-style divisions were built instead; defended settlements become more common, leading to the development of hilltop settlements that were the precursors of the great hillforts of the following Iron Age. The building of round barrows died out, and was replaced by flat cemeteries with cremation burials in urns. In Europe, this Urnfield culture became dominant over much of the continent. Much weaponry is in evidence, with increasingly rapid development of sword and spear forms. The downturn in the weather may have made survival much harder, perhaps for several centuries, possibly leading to an increase in aggression and hostility as each community was determined to protect its food and resources from raids by the neighbours. Nevertheless, there is evidence for an expansion in the number and size of settlements at this time, and an intensification of farming in much of Europe.

Trade and contact with the Mediterranean began to increase, with commodities such as salt, amber and probably furs finding their way southwards. Greek-style bronze buckets and pottery are found coming in the opposite direction. Gold was exported from Ireland, and tin from Cornwall.

Late Bronze Age Europe was dominated by the Hallstatt culture, named after the Austrian site where it was first identified by a mining engineer, Johann Ramsauer. From about 1200BC, new types of metalwork and pottery appeared. Technically brilliant multi-coloured bowls, pots and dishes were made, along with ornate bronze pins, razors and weapons. The importance of trade led to the development of some big defended settlements, usually on hilltops overlooking important trade routes, which held large populations, particularly in the south and east. There were workshops for craftsmen in wood, bone and metals, a range of housing from the very large to the much more modest, and strong palisades and gates. Greek red and black pottery has been found on these sites, along with other Mediterranean artefacts. This type of site spread from southern Germany and the Danube region north and west into France and other parts of Germany and Poland. In the north, however, settlements were much smaller and more scattered. Everywhere, though, there is evidence to suggest increasing social variations and organisations, more social differences between classes and people, more complex tool kits and greater variety of weapons.

Late Bronze Age Britain lacked these 'princely' sites, but elite settlements of much smaller size did appear. There is evidence for the forming of territories by distinct groups of people, and defensive siting of settlements. Weapons became increasingly common, particularly in southern Britain, although burials became scarce. However, large amounts of bronze and other materials, in the form of weapons, tools and ornaments, are found as votive deposits made to the gods, or as sacrifices, in pools, lake and rivers. But bronze itself was becoming hard to find, partly because of over-mining, perhaps, or because the sources of the raw materials were more difficult to reach across other, potentially hostile, territories. Bronze can be recycled – so people began to gather together their broken or damaged tools and weapons ready to be melted down and recast into new objects. Some of these 'founder's hoards' have been excavated (we do not know why these particular caches were never used), such as the one at Petter's Sports Field, Egham, Surrey, with its sword fragments, notched and damaged spearheads, cracked chisels and other pieces. The problem of a lack of metal was solved by the introduction, slowly and piecemeal at first and then more generally, of a new metal – iron. Iron is more difficult to work than bronze, but it is harder and stronger, and, crucially, iron ore is much more common across Europe – so is easier to find closer to home.

The Iron Age began around 800–700BC, although people continued to use bronze for many purposes as it was easier to cast into decorative or complex shapes. By this time, large tribal groupings seem to have come into existence across much of Northern Europe, and in some zones the tribes built massive earthwork enclosures (called 'hillforts', although many are not on hills, but on islands, cliff promontories, or even flat ground) surrounded by huge earth ramparts faced with timber or stone. Some hillforts have two or more concentric circles of these ramparts, the design of which changed over time to reflect changes in use and, in particular, changes in warfare. Complex gates and gate defences were built, demonstrating tactical planning.

In the Early Iron Age, some sites became massive – Manching in Bavaria enclosed nearly 380 hectares and had four miles (7km) of enclosing ramparts. There was dense occupation in the interior, with evidence for large-scale manufacturing and trade. There is also evidence for at least one period of warfare here, in the form of skeletons with weapons trauma – an incident which occurred in the third or second century BC.

This is the period often called 'Celtic', and there does seem to be a common language, which may be called 'Celtic', used over much of the region, accompanied by an art style called 'La Tène' named after a site on Lake Neuchâtel. Place-name studies can recognise early names for landscape features such as rivers and hills across large parts of the continent that have a common language origin. That is not to say that the people across Northern Europe were 'Celts' – the heartlands of the Celtic style were in northern

Germany (the Hunsrück-Eifel-Kultur region, or HEK) and northern France, in the Marne/Moselle area. Beyond these, local indigenous people continued to inhabit their lands, but many adopted 'Celtic' forms of art and artefacts. Local differences continued – and in Britain there are perhaps more differences than similarities, as British-style art developed differently from continental 'Celtic' styles, and roundhouses remained the most popular form of dwelling, along with other purely insular forms of settlement and building. But Celtic-type languages did enter Britain, even if Celtic people did not.

The climate recovered, and agriculture spread on a massive scale, with farms and villages densely scattered over all the lowland areas; the population increased too. New forms of crops and animals were introduced – bread wheat appeared along with older forms of cereals such as spelt wheat, peas and beans were grown, chickens (the Indian jungle fowl) and cats are found at farmsteads, and improved breeds of sheep and cattle, pigs and goats were being bred.

Barrow mounds and cemeteries disappeared from many parts of the region – a few places in Britain have Iron Age burials, such as chariot graves in the Arras culture region of Yorkshire, and isolated examples of cist graves or unusual pit burials from elsewhere, but for most of the population, the method of the disposal of the dead is unknown. Cemeteries are more common in continental Europe, with chariot graves in the Champagne region and some spectacular 'princely' graves in France and Germany. Rich graves only appear in Eastern England at the end of the Iron Age.

As the Early Iron Age drew to a close, in the last decades of the fourth and start of the third century BC, the early large centres began to decline, and the rich graves disappear. The reason for this decline is unknown – it might have been some sort of collapse in the trade networks, or, in some cases, local rebellions against the princely elite class. Many smaller settlements date from this time, with less evidence for differences in social status. The most common burial practice in much of Europe becomes inhumation in flat graves, with around half the male bodies being accompanied by weapons – swords and spears, with occasional shields, and helmets, and items of personal jewellery such as fibulae (safety-pin-style brooches) and bracelets.

European tribes increasingly came under the influence of Mediterranean traders – Greeks, Phoenicians from North Africa and Spain, and Etruscans from Northern Italy. High-quality Mediterranean metalware and ceramics were imported into the great northern hillforts and are found in the richer grave sites, along with, probably, wine, from the fifth century BC onwards. Much was brought by sea – the Veneti tribe of southern Brittany became famous for their large, sturdy trading ships, which brought trade goods into harbours such as Hengistbury Head in Dorset, or along the Channel to Kent and Essex. Exotic goods appeared – dates and olives, fruits and wine, glass for beads and bracelets, amphorae (large ceramic containers) and stemmed pottery jars and goblets. These new products were much in demand for the hillfort aristocracies, and they began to vie with each other for the wealth and prestige to be gained from acquiring and displaying these wonderful new things.

According to Greek and Roman writers, the late fourth and third century BC saw a period of migration of tribespeople across Europe. The movements may have been caused by similar westward movements in Central Asia, possibly as a result of climate changes, creating a domino effect, or they may have been a reaction to the rising populations, leading groups to strike out in attempts to find more land to spread into. Hundreds of thousands of people moved from eastern and central Europe westwards, southwards and eastwards. In 387BC Rome itself was sacked by one such group, and around 279BC the great oracle at Delphi in Greece was raided, possibly by a group of barbarians originally from France. These migrations took European tribes as far as the region of Ankara in Turkey, where they became known as Galatians, as well as deep into the Iberian peninsula.

Classical authors also record the presence of Gallic or Celtic mercenaries at this time, serving in Greek and Carthaginian armies, and recorded in Sicily, Corsica, Sardinia, Greece, Egypt and North Africa. One account records the payment of these fighters in gold coins. The use of these mercenaries seems to have ended by the start of the second century BC, but by then they had returned home with stories and knowledge of Mediterranean civilisations and advances. At the same time, Greek and Roman writers begin to mention and describe the peoples north of the Alps in much more detail.

Further migrations took place later in the second century BC – tribes named Cimbri, Teutones, Helvetii, Boii and Suebii began to move. The Cimbri may have come originally from northern Denmark but they travelled into Austria and across into southern France. Initially these tribes were able to vanquish the Roman armies sent against them, but they were eventually defeated by the Roman consul and general Marius, as we shall see later.

The effect of Rome
The desire for Mediterranean imports, especially wine, was exploited by the culture that conquered the Greeks, Phoenicians and Etruscans – the Romans. People had begun to settle in the area that was to become Rome from about 1000BC, and they fell under the influence of the Etruscan people of North Italy. The Roman Republic came into being in or around 509BC when the Etruscan kings were ousted, and began expanding through Italy in the third century BC; they found themselves in conflict with the Gauls in northern Italy,

and then with the Carthaginians, in a series of wars which ended in the middle of the second century BC. As a result, the Romans gained colonies in Spain, North Africa and Sicily. They went on to take over Macedonia, Greece, Illyria and other regions later in that century. The Greeks had established trading colonies in southern France and Spain – Rome began to take these over in 120BC, creating the province of Gallia Narbonensis. The way was open for Roman merchants to extend their trading activities into the rest of Gaul, Britain, the Belgic regions and Germany, which they did aggressively.

By this time, new centres had appeared in Europe – larger and more complex than their Early Iron Age predecessors. Caesar called these places *oppida*, a sort of proto-town. Towns and cities had been common in the Mediterranean from earliest times, a response to the climate and resources of the region, which necessitated people living in large communities around shared features such as suitable fresh water sources, while the settlement pattern of the north was always more dispersed and rural. But large communities were appearing more and more frequently in the north by the second century BC. They stretch from central France in the west to Slovakia in the east. These *oppida* often housed thousands of people (although some have very little occupation debris), and in the developed centres there is evidence of large-scale manufacturing with increasing standardisation, suggesting the making of trade products rather than ones for domestic use. There were wide-ranging trade contacts both locally and internationally, and the beginnings of a money economy, with each site producing its own coinage. These coins were originally based on Greek gold coins called *staters*, perhaps the payment brought home by the mercenary soldiers, but soon the northerners were making smaller denomination coins in silver and bronze as well. Roman imports are found on these sites: pottery, bronze vessels, and even writing implements. But the most common imports were of wine and wine-drinking equipment.

The *oppida* were assumed by the Romans to be tribal capitals – some tribes had several such centres, although the majority of people still lived in scattered rural farms and villages around them. There is a question here about whether or not these large tribal groupings actually existed in a real sense before the coming of the Romans, or whether people were coming together in the face of a combination of perceived profit and threat. Whatever the answer, the leaders of these tribes were forming aristocracies, who based their power on the ability to provide great feasts for their warriors, and the provision of exotic foreign wine served in Italian containers was the favourite way to display their influence and power.

Hundreds of thousands of wine amphorae sherds of a type called Dressel 1 have been found in southern France dating from the late second to the late first century BC. Two major centres – Tolosa (Toulouse) and Cabillonum (Chalon-sur-Saône) – were both actually built on amphora sherds. It became the habit from the first century BC to ship wine up the French rivers in amphorae to a river port such as Toulouse or Lyon, and then transfer it into barrels, some with a capacity of more than 1,000 litres, for onward shipping by barge into northern Gaul and beyond. In this way, the vast appetite for Italian wine amongst the tribal aristocracies was provided for by the Romans, along with extravagant feasting equipment and other luxuries.

How did the tribal leaders pay for these imports? Apparently, by raiding their neighbours. The Romans had a vast appetite themselves – for slaves. As more and more Roman men were engaged with the armies of conquest, more and more slaves were needed to run the farms, workshops and state services back in Italy. Diodorus Siculus quotes Posidonius and says the Gauls would exchange a slave for a single amphora of Italian wine. The barbarian mania for wine became a marvel to the Romans, especially the way the 'savage' tribes of central and northern Europe liked to drink it neat, unmixed with water, something Romans would not dream of doing. Later, Tacitus suggests that giving alcohol to German barbarians was a good idea for the Romans – because the tribesmen were easier to defeat when they were roaring drunk.

Some of the northern Gauls resisted the Roman trade. The result of the desire for luxury imports in the south had led to tribal chiefs waging war on each other to acquire slaves to trade to the Romans, destabilising the country and paving the way for conquest. The Nervii tribe of Gallia Belgica (modern-day northwest France and Belgium) and the Germans believed wine weakened men, and they were aware of the dangers of the trade; in response, the Nervii and allied tribes closed their borders to Roman traders. This provided Julius Caesar with the excuse he needed to invade the lands of the Nervii and other Belgae, and to destroy the power and wealth of the tribes there. His campaign began in the 50s BC, and within a decade France had become a Roman province.

Late Iron Age Britain
The Later Iron Age in Britain is somewhat different from that of continental Europe. While large hillforts developed, they were never as big or as complex as their European counterparts. Many areas of Britain did not have hillforts, and a number of other types of settlement occur which are not found in continental Europe. In the West Country and Wales, small earthwork enclosures called 'rounds' or 'raths' are numerous. These are, in effect, simply defended farmsteads, often built on hill slopes. The cliff castles of this region

are similar to the promontory forts of Brittany, however – places such as Trevelgue Head in Cornwall and Caerau in Dyfed. Many of them are sited near to accessible beaching places, suggesting that sea trade was an important consideration. Another feature of this region is the *fogou*, an underground passage or chamber, walled and roofed in stone, placed close to or within settlements of stone-built courtyard houses – examples can be visited at Chysauster and Carn Euny in west Cornwall *(Figure 3)*. It has been suggested that these were refuges in times of trouble, but usually they are too small and too difficult to get into to make them effective shelters, and it is more likely that they were either good cool places to store food, and/or local shrines. Elsewhere in the south, small farmsteads within banked and ditched enclosures, possibly with protective hedges or palisades, are common, but in the eastern part of England, wholly undefended farms are found. In the lowland zone of England, it has been estimated that there was a farmstead roughly every half kilometre.

In Wales and Scotland, there are defensible homesteads built on wholly or partially man-made islands – the *crannogs*, one of which has been recreated at Loch Tay in Scotland, and in Somerset there are at least two lake villages at Meare and Glastonbury, where the houses were built on piles, similar to lake villages excavated in Switzerland.

Ireland, Western and Northern Scotland, and the Western and Northern Isles have different forms of defensive settlements. Stone-built enclosed villages and towers were built, often on the coast and at the edge of the limited areas of good farmland in the region. The most visible of these are the brochs, stone towers with spiral stairs within the walls and internal galleries, hearths and storage. The brochs have very narrow entrances and no external openings until you reach the top, and some of the entrance passageways have slots for blocking bars. The tallest surviving example is at Mousa in the Shetlands. There is evidence for encircling villages of connected stone houses, within earth and stone enclosing walls at some of the brochs. At the broch of Gurness on Orkney it has been estimated that thirty or forty families could have been resident by the end of the first century BC. Another form is the wheelhouse – a circular structure with internal radiating walls, dividing the interior into rooms. It is presumed that the whole of the wheelhouse could have been roofed over. Duns are stone forts, a number of which still survive in Ireland, such as Dun Aonghasa on the Aran Islands. Here, a massive stone wall, five metres thick and five metres high, encloses a semi-circle of land on the edge of a high steep cliff that drops vertically into the sea. The siting of these defensive settlements suggests that sea raiding may have been a threat; alternatively, these may have been the bases for the raiders themselves.

Figure 3. Reconstruction of an Iron Age courtyard house at Chysauster, Cornwall.

In lowland England, in the last century or so before the Roman invasion, a new type of settlement appeared – the territorial *oppidum*. Perhaps the best known example is Camulodunum – modern Colchester in Essex, but others existed at Silchester and Chichester. Territorial *oppida* differ from their continental cousins, and from enclosed *oppida* in Britain such as Maiden Castle in Dorset, by being defended not with an encircling set of ramparts, but instead consisting of a number of settlements within a larger area of landscape. Approaches to these settlements are protected by lines of discontinuous and overlapping dykes, with staggered entrances and the utilisation of natural features such as rivers and hills. Defence could be mounted by raids and ambushes through and between the dykes, which would serve to confuse and delay attack – British warriors at this time were still using chariots for war, something that had disappeared from the Continent some time earlier. It is almost as if the Iron Age Britons were creating a forerunner of the garden city – a form of urban settlement that was dispersed in its own hinterland. At Colchester *(Figure 4)* different functions have been identified in various of the settlements within the defended area – an aristocratic centre, a ritual centre, a manufacturing and trading centre, as well as the farms and hamlets that supported the population with their agricultural produce. There is evidence of trade with the Romans, especially in the century between Julius Caesar's campaigns in the 50s BC and the Claudian invasion of AD43 – rich graves in Colchester, Welwyn and elsewhere include amongst the funeral offerings wine amphorae and Mediterranean feasting equipment.

Britain survived independently while France was undergoing first the brutal conquest and then the process of Romanisation and pacification, but it was not unaffected. It is possible that refugees crossed into southern England from the related Belgic tribes (the Romans later called Winchester *Venta Belgarum* – the market place of the Belgae), and for those leaders willing to trade with the Romans, there was profit to be made. The Catuvellauni tribe from Hertfordshire expanded into Essex and south of the Thames, pushing other tribes into smaller enclaves, and dividing loyalties. The Atrebates tribe of Hampshire, Surrey and Sussex (and with links in the Pas-de-Calais) shrank to a smaller aristocratic unit known as the Regni, based at Chichester, and it is here that some evidence suggests the presence of a Roman diplomatic and military mission in the decades before Claudius, at the site that would become Fishbourne Palace.

Late Iron Age Britain was a rich, successful place – not as urbanised or developed as Gaul, but creating its own strong identity. It was exporting goods to Europe – the Roman writer Strabo gives us a list that includes precious metals, iron, wheat (and large storage pits that could have contained many tons of grain have been found at the excavated hillforts such as Danebury in Hampshire), cattle and leather, as well as slaves and hunting dogs. In addition, Britain supplied Gaul with its intelligentsia – the Druids. Druids were the white-collar workers of Late Iron Age society; they were the bards and priests, judges and doctors, lawyers and historians, and advisors to tribal leaders – and they were all trained, according to the records the Romans have left us, on the island of Anglesey – British and Gaulish both. Young men and women of promise studied for many years, committing their knowledge to memory in the absence of writing, and then going out to the tribes to support the ruling classes. The Romans saw this network as a huge threat – it may be suggested that resistance to the Romans in France and later in Britain was orchestrated by these educated people, who may have retained contact with each other after their 'university days'. Certainly, one of the first major actions taken by the Romans when they conquered Britain was to mount a campaign to destroy the Druidic stronghold on Anglesey – coinciding with Boudica's revolt in about AD60.

Nearly a hundred years later, Britain also fell to the Romans, and although the Germans were not conquered, their societies were also changed by the effects the Romans had on the rest of the Continent. Prehistory, for much of Northern Europe, had come to an end.

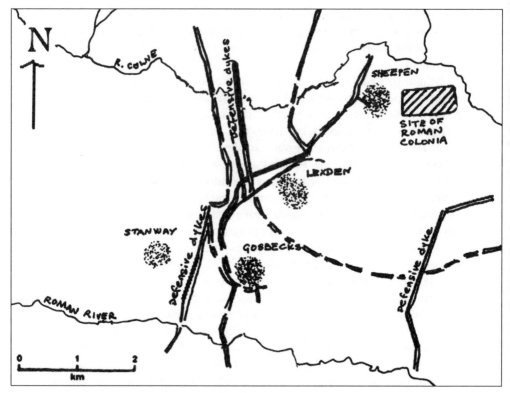

Figure 4. Plan of some of the defences and settlement areas of the Late Iron Age oppidum
of Camulodunum (Colchester).

War in prehistory

At what stage in all this change and development did war begin? That there
had been interpersonal violence from the time of the earliest forms of
hominids is in no doubt, but when does a fight become a battle, or a feud
become a war? Some theorists believe that war as such cannot exist in early
societies without a state level of organisation. They are of the opinion that
warfare is a very complex set of behaviours, and therefore is outside the scope
of 'primitive' societies. They would claim that before the appearance of states
such as Egypt under the pharaohs, or Rome, war did not happen. There might
have been attacks or even battles, but not actual war.

Clearly, this distinction depends on the meanings we give to words. The
word 'war' is used in many ways – we can have 'wars' with our neighbours
over their hedges, we can have 'cold' wars, we can even 'be at war' with
ourselves! Violence in human beings comes in many shapes and forms, and

always has. Various attempts to define levels of violence have been made, and it may be useful to review some of these here, to establish what sort of 'warfare' we are talking about in the societies of Northern Europe before the Roman conquests.

At the lowest end of the scale is one-on-one violence – between siblings, neighbours, man and wife, or as a result of a criminal act – mugging, assault, murder. Archaeological evidence of early murder has been found, but such acts do not concern us here, except to note that such violence and crime can occur *within* a more general state of war.

Moving up a notch, there is what has been termed 'sport' violence, committed by relatively small groups of people on others – think of battles between football fans, or student demonstrations that get out of hand, for example. Once more, this is not war, but rather a form of 'letting off steam', although such violence can happen within a war, or be very hard to distinguish from actual battles in a warfare situation unless you are in possession of all of the facts about the participants. It is also hard to separate the making of threats, or aggressive posturing, or criminal acts such as trespass, which may be part of a war or the means of instigating a war, but on the other hand may be quite unrelated to actual physical aggression.

Physical violence can occur in single combat actions – raids, ambushes and battles. All these can be part of a war, or they can be stand-alone incidents. However, if such raids are repeated over a period of time, or if ambushes are part of a wider strategy of domination by one group over another, then they can be seen as warfare. Feuds are a localised form of war – one village against another, one family or clan at odds with another. These can be relatively short-lived, or they can last for very long periods of time, becoming endemic in a region. A whole series of attacks by one group on another, followed by reprisals and escalation of violence, begins to be a war, even if there are periods of time between the attacks when there is an appearance of peace.

In such situations, one group may call on others as allies, to support their actions against the aggressor, who may then do likewise. These pacts need not be very formal, but they do need to be maintained and they need a degree of reciprocity. They also imply leadership, to make the negotiations, to promise the mutual support or rewards on behalf of the larger community. In other words, society needs to have reached a level of complexity where there are chiefs or ruling elites for this sort of escalation of hostility to happen. But we are still a long way from thinking in terms of political states – such treaties can be made on a much less complicated level, between neighbours and relations.

Levels of social complexity can be categorised as progressing from the very simple to the very sophisticated. The most basic level is that of the family, nuclear and then extended, with the older members probably being the people who get to say what is to be done. A number of related families form a clan, which may cover a much wider geographical area. Clan organisation may require a number of elders to combine to direct affairs. A large clan may start to draw in people who are not blood relatives, but who live within the territory or whose lives are connected to the clan, such as servants, clients, traders and craftsmen, and people who have relatives who have married into the clan – people who cannot necessarily be directed by elders who are not members of their own families. At this level of complexity, there is a tendency for a chief to arise – one person who is more powerful, charismatic or capable than others, and whom everyone else will agree to follow. Chiefdoms also tend to rely on warriors more formally than clans to impose control on outsiders and within the community itself, and a gap opens up between ordinary people and those who are close to the chief. War between chiefdoms becomes a strong possibility.

Competition between chiefdoms may result in one becoming dominant, and being able to impose its will on others. Or several chiefdoms that share an ethnicity, a territory, or resources, or a language or set of beliefs, or any combination of these, can combine for mutual support – they will become a tribe. Tribal organisations can be very large and control hundreds of square kilometres of land, and thousands of people. They are controlled perhaps by a chief, or even a king, or by a council of aristocratic leaders. There will be more pronounced differences between farmers and peasants, craftsmen, and the class of people who make up the tribal government – differences in terms of wealth, power and influence, and material comfort. Such a complex community needs ever stronger government – the tribe may eventually become a state. At these later stages, full-scale war as we understand it today can and did happen.

Modern war is understood as involving political leaders, state mobilisation of troops and materiel, large-scale engagements and the agreement (and often the endangerment) of non-combatants. It is argued that this requires a state level of organisation, but I believe that even small prehistoric wars would have involved similar actions and participation, just on a much-reduced scale. When is a boat a boat and not a ship? When is it a raft or canoe or kayak? Basil Greenhill has said a boat is what people want to call a boat at various times and in various places. By the same token, a war is what people experienced as a war, whatever its scope or duration. A war involving several villages or tribes need be no less devastating, and indeed may often be more so, than a large modern conflict for the people concerned.

Reasons to go to war in prehistoric Europe

There are two levels of conflict to consider – the personal and the communal. War belongs to the communal sphere – the action of the whole social group, or a large part of it. Interpersonal conflict between smaller numbers of individuals, however, is observable from the earliest period of human existence, and there are a number of possible causes for our species' tendency to fight amongst ourselves. It may be part of our genetic make-up; our nearest relatives, the chimpanzees, also fight each other, sometimes with weapons, and have been known to murder each other, apparently in reprisal for trespassing on the territory of a particular band, or as a result of one individual being viewed as somehow 'different' from the others. It has even been suggested that it is this tendency that has helped us to evolve socially and technically to where we are today – as we sought ever more sophisticated ways to fight and win against each other, we developed our bodies and brains, and learned the skills necessary to conquer alongside those necessary to develop technologies and ideas.

Violence against other humans can be caused by enmity and jealousy within and between families, by impulses to wreak revenge on those we think have hurt us, to punish others for what we believe to be crimes and 'wrong' behaviour, to prove to ourselves and others how strong and brave we are, to fulfil certain religious obligations such as gaining victims for sacrifices, to gain power over others (along with wealth and prestige), or to let off steam (especially in the case of young males), quite apart from violence caused by those lacking normal mental stability. These forms of violence can escalate, involving more people in feuds, but are not in themselves causes of outright war in most instances.

The reasons why people went to war in the ancient past seem mainly to do with types of stress that would have created a sense of unease or fear. One common stress factor in early communities would have been climate change. If the weather turned cold and wet, or hot and dry, for long periods, the business of finding sufficient food would have become fraught with difficulties. Many people believe that the rise of war occurs alongside the adoption of farming. People become tied to the land because of the amount of work and effort they put into clearing, making and fencing fields, building houses, barns and byres, sowing, weeding, manuring and so on. Their neighbours will have done the same, and slowly the wild landscape would have disappeared, and all the countryside would have been owned or claimed. So if the crops fail or the herds and flocks die, they have nowhere else to go. They will become more prepared to fight for what they have, or to raid others to gain what they lack.

Over-use of land may also be a factor – if the soil is worn out and less fertile, harvests will be poor and levels of dietary deprivation and stress will rise. Such conditions may create the situation where people are forced to begin migrations in search of new farmland. Those whose land they wish to cross in their journeying may react aggressively to protect their own holdings and chase the incomers away.

Climate changes have occurred throughout human history – from the warming after the last Ice Age to the present day. There have been cooler, wetter periods, and warmer, drier ones. There seems to have been a major climate incident soon after 1200BC, creating arid conditions in the Middle East that led to depopulation and the disappearance of the Greek city states, a cultural vacuum from which recovery took many centuries. In the north in the same period, there is evidence of cold, wet conditions from core samples taken from peat bogs and polar ice which preserve environmental data – long winters and short cool summers, leading to the abandonment of arable fields and a change in farming towards larger-scale stock keeping. We can see evidence for this in the earthworks of the field boundaries – the older field systems in Wessex are overlaid by long 'ranch' boundaries, for example, more suitable for cattle and sheep management. The climate then warmed up, until by the start of the first century AD conditions were much the same as they are today. Then there was another downfall in the climate in the middle of the first millennium (the Dark Ages, as they are known, and at this time there are records of starvation and disease), another rise around the time of the turn of the first millennium, and another fall in the fourteenth century AD (the century of the Black Death), and these changes are, of course, continuing.

It is not clear whether climate stress is a direct cause of an increase in conflict – probably, in itself, not, but it may be a contributory factor. Climate change is visible in the archaeological record – from studies of pollens, molluscs, and other indicators as well as the peat and ice cores already mentioned – although not necessarily easy to date very closely.

Another cause of stress may be demographic change – a rise in population density, creating food shortages and crowding. It seems it is not simply a matter of numbers – societies deal with a rise in numbers reasonably well, so long as there is enough room to accommodate them. The difficulties start when the space begins to run out. Crowding creates psychological stress as well as physical problems. Local resources may become inadequate, fights may occur, and again, there may be a move towards migration – which happened in the later Iron Age, in the late Roman period, and in the nineteenth century across Europe. Other populations today still react with hostility to immigrants (or 'economic migrants') and sometimes oppose them with force.

However, it has been claimed that places with low population density see as much war as places with a lot of people per kilometre, so the situation is more complex than it seems.

A further factor to consider is the fear effect. It is possible that it is the *fear* of shortages that motivates people towards aggression more than actual shortages. When the shortage is real, there may be a more fatalistic or pragmatic mood among the population – more concerned with day-to-day survival than organising for war. Population rise may be something we can recognise archaeologically – an increase in housing, more intensive farming and larger cemeteries may all indicate a higher density of people.

Other subsistence threats may also be a factor – natural disasters such as flooding, volcanoes, the changing of the course of rivers, hurricanes and tsunamis could and do create stress. Man-made disasters could also be involved – such as soil exhaustion caused by over-farming, erosion because of the destruction of forests, or flooding or drying out of land because of changes in water management. Even when nature is innocent, social factors could play a part – land tenure and inheritance systems, for example. If all the land goes to the eldest child, that leaves the others competing for their living; if on the other hand the land is split amongst all the children, over time the plots would become too small to be viable, and conflict may result. Even religion can cause unbearable stress for subsistence – the early settlers in Greenland suffered starvation and disease and were forced to abandon their homes and farms as the climate deteriorated in the Middle Ages, because their bishops forbade them to copy the practices of their Inuit neighbours, practices which, while not Christian, were nevertheless better suited to the environment. Some of these stresses may leave evidence for us to recover.

Changes to access to other resources might also be involved – these might include the failure of mines for stone or metal, the loss of access routes to these from one cause or another, or the loss of trading opportunities with other groups for any number of reasons. Such alterations to the economic picture could result in increased competition between groups, and then the onset of raiding to redress the perceived shortfalls.

As populations grew, societies became more complex, as we noted above. Some people climbed the ladder of social status to the top, while others were left at the bottom. Classes developed – aristocrats and warriors at the top, craftsmen and perhaps traders in the middle, and peasants and slaves at the bottom. Social inequality itself can lead to conflict if there are rebellions and revolutions, and historically it has been seen that those at the top of the pile, who often maintain their position with the backing of armed warriors, are likely to be prepared to go to war against neighbours or incomers to maintain that power.

There is also the formalisation of territories that tends to accompany such changes. Frontiers become permanent and marked, and trespassing becomes a cause for possible armed reaction. Border patrols may be instigated, and arguments about straying cattle or people can lead to trouble. Once politics are involved, peaceful co-existence can become compromised. Evidence for this is less clear cut. We may note differences in wealth and social status within settlements, or even a range of high and low status forms of settlement. The same distinctions may be evident in graves. But how these operated, how people felt and behaved within these systems, is much harder to imagine. The one thing we must never do is to assume that people in the past would have acted and reacted like us – our world is very different from theirs in the level of education and knowledge we have about ourselves and others, our understanding of the natural world through science, the communications we have between us, the historical context of our own societies, our ideas about ethnicity, gender, and age relations and so on. They might have done what we would do, of course, but equally, they might have had very different ideas and priorities.

Early prehistory has provided us with many examples of interpersonal violence, resulting in single victims or in large numbers of dead, and with evidence of destruction of villages. In the next chapters, we will look at examples of archaeological finds that demonstrate the long history of human violence in Northern Europe, starting with what we know from the thousands of years we call the Stone Ages.

Recognising war

But first, how do we go about recognising these various forms of aggression and conflict without written history? Only in the last hundred years or so before the Roman conquests do we have any documentary descriptions of the people of Northern Europe. This is where archaeology becomes vital – but archaeological investigations of prehistoric war face many problems. The next chapter will attempt to discuss these issues and suggest some solutions.

Chapter 2

Evidence for War

The aftermath of a battle is always a terrible thing. Bodies and parts of bodies, human and animal, lie strewn across the ground, perhaps for miles. Groaning and screaming men and horses await either the help of stretcher bearers and medics, a merciful release at the hand of a friend, or a vicious murder at the hands of scavengers intent on robbing the dead and dying. Crows and ravens circle overhead, flies swarm and stray dogs, attracted by the smell of blood, move in to feast. Weapons and armour are gathered up by the survivors unless too damaged to salvage; boots are stripped from the feet of the dead and pockets are rifled. If there is time, perhaps the dead (one's own if not the enemy's) may be gathered together in a mass grave or, easier and less hard work, a pyre. In the next weeks and months animals will hunt for carcasses, insects and bacteria will invade what is left, and the rains and snows will fall, and the shreds of men and equipment will sink into the soil. Even there, the process of disintegration will continue, in the shallow earth, until almost nothing remains. Those few survivors who leave the battlefield will take with them only the hazy memories of pain, terror and confusion of the small part of the conflict that they themselves witnessed; few, if any, will be able to record their impressions in writing. None will have seen the whole battle – its beginnings, actions, developments and endings. And so all that enters history are old men's uncertain testimonies and perhaps the tidy accounts of chroniclers who were not there, and who serve only the political aims of the victors.

Archaeology and warfare

It is notoriously difficult to identify battlefields with precision – even sites from relatively modern history can disappear. A battle is an ephemeral event; few battlefields have visible structures to locate them, and even when there are historical records, they can be misleading, based on faulty recollections or on third- or fourth-hand information. Just because a site is said to have been one where a battle took place doesn't mean it is the real location. Wellington had a habit of naming battles after the place where he spent the previous night – thus the battle at Belle Alliance in 1815 became known as the Battle of Waterloo. There has recently been much interest in efforts to establish the site of the penultimate battle of the Wars of the Roses, fought on 22 August 1485 – Bosworth Field. This was the battle that paved the way for Henry Tudor to become king and found a famous dynasty, but very little is known about the battle or its location. Some 20,000 men or more fought in this engagement, which was pivotal in English history, and yet its site was lost. An extensive programme of survey and research, which included landscape survey on the ground and from the air, cartographic and documentary study, the taking of hundreds of soil samples to reconstruct the contemporary landscape, metal detecting exercises and place-name studies, has eventually succeeded in identifying the most likely site for the battle, some two miles from the Battlefield Interpretation Centre that had been built before the research took place!

Until relatively recently, no one looked for evidence for war in the prehistory of Northern Europe in any scientific way, and warfare was not a very popular topic among archaeologists in the later part of the 20th century. Many people believed in a prehistoric past where lives were 'nasty, mean, brutish and short' – the Hobbesian view of society. It was, after all, the belief of the Victorians (like the Romans before them) that it was they who were bringing 'civilisation' to the barbaric native peoples of the world, and that all societies before the nineteenth century were 'primitive'. After the Second World War, a new generation of archaeologists had a tendency to prefer more pacifist and positive explanations for the past, choosing to look for ritual or political explanations instead of military ones. But here, too, some went too far, trying to create a 'golden age', in some cases influenced by Marxist ideals. Over the last twenty years or so there has been more interest among archaeologists in the topic of war, and more balance in theoretical approaches; in addition, advances in scientific forms of research have paved the way for achieving a more informed basis for interpretations. This is continuing – there is still a great deal of work to do before we will be able to say that we can definitely identify the occurrence of conflict in the past, and to trace its effects.

If it is so difficult to find evidence for an event that happened a mere 525 years ago, what chance do we have of finding the traces of battles and wars that occurred thousands of years in the past? The problems are magnified by the attitudes that have been held about the whole notion of warfare in ancient times. Victorian (and later) antiquaries and archaeologists were often themselves military men, who had been trained to see the landscape and to view the past in terms of warfare and classical cultures. As a result, they tended to adopt military explanations for monuments and objects perhaps too easily, assuming invasions and conflict were the reasons for all changes in society. They identified and named features in military terms, in line with their own perceptions and experience. (For example, there is a modern uneasiness about using the term 'hillfort', which was given in the antiquarian period to the large ramparted enclosures of the Iron Age, as later research has tended to reject a wholly martial explanation for these prominent landscape features in favour of more complex interpretations).

Indicators for war

Traditionally, archaeologists have relied on a handful of possible indicators to identify war, all of which are themselves fraught with difficulties. These indicators are generally thought to include:

1. Fortifications	structures built or modified by people which appear to provide defences and/or bases for attack;
2. Weaponry and armour	the presence of martial equipment of various types;
3. Skeletal trauma	evidence of weapons injuries on human bones, and incidences of mass graves;
4. Iconography	paintings, carvings, drawings and other forms of visual representation of warriors and battles;
5. Burning	evidence for wholesale destruction by fire of houses and villages.

These headings appear to be sensible – until one looks at them in more detail. Then the cracks in the theory appear – and they can be very large cracks indeed. In this chapter, we will look at the problems they present, and consider some alternatives.

Fortifications as evidence

It may seem obvious that the presence of a fort or a castle indicates conflict – but does it? Quite often, these structures are built to make sure conflict *doesn't* happen – as a deterrent to war, in the same way that stockpiling nuclear weapons in the 1950s was thought to prevent a nuclear holocaust. Castles can have many functions – they are residences, gaols, treasuries, courthouses, garrisons, administrative and governmental centres, and symbols of identity and status. Many castles have never seen a shot fired in anger. So their presence cannot be seen as evidence of war itself, any more than the presence of walls and ramparts in the prehistoric past can, although

29

they do demonstrate that people had knowledge of forms of attack and defence.

When did defences begin? In Northern Europe, defences can be traced back to the Early Neolithic period. The first farmers constructed banks, ditches and fences around their dwelling and fields, such as those excavated at Darion, in Belgium *(Figure 5)*. It is possible that these 'defences' were intended to keep out marauding groups clinging to the older, Mesolithic hunter-gatherer way of life, and that there was conflict between the two. Masai farmers have historically been involved in conflict with nomadic Bushmen hunters in southern Africa in the same way. For the hunters, the fences and fields are alien – why should they not be able to wander over the landscape wherever they wish, as they have always done? Why can they not kill a cow for food if they see it, or gather the corn that is growing in front of them? The farmers, of course, tend to see things differently. On the other hand, these banks and fences may simply have been intended to keep stock in and predators such as wolves and bears out.

Palisaded enclosures have been excavated in Britain (at Orsett, in Essex, for example), but Britain also has examples of defended Neolithic sites that certainly did see aggression, or where conflict may have occurred. These will be detailed in the next chapter.

Much discussion about fortifications before the Romans has centred on the hillforts. These huge structures began to be built in the Late Bronze Age, and were enlarged and developed through much of the Iron Age. A vast amount of organisation, effort and material went into their construction. It was clearly not a light undertaking to build a hillfort – the importance of the monument to its community must have been enormous. It has been estimated that the hillfort of Ravensburgh Castle in Hertfordshire would have required the cutting and transporting of 19,040 timber posts and 175,045 man-hours to build the 1,190 metres of 14-metre-high rampart around the site. Some 3,840 hillfort sites have been identified in Britain, representing a huge investment in labour and resources. So what were they for? We have seen that the immediate interpretation of earlier antiquarians was that they were looking at military structures, and much about their design and the changes they underwent over the centuries would confirm this impression. But there is also much about them that does not work so well in a military sense – the length of the walls to be defended, the lack of access to water in many examples, making them unfit as refuges for any extended period of time, and the fact that in some cases the interior is visible from outside. Alternative explanations for hillforts include use as a market place, for ritual and ceremonial events, as a collection point and place of safety at harvest time, and as a 'central place' – a symbol of the power and pride of the community.

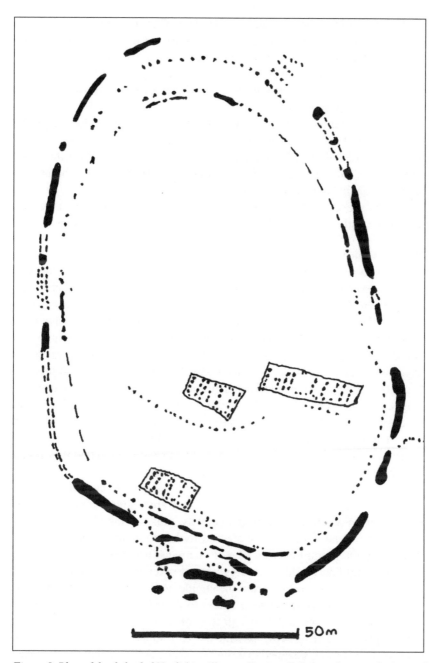

Figure 5. Plan of the defended Neolithic village at Darion, Belgium, showing the lines of ditches and postholes.

The probable answer is that hillforts were *all* of these things in different places and at different times, in the same way that castles fulfilled a wide range of functions. Their size and apparent strength may also have served as a deterrent to would-be rivals. Hillforts were attacked; conflict did happen, but whether the *building* of a hillfort constitutes evidence for war or not is another, thornier question.

It is worth remembering that not all defensive strategies depend on the construction of a fortification – or at least one that might be recognisable in the archaeological record. Hiding in the woods, or adapting other structures temporarily, can also occur, but we would be very unlikely to be able to recognise or find evidence for such strategies.

So, the presence of a fortification on its own cannot prove that warfare took place, only that it could have done. We need something else.

Weapons and armour
People who equip themselves with a variety of weapons and body armour might be expected to engage in conflict. It seems obvious – but once again, there are problems. First of all, there is the recognition of what makes a weapon. The simplest, and probably the earliest, were likely to have been 'found' weapons – sticks and stones that did not necessarily require any human modification to become objects of lethal force *(Plate 1)*. Chimpanzees have been seen using sticks to attack rivals. Rocks and sticks could produce blunt force trauma, and if split, then they could also inflict soft tissue damage. How could an archaeologist determine whether a particular stick (always supposing one could survive for thousands of years) or a rock had been used as a weapon? Only if we discover large caches of rounded, similarly-sized stones, as at Danebury hillfort, can we make the assumption that they might have been used as weapons – in this case as slingshots.

These objects can, of course, be modified – a stone can be shaped, a stick sharpened – to produce axes and spears. These are among the earliest forms of weapon known to have been deliberately made by the human species – but are they actually weapons, or are they tools – for hunting and other uses? Axes were the ubiquitous tool of early humans, used for everything from carpentry and boat-building to digging and butchery. The same is true of arrowheads and spearheads, from the simple point to sophisticated barbed-and-tanged forms, from throwing lances to thrusting spears. Their first use must surely have been for the procurement of food. Arrowheads are sometimes found in graves, as with the Amesbury Archer mentioned in Chapter 1. It is often assumed that their presence indicates that the deceased was a bowman, but further research has suggested that, in some cases at least, the arrowheads indicate the cause of death of the individual.

The 'Iceman' found in the Italian Alps was found to have an arrowhead embedded in his body, where it could have severed a vital artery, causing him to bleed to death; he also had his own arrows which retained traces of human blood from several other individuals. Here, the ice had preserved the soft tissue, and the original position of the arrow; much more usually the body has been reduced to bones and the shaft of the arrow has rotted away, so that the arrowhead has fallen to the bottom of the grave, where it might easily be mistaken for one of the grave goods placed there as part of a funeral rite, especially if the arrow did not damage any bones or if the contents of the grave have been later affected by animal burrows or earth movement.

Some stone axes seem never to have been intended for any type of actual use – the finely polished axes of the Neolithic for example. Many of those found show absolutely no signs of use at all, and some are made of exotic stones too brittle to be used in anger. Miniature examples have also been found, as well as giant versions, none of which would have been at all practical. It seems more likely that these artefacts were made and collected as some form of wealth or status symbol.

Many blade weapons are similarly ambiguous – knives, dirks and daggers are useful tools. Only when the rapier or sword develops can we be sure we are looking at a weapon designed for interpersonal combat. Hunting cannot be done with swords very easily! But swords can also be sport weapons and ceremonial objects. Early Bronze Age rapiers have been characterised as weapons for duels, perhaps champion versus champion, unlike later swords, which are more clearly weapons for war. However, swords as ritual objects are also found – such as the modern Great Sword of State. This is a symbolic weapon – the Queen is not expected to actually swing it at her enemies!

Another consideration is that of training – weapons might have been made and used in practice fighting, but never actually in real combat situations, or used only for sporting contests to demonstrate skill.

Armour, too, can be more of a status symbol than practical equipment. The bronze shields found in watery deposits dating from the Bronze and Iron Ages are often very fine and expensive pieces of kit – perhaps too fine for actual use. Some are inlaid with glass and coral decoration and finely worked designs, like the famous Battersea Shield found in the River Thames, surely too valuable to be risked in combat (although studies of some shields do show weapons damage). Helmets, too, are often highly decorated – such as the gilded Agris helmet from northern France; some are impractical – the horned helmets from Viksø in Denmark *(Plate 8)* are thought to be too top-heavy to wear in battle, and while the wonderful helmet found in Romania, which is surmounted by an iron raven with red glass eyes and flapping, clanking wings, might have put the fear of death into an enemy, one cannot help feeling that the wearer could have been put off his stroke quite easily, or at least ended up with a bad headache!

It is probable that these items were worn on 'state' occasions, rather than in real war, most of the time, as a proclamation of the status and importance of the wearer. This notion is reinforced by the fact that most finds of these artefacts come from votive deposits or from graves. In the case of the votive deposits, they would represent highly valuable offerings to the gods; in graves, they would be a recognition of the importance of the deceased rather than directly of his prowess as a warrior, especially as weapons are also sometimes found in the graves of women and children.

Weapons may also be used for other purposes – to commit criminal acts, for example, or to exact judicial punishment. Publicly visible possession of weapons may in itself be a deterrent against their use – this is an argument used by pro-gun lobbies in the USA today.

Therefore, the presence of weapons and armour need not mean that there was war. It certainly means that there is knowledge of conflict, and even preparedness for it, but not that it actually happened.

Skeletal trauma

Identifying war through skeletal trauma presents even more problems. The first, and most obvious one, is that we simply do not have enough bodies in most instances to tell us anything useful. Perhaps fewer than 0.1 per cent of all the people that died in the past have left any physical traces of themselves – because their bodies were cremated, or buried in shallow graves that have been built over or ploughed out, or destroyed by scavenging animals, or because they were buried in acid soils that quickly destroyed all traces. A human body can completely disappear in six months in some soils. Bodies may have been committed to rivers or the sea, or placed in deep lakes. In wars before modern times, the dead may have been either left to rot where they fell, or gathered into a single pyre for burning. Even mass graves disappear. Bodies from the First World War are only now being discovered, with little remaining to tell who the soldiers were or how they died. Only a few instances of 'war graves' from the ancient past have ever been found. So our sample of evidence is extremely small.

To assume that a person died in a war, we need either a mass grave indicating multiple deaths in a single incident, or evidence of weapons injuries or mutilations. Rarely, a weapon remains embedded in the body of an individual – such as the Roman ballista bolt in the spine of a man found at Maiden Castle hillfort in Dorset, or bronze spearheads found in the remains of bodies in Aveyron in France, Over Vindinge in Denmark or Tormarton in Gloucestershire. Arrowheads have been found in many graves; examples

34

where they are clearly the result of injury are less common, but include the Iceman mentioned above, and other examples from Britain, France and the Netherlands. Cut and crush marks on bone caused by axes, maces or swords have also been found, as well as healed trauma.

Some apparent injuries are in fact the result of post-mortem funerary rituals – such as the removal of the head after death to allow the spirit to leave the body, a custom apparently followed by some Late Iron Age peoples, and which appears quite late into the Roman period in both France and Britain. Other factors may cause what appear to be injuries unless investigated in great detail – the weight of the earth above a body may fracture bones and crush the skull, and scavenging animals can do similar damage if they have burrowed into the grave. Body parts may be removed or modified for other reasons too – ritual eating of the dead to ensure the survival of their life force within their friends and relatives is not unknown. Cut marks and removal of body parts could also be the result of medical interventions unrelated to combat – surgical procedures of this type were being undertaken very early in human history, such as trepanning – the boring of holes in the skull to relieve depressed fractures, migraines and even madness! It is not necessarily easy to separate holes of this type from holes made by weapons, especially if the bone has deteriorated in the soil.

It is also likely that many, if not most, victims of war will not show this kind of trauma on their skeletons at all – most injuries would not have been forceful enough to mark the bone, but would have destroyed soft tissue, leading to blood loss and rapid death, or to infection and a slightly delayed death. However in many such skeletons we find, the evidence for violent death will simply have decomposed, leaving us with nothing to go on.

To establish whether any visible skeletal wounds were caused in war is extremely difficult – we need to rule out the other possible causes, such as judicial execution, accident, or murder. So a single body, no matter how clear the nature of the wounds might be, cannot be taken to prove that war was a factor in causing death.

Mass graves are more useful in this respect. Examples of mass graves have been found dating back to the Mesolithic period; a particular feature of the nature of mass graves is that many do not only contain people who were possibly warriors – the adult males. In many cases, the majority of victims are women and children. This is a phenomenon of modern wars as well as ancient ones. To attack and slaughter the families of fighters is a common way to demoralise the enemy and to satisfy blood lust. One only has to look at more recent events in Rwanda, El Salvador and Bosnia to see how this horrifying scenario is repeated again and again in human history.

There are other causes for mass graves than warfare, however – natural disasters such as floods, fires, and famines or mass epidemics may create the situation where carrying out normal individual burial rites no longer becomes possible for the survivors, although such graves might contain a more balanced number of males and females, adults and children. A possible explanation for some mass graves, or sites with multiple graves, in prehistoric Europe is that human sacrifice was part of established ritual in some societies; eight bodies found at Friebritz in Lower Austria were placed in the centre of a ritual enclosure, and one explanation of a mass grave at Esztergályhorváti in Hungary also claims that this was a cult site.

There are numerous other considerations that have to be taken into account in studying skeletal evidence: suffice it to say, apparent weapons trauma on a skeleton cannot, on its own, prove that warfare happened.

Iconography

Iconography means pictorial or symbolic representations: artwork, decoration, stone settings and other forms of making a picture of the world and passing on information visually. Those from the distant past may be very hard to interpret, because we lack the key to crack the code. Lines and hollows scratched into rock look like nothing at all to us – just idle doodlings, but it may well be that in fact we are looking at messages full of meaning. We use symbols all the time in modern life – traffic signs, warning signs, symbols that denote particular interests or facilities, and so on. We all know what they mean – an exclamation mark warns us of a traffic hazard ahead, or a table under a stylized tree announces a picnic area, and we have learned to recognise that a lightning bolt warns of high-voltage electricity. But what would archaeologists several thousand years in the future make of these symbols, if all our written information had disappeared by then? They might come up with some very strange ideas!

The way in which symbols can convey hidden meaning is illustrated by the signs used by the Blackfoot tribe in Canada, and those used among the Pueblo peoples of the southwest United States. Here, the sign for 'battle' was a drawing of the bare soles of the feet – which derived from a notion of being 'stripped for action'. Triangles mean arrows, and also conflicts in which arrows are used. It is hard to know how we could have recognised these meanings without the testimony, recorded by anthropologists, of people who were living while the signs were still understood.

In the context of northern Europe, the amount of war-related iconography is very limited. There are a number of different types of rock art, and some scenes etched on scabbards, some carved wood and stone figures, and perhaps some war memorials, but little else.

Among the symbolic rock art of Europe are carvings that may represent the rounded caps of leaders in the Scandinavian Bronze Age, which also appear as pommels on swords and as individual carvings. These often occur in pairs, and it is suggested this represents a dual leadership – warrior-kings and priest-kings – the caps being protective headgear that gained the status of an early form of crown.

In Brittany and other parts of France and Europe, there are 'statue-menhirs' – large carved stones which seem to show shapes representing the torsos of warriors wearing padded tunics, baldrics and weapons, like the example from Les Pierres Plates in southern Brittany, or the one from Petit Chausseur in Switzerland, or others found in France *(Figure 6)*. More schematic shapes that include axes and possible armour are found on stones in passage graves of the Neolithic, such as at La Table des Marchands, Locmariaquer. Axes are often carved into Neolithic monuments – at Gavrinis in the Bay of Morbihan, for example, and on the uprights of the trilithons at Stonehenge. We can perhaps presume that these carvings represent the interests of warriors, or perhaps warrior gods.

Figure 6. Chalcolithic statue-menhir depicting a warrior, Tarn, France.

In southern Sweden, and elsewhere in Scandinavia, are rock carvings of boats and warriors that are easier to understand, at least to some extent *(Figure 7)*. Here there are depictions of boats, perhaps for raiding, and scenes that appear to show mounted warriors armed with shields and spears engaged in battle. Many such representations date from the Late Bronze Age, as do the unique Roos Carr wooden figures from Humberside, which show naked warriors armed with clubs, carrying round shields, and apparently standing in boats. Gods or warriors? Perhaps they fought with the Scandinavian boat raiders – or against them?

War memorials are of course common today and take many forms. It seems highly likely that similar commemorative structures were erected in the past, but they lack plaques and inscriptions, and so are very hard to identify. One form may be the 'centotaph' barrow. In a number of barrow mound cemeteries of the Bronze Age, it has been found that some barrows

Figure 7. Scandinavian rock art scene depicting a fight aboard a ship.

do not have, and apparently never did have, burials within them. Were these monuments erected to those who died fighting far from home, whose bodies could not be brought back for burial? Examples have been suggested at West Heath in East Sussex and Deerleap Wood in Surrey. If a more modern hill could have been constructed as a battle memorial, such as the Butte de Lion at Waterloo (commemorating the Dutch dead in 1815), what might Silbury Hill in Wiltshire have represented? These are just guesses – there is no way to be sure that these monuments were built for such a purpose, but the thought is intriguing.

Memorial sites that are more clearly related to warfare have been found in Denmark and France. At Hjortspring in Denmark, large quantities of weaponry and armour were placed in a bog around 300–400BC and seem to represent the arms and accoutrements of a war boat, which was also immersed in the bog. In France, among other interesting examples that may relate to a warrior head cult, there are also the extraordinary sites at Ribemont-sur-Ancre and Gournay-sur-Aronde, which will be described in more detail later.

Art can be misleading, however. Representations of battles, warriors and armour may be antiquated and symbolic – a habit that recurs throughout history. Twentieth-century war memorials abound with Greek helmets, Roman armour, medieval tilting helms, and naked sword-bearing warriors, bearing little relation to the actuality of the arms and styles of fighting of the two World Wars. Nor can we be sure that representations of war mean that war happened at all – such scenes might be intended to represent political ambitions and propaganda, or stories and figures from myth and past history.

Burning and destruction

To find a whole settlement that has been completely burned in a single incident is rare – indeed, no such examples are known from northern Europe before the Roman period as far as the author is aware. To excavate a whole settlement is also rare – usually only a section can be examined, due to later erosion or damage, time considerations, or financial constraints. Burned houses are more common, but we are back in the morass of problems of evidence and interpretation. It seems in certain places and times that it was the custom to burn down the house of someone who had died, perhaps to discourage their spirit from haunting the living. Houses might have been deliberately burned as a cleansing act after sickness, crime or misfortune. If a whole settlement decided to move, perhaps to more productive farmland, they might have decided to burn the old village or farm down to clear the land for future use. And, of course, in a world where people live with open fires in timber and thatch buildings, accidents must have been common. Fire could easily have spread to several buildings if fanned by the wind. So, how could we establish a deliberate, aggressive act of arson? The pattern of the burning might help – houses burned on the periphery of a village where the wind would not necessarily have spread the flames might seem to represent a non-accidental incident. But as noted above, the occasions where such a full picture of a settlement can be recovered are vanishingly scarce.

Crops may have been burned in fields – a common act in early Greek warfare – but very little evidence would be left behind, and how could this be differentiated from normal stubble-burning?

So the archaeological indicators of war are unreliable. But how much can we put our faith in the written evidence, where it exists?

Was there ever a Roman Conquest?

This is the title of a paper by Elizabeth Hamilton of the University of Pennsylvania, published in 1995. In the paper, she took the written record of the Roman Conquest of Belgic Gaul, and examined seven sites to match the archaeology to the history. She was trying to judge whether, if there were no documentary account of the conquest, archaeology alone would indicate that it had ever happened. She considered evidence from a major hillfort, the Titelberg, from grave sites at Clemency in Luxembourg, Schankweiler near Bitburg, Goeblingen-Nospelt which lies 17 kilometres from the Titelberg and Wederath-Belginium near the city of Trier, the city of Trier itself, and a defended hilltop called Wildenburg in Hunsrück.

At the Titelberg, there was evidence of repeated sequences of fortification – the earliest three phases had been destroyed by fire, while the fourth phase had simply rotted away. The final phase, of earthwork walls built in the middle of the first century BC, still stands today and shows no evidence of destruction. Up until the third quarter of the first century BC, the site appears to have been thriving; around 20BC the population seems to have declined and so did the site's prosperity. After that time, there is a small number of finds that might be associated with the Roman military, and a change in building styles that reflect Roman preferences, which could as easily be a change in fashion as one caused by warfare. So here there is no direct evidence of warfare contemporary with Julius Caesar's campaigns.

The defended hilltop at Wildenburg included sections of *murus gallicus* walls – constructed of stone with timber interlacing. Again, there was no sign of destruction; the site was abandoned at the start of the first century AD, but there is no sign of any fighting or military occupation.

Of the various grave sites, the one at Clemency dated from between 70–50BC, just before the coming of the Romans. This was a rich aristocratic grave, possibly associated with the ruling elite at the Titelberg. Along with local pottery and goods, there were seven Italian amphorae, a lamp, pottery and bronze vessels also from the Mediterranean world. The kinds of artefacts that we might associate with the arrival of conquerors were therefore already infiltrating the region long before the military presence. At Goeblingen-Nospelt, the grave which can be dated to the third quarter of the first century BC also had imported Roman and Roman-style artefacts of the type associated with the luxury trade. Wederath-Belginium is a large cemetery – over 3,000 graves – in use from at least the fourth century BC to the fourth century AD. Swords appear in graves from about 150BC onwards, along with female jewellery and other goods. Around 20BC there is an increase in the number of graves, suggesting a rising population or an increased death rate, but the grave goods continue to represent the older tradition. The style of graves does not change until the second century AD, when more simple urn graves appear. More Roman-style (though apparently often locally made) goods are included in the graves during the first century AD. In other words, there is little evidence of any major cultural or political change around the time of the Roman Conquest (in the 50s BC). The Schankweiler site was much smaller and dates to between 1 and 70AD. There are few social differences evident in any of the graves; the only discernible change is a replacement of locally made goods at the start of the century by Roman artefacts towards the end of it. The city of Trier itself was a Roman foundation at the very end of the first century AD, and became an important outpost of the Empire. It was laid out with a symmetrical street plan, but it was some decades before buildings with stone foundations were put up. A forum and basilica, the central buildings of any Roman town, do not appear before the early second century, although wooden predecessors may have existed. There are Roman tombstones commemorating Spanish cavalry soldiers, but no evidence of a fort. The town may have been a Roman foundation, but there is little to suggest that it looked much like a typical Roman site until much later.

Yet this region saw, according to the written records, some of the most sustained military campaigning of the entire conquest of Gaul. Caesar writes of the decimation of local tribes, of thousands of deaths, of the destruction of settlements. But archaeologically, the evidence simply is not there. Nowhere in the Belgic region have mass graves, battle sites, or incidences of skeletal trauma been found to confirm the written record. All the evidence of change in the period could equally well be explained by changes in fashion and trade rather than conquest.

So the traditional indicators of war have all been found wanting. Other less obvious forms of evidence for war could be considered.

Archaeological methods
In Chapter 1, brief reference was made to the things that modern archaeology can do. It is worth at this point describing archaeological methods in a little more detail, for the benefit of non-specialists. The perception of archaeology given by television and other media is that it is all about digging holes, but in fact excavation is a minor part of most modern archaeological research – the ten per cent of the iceberg above the water. Most work is generally unseen by the public, and perhaps not as well understood as it might be. Of course excavation is important, but nowadays it is often seen as a last resort. This is because we are well aware that archaeology is a diminishing resource. Excavation equals destruction. Once we have removed the evidence from the ground, we can never put it back the way it was.

We are very well aware that great changes have occurred in our discipline over the last hundred years; we level curses at the damage done by our predecessors with their rough and ready methods, the information lost or damaged, the sites that now can never offer up all their secrets. And we are also painfully aware that in another hundred, or thousand, years, archaeologists of the future might well be cursing us too for *our* primitive methods. So whenever possible, we choose not to excavate, or only to excavate a small sample of the site, so that those future archaeologists with whatever new and exciting methods they have developed, will have untouched evidence, uncontaminated by our clumsy twenty-first century efforts. It is generally the case that only sites threatened with total destruction by commercial developments will be totally excavated; in addition, a few academic excavations are permitted on a larger scale to try to fill in gaps in our knowledge, but every excavation now is required to have a tight research design, that enumerates exactly what we are trying to find out and how we propose to do it. The old ways of 'just dig a hole and see what's in it' are long gone.

Many sites will only be sampled – small test pits will be dug to see whether archaeology remains, and what condition it is in. Then decisions can be made about whether development for housing or industry should go ahead, or whether the site requires protection and preservation. In all cases – large open-area excavations or small test pits – the emphasis is on recording; our paper, digital, photographic and measured archives will be all that survives of the site once we have completed our work, and they must be of the highest standard possible.

Many sites are not excavated at all – we are now able, using geophysical methods, to record a great deal of information without ever having to stick a spade in the earth. There are difficulties – soil types and conditions, confusion with natural features and so on that have to be taken into account, but techniques such as ground-penetrating radar, magnetometry and magnetic susceptibility surveys and resistivity surveys can often provide us with a picture of what is going on under the ground surface, mapping pits, ditches, walls and other structures through readings of their electrical resistance levels, or different magnetic signals compared with the natural ground levels. The readings are taken electronically and mapped digitally to create a plan that is often identifiable as a particular type of site – a Roman villa, or a Bronze Age farmstead, for example, recognisable by comparison with sites that *have* been excavated in the past.

Much information is also gained from aerial surveys. Slight changes in ground level, invisible when standing next to them, can become obvious from the air, as shadows, or crop growth, or light snow reveal them. From the 1920s onwards, aerial photographic surveys have rapidly become a vital part of archaeological research. To these have been added ever more sophisticated means of recording the earth's surface, using infra-red and ultra-violet light, heat sensing equipment, and lidar, a relatively new methodology which can, by sending and receiving pulses to the ground as the aircraft passes overhead, record changes in levels of ground that reveal banks, ditches, hollows and mounds even through tree cover.

Surveying on the ground is also an important tool, using tapes, compasses, levels to record heights, and electronic distance meters. Experienced surveyors can recognise and record tiny changes in ground level that, once plotted on a map, reveal complex subterranean structures and features. Botanical and soil surveys on the ground can also be used – the plants that grow on, and the soil structure within, a buried ditch are often different from those sited over a buried wall. There is a site in Surrey where, at the right time of year, the whole layout of a now destroyed medieval monastery is revealed in the grass by lines of white clover flowering over the buried foundations of the walls.

Much archaeological work is done in libraries, archives and record offices – looking at old maps and plans, reading old documents such as wills and inventories that describe things as they were hundreds of years ago, researching the clues hidden in place-names, and looking for old drawings and sketches. Even prehistoric features can be identified in these – things that still existed a couple of hundred years ago but have vanished under modern town expansion and countryside developments.

When we find artefacts in the soil, we do not simply clean them up and store them in a museum. That is only the final end of a much longer and more detailed process of study and analysis. Advanced techniques are used to identify the individual components of an object – the clays and temper that make up a pot, the paint used on a wall, the metals brought together to make a tool. There is a list of things we want each artefact to tell us. Learning what it was made from, and where the raw materials were found, can identify not only ancient mines or quarries, but also give us information about trade and cultural contacts between peoples. An example of this would be pots found at Hengistbury Head in Dorset which were made using materials containing micaceous clays from Brittany – proving cross-Channel contact between the two areas in the Iron Age.

We also want to know *how* the object was made – what level of technological skill was employed, what equipment was needed, how long it took to make the object, how expensive it was to make (and therefore, perhaps, how valuable it was to its makers and users). We want to know what exactly it was used for – what actions were performed with the object, what did it contain, and so on? Was a pot used just for storage, or for cooking? That gives us extra information about dietary practices. We also want to know why it was thrown away – what caused it to become damaged or obsolete? Was it a matter of necessity, or of preference? Some objects go on virtually unchanged for centuries; others are replaced rapidly as things go in and out of fashion.

These researches involve complex scientific methodologies, studying artefacts down to their molecular level in many different ways, allowing us to understand far more about past peoples and their lives than has ever been possible before. Further, we can make exact replicas and test them against the original through experimental archaeology, to find out how effective they were. We can test hypotheses about buildings (their form, durability, practicality and so on), farming and industrial methods, and much more. We do not try to re-enact the past, but to assess whether or not our assumptions might be sensible ones that could work. But we cannot tell whether they *did* work in the ways we surmise – that would take the one thing every archaeologist would dearly love to have – a time machine!

The study of war and weapons involves all these methods and more. Microscopic studies of metal stresses, for example, can suggest whether or not a weapon could have been used in combat, or whether damage to a shield has been caused by its burial over time, or by an ancient spear thrust. Surveys of sites can reveal changes in their history – decay, refurbishments, changes in strategic thinking, occupation levels and activities that went on there. All these are necessary parts of a search for the evidence for ancient conflict.

Looking for different clues for warfare

To answer the question 'was there warfare here in the ancient past?' there are a number of other approaches. We could look at the *causes* of war and decide if there are any indications that these were operating in a particular time and place. We could also look at the sort of preparations people make when they think war is imminent. And we can look for the results of war – the changes that happen as a result of conflict.

Causes have been considered in the last chapter, and will be referred to as we look at the evidence for very early conflicts. But to start with, what sort of preparations do people make, if they think war might be inevitable? The first thing is that they might build fortifications to protect themselves, but we have already looked at the problems those pose. They might also step up production of weapons and armour; interpretation of these artefacts is problematic, as we have seen, but there are periods when it is clear that more weapons, and more types of weapons, were in circulation.

For example, in the Late Bronze Age there is a proliferation in the types of swords and spearheads produced – straight swords, end-weighted swords, different forms of hilt and different sizes of sword were being made. Spearheads range from small, relatively simple lanceheads for throwing, to heavy, extremely long thrusting spearheads more like the assegais of the Zulus *(Figure 8)*. Varying shapes and details were tried, and as also happened with axes, simple hafts were replaced by socketed ones, very much more secure during use. These changes must be a result of experiment and use, trying to find the most efficient and effective forms. There is also an increase in the number of workaday weapons (rather than special, decorative versions), which might suggest a change from duelling to more general conflicts, and the end-weighted swords might suggest an increase in the use of horses in battle, as these weapons seem to be designed to be more dangerous when used with a sweeping, downward-cutting action. There is a

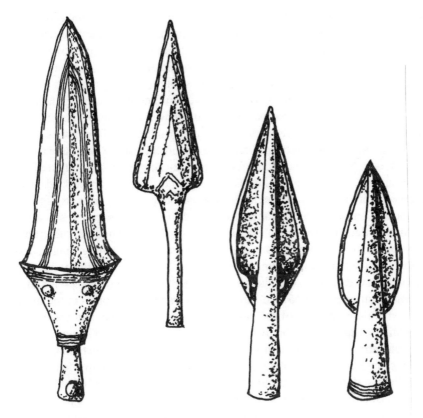

Figure 8. Various forms of Bronze Age spearheads.

strong practical element to many of the developments, which at least suggests real combat experience.

Another response to the threat of war might be selective abandonment – of farmlands and settlements. Some places may have seemed too difficult to defend, and too risky to continue to use. This might be particularly important where the pattern of aggression is one of raids and ambushes, often directed at parties of workers going to or returning from distant fields. This type of evidence has been found at a number of sites, suggesting a sustained series of acts of attrition by one group against another. A further skeletal indicator here is graves with bodies that show signs of gnawing by wolves, dogs or other animals, possibly a result of a delay in recovering the bodies of those killed out in the fields.

It may be possible to tell if people left a village rapidly, or in a more planned and leisurely fashion. If rapid, the evacuation would tend to leave much behind – all the non-essential or heavy equipment that they could not carry, although more modern wars have shown that evacuees will sometimes try to remove items that seem quite useless and which slow down their attempts to escape. Belgians fleeing the advance of the Germans at the start of the Second World War were observed attempting to drag with them pianos and bedsteads on handcarts – sentiment and sense do not always go hand in hand. But if the preparations for war were made well in advance, the valuable larger items (ploughs, millstones etc.) would also have been removed.

The alternative would be to change the settlement's shape to make it easier to defend. New, perhaps hastily built, houses might be erected to accommodate displaced families. Outlying farms might be abandoned, with everyone moving in to the centre for mutual support, and perhaps digging ditches or building walls around for protection. In some cases, so-called 'guard' settlements might be established – small units sited on vulnerable approach routes, whose job is to alert the centre to approaching danger, and perhaps to try to hold up an enemy's advance. Settlements of this type have been observed in the southwestern United States, where the prehistoric Puebloan cultures created small strongholds on approach routes to the mesa tops where the majority of the population had congregated, and there may be similar evidence from the British Late Bronze Age in the Thames region.

Relocating settlements entirely is a more common response to threat, and for this there is quite a large body of evidence. People moved up into hillforts or hilltop settlements, or on to cliff edges, or out into lakes, or onto river islands. Such relocation may simply be a matter of choice, or a perception that subsistence strategies might be improved (the increased range of food in a lake, for example, with the ready availability of fish, shellfish and waterbirds), rather than being caused by fear of attack. But it can also seem to have been counter-productive – making it harder to obtain fresh water on hills, and having to slog up and down steep slopes to reach fields and pastures, or being cut off in damp, misty places during the winter, when house timbers will rot and the peoples' health will be compromised. If we can observe a move that seems to be counter-productive in this way, we have to ask ourselves, what made them do it? The threat of war is at least one possible explanation.

Organising neighbouring settlements in such a way that approaches are visible and each settlement can warn its neighbours of threat also seems to have occurred – they could have used visual signals of fire or smoke, or audible ones – the blowing of horns, for example. They might have had mutual agreements that the men of each settlement would rush to the aid of its neighbour if the warning was heard, while the women, children and elderly could take the opportunity to hide in forests or caves.

Once settlements start to aggregate together for defence, they can then create 'no-go' areas around them – apparently empty landscapes that can be patrolled and which would make any attempt at infiltration by stealth harder to carry out. The Roman writer Tacitus tells us that the German Suebi tribe employed this tactic, both for defence and, in their ability to maintain this region without trespass, a demonstration of their power and readiness to respond to attack.

These changes may well also result in an alteration in the way the people gained their food and other resources, and in their trade relationships. Stock might be pastured much nearer the settlements than before, to protect the herds from raids, and pens and barns for their accommodation might be created. More food might be stockpiled rather than exchanged. Links to other settlements might be severed by the relocations, so that trade between them declines or ceases, which might be visible in a change in the types of tools and equipment being used – a greater reliance on homemade items.

There are a myriad of other possible causes for changes such as these – declining weather patterns, loss of soil fertility, diseases among people and stock and so on. War is just one possible explanation, but it should be considered.

Many other changes might occur *after* a war, varying according to whether one is studying the winners or the losers.

In the case of the losers, if settlements have not been completely destroyed, then they might have shrunk, perhaps becoming run-down and decayed. These themselves might later be abandoned – perhaps because too many people were lost for them to remain viable, or because there are too many bad memories associated with the place. On the other hand, if the winners take the settlements over, we might see new types and styles of building appearing (as with Norman castles after 1066), and new forms or styles of artefact being introduced. There may be changes in more than just the material culture – the introduction of new forms of worship and new burial practices, for example, which suggest that the occupants have different origins from the original inhabitants. All these may be visible in the archaeology.

As we have mentioned, there are many possible causes of people leaving a settlement – it is harder to understand why they should abandon developed fields. Making a field is hard work – there are stones and trees to be uprooted, the subsoil must be ploughed with rip ards (primitive ploughs), and fences and hedges must be put into place. Fields and field systems are among the oldest surviving monuments in our modern landscapes. Some of today's field boundaries and the lanes between them were put into place at least two thousand years ago, and there may be some that date back twice that long.

And some would say that farmers are an inherently conservative breed of people. They face disasters every year but they tend to hang on, pick themselves up and start over. What would force the abandonment of land that so much time, effort and family history had been invested in? It would have to be a very major upheaval, and the choices of those are much more limited. Widespread plague might do it, as it did in the fourteenth century AD after the Black Death, because there were simply not enough people left to work the land in the old way.

We should then see an accompanying reduction in the number of houses and graves for several generations, and evidence for new forms of land management, such as provision for larger herds of stock, which need fewer people to work them than is the case with arable farming. Natural disasters could do it – floods, volcanoes, or long-term climate change – but these should be accompanied by environmental evidence. And war can do it.

As far as the human evidence is concerned, we are still hampered by the scarcity of examples. But after a war, we might expect to see a reduced population, a population whose distribution is skewed, and one whose standards of living have drastically altered. Obviously, many might have died or been removed as slaves. There may be a lack of a whole generation of young adult men and women, leaving just the very old and very young to try to continue. For them, life would have become very hard, both mentally and physically, and we might see evidence of famine and disease more frequently. It is a commonly accepted fact that victims of trauma and grief are more prone to disease than others. In Gaul, after the Roman Conquest, it has been estimated that the population fell by between 14 per cent and 28 per cent; in part this was due to loss of life and enslavement, but it was also combined with a number of years of disastrous harvests (again to some extent connected to the loss of manpower), leading to widespread famine.

Livestock also tend to suffer in these situations, through neglect and enforced changes in their management, as animals are slaughtered before time, or others are killed for food that might otherwise be kept for breeding. The loss of livestock during the Second World War in Yugoslavia was enormous – in one region, 60 per cent of horses, 63 per cent of sheep, 55 per cent of cattle and nearly 59 per cent of pigs died. In the more recent conflicts in Bosnia, similar losses were recorded – the Lika region lost 120,430 cows, 65,280 pigs, 8,042 horses, 231,000 sheep and 2,648,000 poultry birds, either killed or stolen.

After such traumas, we might see behavioural changes such as abandonment of old religious practices – after all, if the gods had failed the people, why should folk continue to maintain their temples or make offerings to them? Burial rites might also be altered to more simple, even cursory, forms, partly because the society can no longer afford elaborate rituals, and partly because the survivors have to deal with too much loss too often to make extravagant rituals bearable.

It may be possible to trace the movement of refugee populations – through the changes they make to the natural environment and through analysis of isotope evidence from bones and teeth that prove distant origins other than where they were eventually buried. Refugees can devastate the landscapes through which they are forced to move – cutting down trees for fuel and shelter, hunting wild animals for food, and even, in extreme cases, altering the very ground they walk over, as has happened in Azerbaijan and Afghanistan in this century, where the tramp of hundreds of thousands of refugees has worn the very soil from the rock.

There are other forms of evidence that it may be possible to acquire, but my main point is that no one indicator is enough. If we are going to be able to study warfare in northern Europe before the Romans, we need to gather and compare all sorts of different clues, understand their potential and their drawbacks, consider all the possible alternatives, and feel our way cautiously towards the most likely conclusions. Therefore, evidence from settlements and fortifications, human bodies, weapons and armour, and historical accounts will be brought together in the following chapters.

Chapter 3

Early Warfare

For the small groups of early humans who moved up from the African savannahs into Europe, violence, injury and death would have been ever-present parts of their lives. They had learned to make stone and wooden tools – spears and axes – to help them to hunt for food, but a stone spear tied on to a wooden haft is not a powerful weapon, however much skill the hunter has acquired. The huge animals they hunted had their own weapons – teeth and horns, hooves and tusks, and the sheer bulk of their bodies. It would be no mean feat for a half dozen humans to bring down a mammoth, a rhinoceros or an aurochs, the huge 'first cow' which stood six feet high at the shoulder and was equipped with a pair of massive and sharp horns. Hours, perhaps days, of careful stalking were needed, to track the beasts, to identify a suitable target, perhaps among the older and slower, or younger and less wary, individuals in the herd. At any time, the other animals might become aware of their presence and turn to attack. Small wonder, then, that if another group of humans were to appear, intent on stealing their hard-won prey, they would use those spears and axes to defend the prize, which probably represented food for many days for their family.

Evidence for the earliest forms of warfare is based on finds of weapons and on the rare discoveries of skeletal remains which show evidence of damage associated with weapon use. Not until the Neolithic period were there houses and farms – more or less permanent sites in the landscape. It is probable that until that time, war as such did not exist – but there was certainly violence and killing in some places. There is a tendency to assume that life was more simple for our early hunter-gatherer ancestors, but it is likely that needs and emotions created as much stress and tension for them as they do for us today. The people of Europe during the Stone Ages were in virtually every respect exactly the same as us, with the same intelligence and abilities, needs and emotions. They were not primitive 'cavemen', but highly successful family groups who knew how to survive in their landscapes against all odds.

Violence in the Paleolithic (Old Stone Age)
There is very little evidence of interpersonal conflict in the Paleolithic period, partly because, of course, there are very few remains that have survived to

be studied. The world population of hominids was very small, and it was probably much easier to avoid aggression. We have to imagine small family groups of people, wandering across southern and central Europe, and more rarely, into the northern parts of the continent when warmer periods occurred. They followed the deer and the aurochs, the giant elk, the wild horses and mammoths. They also hunted rhinoceroses – at La Cotte de Sainte Brelade in the Channel Islands they drove mammoths and rhinoceroses over a cliff, and then butchered the animals on the beach below. They would also have been prey themselves, at risk from attacks by wolves, hyenas, bears and lions. These animals were all represented in the cave paintings that they made and the carvings that have survived *(Figure 9)*.

There is plenty of evidence for tools and weapons, including projectile weapons, which would have been used for hunting the game. Wooden spears have been found near Schöningen in Germany – between 1.82 and 2.60 metres long, these seven spears were discovered alongside the remains of over fifteen butchered horses, and stone tools were also found at the site.

Heavy stone axes were an essential part of the tool kit for both early humans and our close relatives the Neanderthals, and were used for butchery, working wood, and a host of other tasks. Therefore the possibility of weapons-related violence exists, but any clear incidences of it are very rare. In looking at skeletons to assess whether violence was the cause of death, there are a number of markers we look for. These include the marks of weapons themselves on the bone, cut marks on bones suggesting scalping or

Figure 9. Paleolithic cave painting – lioness heads in the Grotte de Chauvet.

removal of flesh, trophy removals (heads or hands cut off), deliberate damage to the face, and defensive wounds on the arms.

There are a number of examples of what appears to have been the practice of cannibalism in this period – in Africa, Spain, Croatia, the Netherlands and France. Here there is a problem. If people were eating other people, were these victims of violence, hunted like animals, or were they the community's own dead, being eaten as part of a funeral ritual? People at Moula-Guercy in Ardèche, France, butchered human remains as if they were animals, and smashed the bones to remove the marrow and extract the brain. The cut marks were more similar to those used in butchery of animals than in defleshing rites for funerals. Two adult men and two adolescents were represented here, among the bones of deer and ibex. In contrast, in Croatia, at Krapina, bodies were also butchered, although the marrow was not removed. In the latter case, it is suggested that this activity was in preparation for burial of the defleshed bones. There have been some misdiagnoses of cut marks on bones of this era, between marks made in the distant past and marks caused by later damage, but the use of modern high-powered microscopy is clearing up some of the past confusion.

Violence is also likely in the case of a young adult Neanderthal found at La Roche à Pierrot, St Césaire, Charente Maritime in France. This person has been dated to about 36,000 years ago. Neanderthalers lived alongside modern humans for a long time until they died out as a separate species. They had fire, they made tools and artworks, and it is probable that they had a language as well. From various sites there is evidence that they cared for less able members of their groups, and practised funeral rituals with care and, probably, love, scattering flowers on the graves and placing special objects with the dead. At one time it was thought that all traces of Neanderthal man had gone, but modern studies suggest that some of them interbred with modern humans, and so traces of their genes live on today.

Although much of the skeleton from La Roche à Pierrot was either missing or badly eroded, study of the body found a healed fracture on the right side of the skull, the left side being missing. It was possible to suggest that the injury was caused by a sharp 'blade-shaped' object, creating a fracture around 70mm long. One would expect accidental damage to the skull to be different, with patterns of bone deformation indicating crushing, which this example did not have. Terrible though the wound was, it was not sufficiently deep to kill – the bones showed signs of healing, and it is thought the injury occurred some months before death. It is possible that this individual was female, and a facial reconstruction has been made of 'Pierrette', as she has been nicknamed *(Plate 3)*.

The Châtelperronian stone tools from the site are quite small and relatively blunt. If any of these had made the wound, they would have had to be set in a haft and wielded with considerable force. In other words, a 'tool' became a 'weapon'. The scientists who studied the bones thought that 'Pierrette' was probably standing when attacked. They do not believe that it is likely the damage was accidental and think interpersonal violence is the best explanation. The victim had suffered heavy bleeding, concussion and may have been impaired in thought and movements, at least temporarily. However, the fact that she survived for some time afterwards suggests that her community provided care and support for her.

Another example of Neanderthal violence comes from the Shanidar Cave in Iraq. An individual buried there 50,000 years ago or more had been stabbed in the side with a sharp implement that left marks on the ribs. Many Neanderthal bones show evidence of trauma, especially to the upper body and head, much more often than those of early modern human specimens, even on the bones of children. It is thought that the lifestyle of the Neanderthals was particularly hard and dangerous, and that it was common to sustain injuries while hunting, or climbing trees or rocks to search for food. The lighter, faster Homo sapiens seems to have been less vulnerable to such damage.

Further evidence for non-accidental wounds comes from Grimaldi in Italy, where a small child was stabbed with a spear that lodged in its spine about 30,000 years ago, and from San Teodoro, Sicily, where the body of a woman with a flint point embedded in her pelvis was found. At Montfort-sur-Lizier in France, a quartzite blade was found lodged in a human vertebra, in a deposit dated between 13,000–8,000BC.

The only other evidence of Paleolithic interpersonal violence is from cave paintings that show people being killed with arrows and spears; examples have been found in Italy, France and Spain. In a scene from the Cosquer cave (Bouches-du-Rhône, France) dated to 20,000BC, a falling human figure is shown pierced by spears; further scenes of humans apparently struck by spears or arrows are found in the caves of Cougnac, Pech-Merle, Gourdan and Combel.

The bow is thought to have been invented at the end of the Upper Paleolithic, between 20,000–12,000BC, and joined the arsenal of weapons available such as clubs, spears, sticks, rocks and so on. A useful hunting weapon, its potential as a weapon to be used against other people seems to have been quickly exploited, although such early bows probably had very limited ranges and strength.

Violence in the Mesolithic (Middle Stone Age)
By this period, around 13,500 years ago, the ice ages were over and much more land was available to the roaming groups of humans in Europe. The

forests of the north were now large and dense, and there is some evidence to suggest that Mesolithic people preferred to stay near shorelines and river banks, rather than penetrate too deeply into the woods. There were more people, too, and it seems possible that it became necessary to define territories. Each group would have a region around which they moved as the seasons changed, following animal migrations, or ripening fruits, nuts and other plant foods. This may have contributed towards a rise in violence, as they acted to stop trespassing by neighbours or migrating groups.

From time to time, these humans actually began to build shelters and make camps, which they lived in for some months at a time – such a camp has been excavated at Star Carr, in Yorkshire, on the banks of a now-vanished lake. The people there made use of the resources of the lake over the months of summer. They used antler projectile weapons and harpoons, and turned antler skulls into masks or headdresses, perhaps for hunting magic. Here they also built a structure made of wood, perhaps covered by hides, with a floor of moss and reeds. They had a boat and they made a timber trackway out to a jetty or fishing platform in the lake. The site was used for between 200 and 500 years, periodically, from around 8770BC.

There is no evidence for violence at Star Carr, but in contrast to the limited amount of material from the Paleolithic period, there is a growing body of evidence for violent encounters in the Mesolithic period elsewhere. At Jebel Sahaba in northern Sudan, in the earliest part of the period about 13,000 years ago, about half the fifty-nine bodies excavated showed evidence of having been killed by weapons, including arrows. Some of the children in the cemetery had been executed by arrows deliberately aimed into their necks. There were multiple burials and evidence of multiple wounds on single individuals. In Europe, there are other examples of mass graves – in Germany, Bavaria and France, and from eastern and southeastern Europe.

At the Iron Gates Gorge and the site of Lepenski Vir on the River Danube, a number of cemeteries and burials have been discovered. They include individuals from the Mesolithic and slightly later Neolithic periods, from around 7600–7000BC. Among these, there are examples of injuries caused by projectile points – at one site, a bone point was lodged in the pelvis of a teenage male. There was also blunt force trauma – a crush injury on the front of the skull of an older man, and 'defence' injuries on the right arm of an adult female. Another adult male had a number of depressed fractures on his skull, and such fractures were also found on two further individuals. At other sites in the region, there are several more examples of fatal and multiple projectile wounds, embedded projectile points, and defence injuries – in up to a quarter of all the people whose remains were found. It is thought that these cemeteries represent a series of bouts of fighting over time, rather than any endemic warfare. This may be the kind of inter-group violence that should be expected from small, relatively isolated human communities who occasionally clash with others, but whether the injuries are a result of murder, fights within the family or war is impossible to tell.

Across Europe there are examples of bodies with projectile points and other evidence for violence – among these are flint projectile points in the spine of a man at Téviec in Brittany, and in the pelvis of a man in the cemetery at Skateholm 1 in Sweden. Sites in Sweden and Denmark also bear evidence of possible cannibalism, with cut marks on bones, and bones split to extract marrow. At the Grotte des Perrats cave near Angoulême in France, at least five adults and three children were represented among scattered bones of animals, fish and birds, all apparently killed for food. Bones that contained marrow had been broken open, while bones without marrow had just been discarded among the other rubbish. There was evidence that the skulls had been opened to remove the brains. Careful study of the remains has suggested that these acts were not part of some careful funeral ritual – this was butchery in the most literal sense, and it was even observed that human tooth marks were visible on some bones. It would seem that some human groups preyed upon others for food, in the same way that they hunted deer and other animals.

Other graves have been found in Denmark that might suggest cannibalism, with split bones for marrow extraction, and possibly scalping. A man whose remains were found in Gough's Cave, Somerset, may have died from violence around 7150BC, as there was a hole in his skull possibly caused by an attack, which formed an abscess that may have been the eventual direct cause of his death. Earlier, less complete skeletal remains from the cave suggest that cannibalism had been practised – parts cut from skulls, blunt force trauma on adult and child skulls, and some evidence that might suggest the cutting away of their tongues. Animal carcases in the cave had received similar treatment. Cutting away of part of the skull to form a cup is suggested here, and at nearby Aveline's Hole, another cave in the system.

Late Mesolithic sites in the Netherlands also have evidence for violence – a depressed fracture from a wound made by a club on the skull of a man from the site at de Bruin, and a severe skull injury on one of two men buried in a single grave at Schipluiden. There is a multiple burial at Vedbaek of a man, woman and child, with a bone point lodged in the man's neck. There are more sites further afield with similar discoveries, in the Balkans and the Ukraine.

Depressed skull fractures, some healed and some possibly fatal, have also been observed on many skeletons – including male bodies in Denmark and

Sweden, and a female, aged about forty and buried in the same grave as a young child. Such fractures could be the result of falls, or blows from clubs or thrown stones.

Ofnet, in Bavaria, is the site which gives us the first evidence of mass murder. It has been dated to around 7,720 years ago, and what was found there was a macabre collection of human skulls carefully stacked like eggs in pits *(Figure 10)*.

These people seem to have died violently. Marks on the back of the heads suggest some may have been battered to death with heavy stone 'shoe-last' adzes or maces and the male adults and two of the children had been hit on the back of the head with axes; all the bodies were decapitated with stone knives, as cut marks on the vertebrae demonstrate. The skulls had been covered with red ochre, an earth pigment that is frequently found on burials across the world, from the Paleolithic era onwards.

Most of the skulls (some twenty of them) belonged to children, and two-thirds of the adults were women, and with the women and children were some deer teeth and shells, possibly worn as ornaments around the neck and in the hair. It seemed clear that the four adult males in the group had received more wounds than the others, perhaps because they had been trying to protect the women and children. It has been suggested that placing these skulls in the pits was some sort of 'trophy' display after a massacre. There was no trace of the remainder of the skeletons, which were presumably discarded or buried elsewhere. A smaller, similar deposit was found at Hohlenstein Stadel in Germany – three individual skulls, two of which showed evidence of blows to the head with an axe.

The Ofnet site seems to come closer to revealing an act which might be defined as war – clearly the weakest members of a group had been targeted, perhaps while the rest of the menfolk were away hunting. This is a pattern that repeats itself across the world and across time, even to the present day. The killing of the women and children can be a form of genocide – wiping out the reproduction potential of the group, as well as a way to destroy the morale and courage of their husbands and fathers.

As the skeletal evidence demonstrates, by the Mesolithic period there was a range of 'tool-weapons' that could be used for interpersonal violence. Some of these survive, some may not – the effect of a sharpened wooden spear or arrow can be as lethal as those of bone, antler or stone points, but we will never be able to find such a weapon, as the wood will have decayed away completely. The range of stone implements includes mace heads with holes drilled for hafting, and 'hammer-axes', some of which are decorated and may have acted as status symbols. Many of these tools are blunt-edged, and it is hard to think of a practical purpose for them in food preparation or wood-

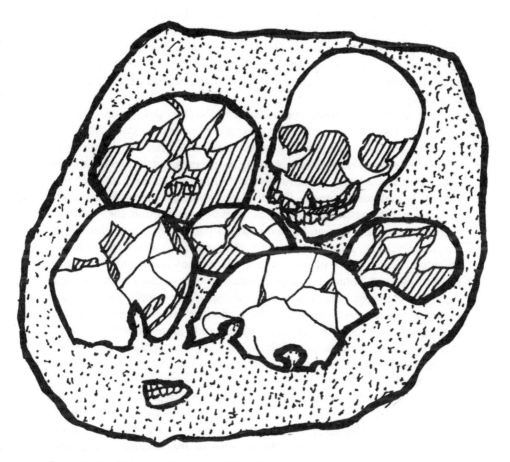

Figure 10. Skulls arranged in a pit at Ofnet, Bavaria.

working, so we may be able to consider them as being more likely to represent the weapon end of the tool-weapon spectrum. There is also a wide variety of tools made from antler – hammers, adzes and axes, some with drilled holes for shafts to be fixed. They could have had many uses, for mining, digging, and cutting meat. Antler was also used to make projectile points, as was bone. It is not always clear whether a projectile point (especially if broken) was attached to a spear or to an arrow.

Composite tools also appear in the Mesolithic – numbers of tiny blades hafted together to form saws, harpoons, and sickles, all of which could also be used as weapons. Archery also became more important. Mesolithic bows have been found at a site on Zealand, in Denmark, the largest surviving one being 180cm long, and there are other examples from Scandinavia and

Russia; about 100 arrow shafts, some still with their flint arrowheads attached, were discovered at Stellmoor in Germany, along with fragmentary remains of two further bows. Outside our area, in the Spanish Levant, there is rock art with many representations of bows of different sizes and forms, and at the Minateda rock shelter, at Albacete in Spain, there is a depiction of an archery battle.

Why are there so many more instances of violent death in this period? Of course, there are more bodies to examine than in the Paleolithic, and communities were larger. There is some evidence that nomadic hunter-gathering as a way of life was becoming more restricted, with more groups competing for territory, and probably a dividing up of the landscape into separately claimed territories. Trespass into another's piece of land might have been the reason for attack, as well as competition for particular resources available only in limited places – particular fishing grounds, or hunting places on animal migration routes, or places where less common fruits and plants grew, or particular kinds of preferred stone were to be found. It is worth noting that some researchers believe that a connection can be drawn between places where evidence of Mesolithic violence has occurred, and natural boundaries in the landscape – rivers, rapids, mountain passes and other such 'breaks' in communication routes. It seems possible that it was at these 'break-points' that there was more chance of running into another group of people, and therefore more likelihood that arguments would break out.

By the end of the period, from about 7500BC onwards, a new explanation for violence has been offered – competition between these semi-nomadic communities, following animal herds and collecting plants in the ancient fashion, and the newcomers – the farmers of the Neolithic, who were beginning to cut down the forests, plough and fence the land, and introduce domesticated animals.

Violence in the Neolithic (New Stone Age)
The potential for conflict between nomadic and settled groups exists and is well known from more recent historical and ethnographic accounts. Each side would have very different concepts of the ownership of land and the food resources it held. The notion of ownership itself in respect of territory is thought by some to be a major change in human thinking during the Neolithic period. It is hard for each side to appreciate the other's position. Not so very long ago, one man said 'What is this you call property? It cannot be the earth, for the land is our mother, nourishing all her children, beasts, birds, fish and all men. The woods, the streams, everything on it belongs to everybody and is for the use of all. How can one man say it belongs only to

him?' He was a Native American, speaking about the spread of white land ownership in the United States.

It is possible that early farmers began to fortify their homes against incursions by the people still clinging to the old ways. This was claimed for sites in Belgium, including Darion *(Figure 5)*, Oleye and Longchamps, where deep ditches and palisades had been constructed about 5000BC. One of the excavators believed that these farmers were living on the frontier between the Mesolithic and Neolithic transition, and felt the need for protection from roaming bands of hunters. Burned houses and Mesolithic projectile points found at the sites reinforce this opinion, although others question whether the evidence is strong enough to confirm aggression at these places.

It is still not clear whether the early farmers were indigenous people who adopted the new way of life, or were incomers, spreading as colonists over northern Europe – there is evidence on both sides of the debate. It is likely, however, that conflict between Neolithic groups themselves also occurred.

Evidence of massacres comes from a number of places in the Early Neolithic of Northern Europe. Mass graves have been found – in around 5000BC at Talheim in Germany thirty-four people were buried together. Sixteen of them were children, seven were women and nine were men. Their bodies had been thrown without any care or respect into a pit. Many of them had suffered blows to the head with a heavy tool, and a few had been hit by arrows. Forensic studies of the remains show that many of the victims had been attacked from behind, and then struck again as they were kneeling or lying on the ground. Different types of axes had been used – thin and thick blades – and possibly wooden clubs, suggesting a group of attackers. Some individuals had suffered multiple wounds to head, arms, legs and pelvis.

It has even been possible to link some of the children with particular adults and it is suggested that the victims were from two extended family groups. Interestingly, isotope tests of the teeth and bones showed that the victims were not necessarily local to the area in which they were found, although the material culture – their tools, decorations and other possessions – found with the bodies (pottery in particular) shows no difference from the local forms.

A site surrounded by a ditch in Austria, Schletz-Aspern, had a much larger cemetery population – perhaps 300 individuals. Of the sixty-seven excavated, a similar pattern of injury was found; here there were twenty-seven children (including a newborn), twenty-six men and thirteen women, and it was noted that many of the adults were relatively old. They were local. The bodies seem to have been left to decay for some time before the remains were collected and buried, as small bones were missing, and animal tooth marks were seen on some bones. It is thought likely, based on the pattern of the wounds, that most of the victims had been attacked from behind, as they were trying to run away. Of the forty skulls found, thirty-nine had been smashed. The village at Schletz had been fortified, so attacks had been expected and seem to have occurred fairly often over time.

Another site with evidence of violence is Vaihingen, near Stuttgart in Germany – here twelve bodies were dumped in two pits outside a village, some showing evidence of violent injury. Just over a third of the dead were non-local. Tensions between locals and migrants may have erupted in these cases.

The weapons used were those typical of the farming communities of the time and place – in other words, this was conflict by Neolithic groups with other Neolithic groups. Some have suggested that there was a pattern of raiding between villages – perhaps for booty, and perhaps for women (there are very few young women represented in the burials) who would have been carried off. Alternatively, there could have been some form of 'ethnic cleansing' – the removal of people who were seen to be foreign or different in some way, as occurred in Rwanda and in the former Yugoslavia in more recent times.

The bodies found at the Jungfernhöhle cave in Bavaria were also mostly either female or children – a minimum of twenty-three children or adolescents and nine to eleven young women in a group of at least forty people. It seems here that the long bones had been deliberately broken, and possibly teeth had been removed for trophies (a necklace of human teeth from the same period has been found in Slovakia). The site also contained the bones of other animals and general rubbish, and the suggestion is that cannibalism could explain these remains.

More evidence suggesting the eating of humans by humans has been found at Fontbregoua in France, where human skulls show cut marks made when the skin and hair was cut away, at Zauschwitz in Germany, where six bodies with broken long bones and skulls were found in a rubbish pit, and at Fronhofen on the Bavarian border, where a pit contained the broken and partially burned bones of at least five people.

The Fontbregoua site is a cave where a large number of shallow pits were found; ten held animal remains – only boar in three of them, and in others the bones of now extinct fauna as well as foxes, martens, badgers, deer and a wolf. Three pits also contained human remains – a total of perhaps ten adults and six or seven children. It was clear that the bodies had been dismembered in the same way as the hunted animal carcasses, and marrow had been extracted from their bones. Stone tools that had been used for the purpose were found scattered among the bones. At Hohlestein the remains of thirty-eight individuals, including children, found in a pit amongst animal bones, also had broken and split long bones and skulls cracked open. It is hard to escape the conclusion that cannibalistic practices had survived among these early farming communities, but whether these derived from aggressive attacks, were part of a normal funerary or ritual practice, or were evidence of an extreme reaction to a period of starvation is impossible to say.

Slightly different evidence comes from another German site – Herxheim. Partial remains of over 400 bodies were found, including many cut-off skull caps; there were cranial wounds, though in many cases these had not been fatal, and had healed over. An alternative explanation, other than conflict, is offered here by most people who have considered the site – this was a ritual place, used over a longer period of time, and the treatment of the skulls may have been part of funerary or sacrificial ceremonies. We cannot assume that people in the past would have had the same attitudes towards the bodies of the dead that we do – to incorporate the remains into cannibalistic or other ceremonies may have been a mark of respect, even a way of ensuring a degree of immortality for the deceased, as part of their body would live on, either nourishing the living, passing on the essence of the dead person, or using their skeletal remains to create an object of veneration.

Further evidence for Neolithic conflict has been found in other parts of Europe – the Balkans, the Ukraine, Greece and Macedonia, with weapons trauma, massacres and destruction levels. More weapons trauma is also found – in addition to the stone axes and adzes, clubs and probable sling stones, finds of arrowheads in tombs of the period are fairly common across Neolithic Europe, although in France there is an interesting regional pattern – a large number of examples from the south, a few from Brittany, and a group of examples in the Paris Basin, but fewer elsewhere. There is also evidence of trauma caused by flint knives, which leaves a different kind of trace on the bone from that left by arrowheads.

Enclosed or defended settlements have been excavated in many places. The presence of very deep (some over two metres) V-shaped ditches is thought to indicate a defensive intention – this shape is perhaps more difficult to dig than a flat-bottomed one, and is not necessarily suitable for purposes such as drainage. If the earth was piled up on the inside of the ditch, and/or a palisade was erected, then the defensive nature is possibly more intentional. Complex entrances also suggest defence – screened openings, or funnel-shaped access-ways, would seem to make peaceful movement unnecessarily difficult, but would help to prevent, or at least slow down and fragment, an aggressor force. About eighty-four sites across Europe are known to have had some form of defence, and they seem to have been more common as time went on.

Examples found in Germany, Belgium and the Netherlands combine timber palisades with earthen banks and ditches, and are mostly connected to settlements; in France they surround timber longhouses. At Cateny in the Oise region, a site called Le Camp de César enclosed five hectares on a strategically placed spur of land. It was surrounded by a wooden palisade, and a rampart and ditch protected the access across the neck of the spur. A number of the French sites are surrounded by interrupted ditches and palisades on rising ground behind them. The site of Champ-Durand, in the Vendée, had three concentric rings of interrupted ditches around a three hectare plateau. The inner ring had the largest ditches – between five and seven metres wide and around two and a half metres deep. At some later period, a dry stone wall was added to the inner face of the ditches as a revetment. Five human bodies were found at this site, but no evidence of trauma.

In Bavaria a similar defended site was found at Galgenburg. This enclosure was built on a slope and surrounded by interrupted ditches and a palisade that had been faced with applied daub. The main entrance was fronted by two slanting ditches, creating a funnel effect. A concentration of flint and bone projectile points was found around the entrance.

Defended settlements also appeared in Britain. A form of structure associated with the period is the causewayed enclosure – an area of land enclosed by a series of interrupted ditches separated by 'causeways' or undug passages, similar to those of France and Germany. These appeared in the early part of the Neolithic period, and a number of different purposes for them has been suggested. They could have been market places, ritual sites, places to put the dead for natural defleshing before interment of the bones (a process called excarnation), feasting sites and so on. However, some became settlements over time, and were given defences.

At Hambledon Hill in Dorset, excavations showed that causewayed enclosures on the hill were surrounded by three kilometres of timber-reinforced earth ramparts, and massive oak posts lined the three entrances. Two enclosures survived the later building of the Iron Age hillfort at the site – the smaller Stepleton enclosure on a spur to the southeast, and the Main enclosure on the eastern side. The Main enclosure was eventually surrounded by three sets of non-connecting ditches, each backed by a low rampart and palisade. The Stepleton enclosure was also further defended over time, and on one occasion part of the rampart and palisade had been catastrophically burned. New ramparts and palisades were built over the remains of this inferno, involving the use of at least 10,000 large timber posts. There is evidence of domestic occupation, despite the lack of water within the enclosure, as well as traded goods from as far away as Cornwall and Brittany.

It may well be that these exotic objects had something to do with the fact that around 3500BC the site was attacked again. A large section of the Stepleton defences was set on fire, burning the oak beams and posts in a fierce conflagration. The core of the rampart collapsed; underneath it were found the bodies of two men, both with arrowheads in them. They may have been trying to escape from the attack – one of the men had been carrying a small child in his arms when he was shot in the back, the arrow piercing his lung. He fell, and the child was crushed beneath him. Two other skeletons were found where they had fallen, one of which was incomplete, having been scavenged by wolves or feral dogs. Two more burials outside the enclosure may have been those of members of the attacking force, as one young man had been carefully buried in a pit and covered with a layer of the burned chalk rubble from the rampart, unlike the more casual disposal of the other victims.

The Neolithic site on the prominent hill of Carn Brae in Cornwall had a wall of great granite blocks, some weighing more than two or three tonnes, possibly two metres high or more. Around 2700–3000BC there had been a number of houses in the interior, surrounded by nine acres of land within an outer wall, home to 100–150 people. This site also had evidence of long-distance trade, and the visitor today can well appreciate the distant views the hilltop location offers, which would have increased the safety of the occupants. The entrance was further defended by a ditch and a sort of barbican. Nevertheless, the site was attacked. Many of the houses had been burned down, and some 800 arrowheads were found in and around the village, large numbers of them affected by fire. Hundreds of other arrowheads have been found surrounding the area, with a dense concentration around the entrance in the wall, some embedded in the wall itself. The wall seems to have been deliberately destroyed at this point; no evidence of bodies was found here, but the acidic soil makes survival of bone unlikely in any case.

At Hembury in Devon, another causewayed enclosure also showed signs of being burned, and there was a concentration of arrowheads, many damaged by fire, found around the entrance. An enclosure at Billown on the Isle of Man also produced a large number of arrowheads in the ditch and may have been the subject of an assault. The site at Thornhill in Northern Ireland also had a burning episode associated with arrowheads.

Another attack took place at Crickley Hill in Gloucestershire; again a causewayed enclosure, this too had been modified for defence. The two concentric rings of ditches lay in front of a low rampart and palisade. Inside were the probable remains of houses that had burned down. A little later, the site was reoccupied, and this time a large continuous ditch was dug, backed by a massive stone-faced rampart and palisade. A new, larger settlement filled the interior. This came under assault – the evidence comes from the excavation of a section of the defensive rampart and two of its entrances, where over 400 arrowheads were found, the patterning of their locations clearly indicating that a sustained archery attack at the gates had occurred. More arrowheads in the interior were found in the ashes of a burned building – it is possible that this was the defenders' weapons store. Phillip Dixon, the excavator, believed that the defences were designed to defend against an archery attack – an assault would be slowed down and broken up by the ditches, and the defenders could have used the low rampart as a killing ground as the attackers climbed out of the ditch.

There is not a clear distribution of these sites in Britain (enclosures have been found on Dartmoor, in Sussex, at Abingdon on the Thames and in Wales, and an island settlement reached by a causeway in Scotland), and some of them have exotic trade goods within them. It is possible that these communities were particularly wealthy, profiting from trade connections by river and sea, and that they therefore attracted envious attackers – less wealthy neighbours, perhaps, or foreigners who preferred to take the goods the people of the fortified enclosures had to offer without paying for them.

Chez-Reine in France *(Figure 11)* also has a barbican-like entrance like Carn Brae, and the French sites, like the British ones, have evidence of long-distance trade. Sites with ramparts, ditches and palisades are recorded in the Balkans too. Even more complex stone defences appeared in south-western Spain and Portugal towards the end of the Neolithic period. Early villages surrounded by complex stone walls are known from Macedonia and Greece, although often considered not to be defensive.

Five palisaded enclosures are known from Scotland, consisting in most cases of concentric rings of timber posts, sometimes linked by planking and, at Blackshouse Burn, south Lanarkshire, by a bank of stone between two such circles. At this site, the bank was enlarged to cover the wooden posts. These sites do not seem to have been settlements, but are perhaps best seen as local focus monuments. Their scale demonstrates their importance to the local communities who built them, and it is this role as a focus or symbol of the community that might explain why they were destroyed.

A similar lack of settlement evidence is found at a number of Later Neolithic enclosures in Europe, such as the vast enclosure at Urmitz on the Rhine, which encloses an area of land measuring 1.2 kilometres by 800 metres. The same is true of a number of Scandinavian sites such as Bunkeflostrand and Hyllie in Sweden, and Rispebjerg in Denmark, except for numbers of axes or axe production debris (possibly the very axes used in the construction of the enclosures). The Scandinavian examples have elongated skewed entrances, similar to those in Scotland, and are also found

Figure 11. Plan of the Chez-Reine defended Neolithic site in France.

100 m

close to other monuments such as causewayed enclosures, timber circles and tombs. Like the Scottish ones, they are about 3.5 hectares in area.

In these cases, it is believed that the enclosures are not defensive but ceremonial, the various post settings creating a bounded space for ritual and meetings, and the arrangement of the posts in the landscape suggests that social hierarchies were operating, with access becoming increasingly limited to the special few as one moves further inside them. They probably bear more relationship to sites such as Avebury and Stonehenge than the defended settlement sites such as Crickley Hill, although these settlement sites may have begun life as similar ceremonial centres.

Evidence from Neolithic graves
More individual evidence of conflict comes from graves. There are many examples in Britain of Neolithic people killed by arrows – actually in bones from Fengate in Cambridgeshire, Ascott-under-Wychwood in Oxfordshire, Penywyrlod in Wales and elsewhere, and at many other sites arrowheads

found within graves may have been present in the body of the deceased when they were interred. Sites dug before modern methods and scientific aids were available are likely to have missed the significance of projectile points found in graves and the clues left in the bones they found (which earlier antiquarians often just discarded, although some did make notes in their written records of traumatic injuries they had seen). One such record left by an antiquarian, a Mr J. Thurnam, in 1869, records that he had noted very many examples of skulls appearing to have been damaged by clubs or stone axes in the long barrows he had excavated. (He had conducted excavations at Littleton Drew long barrow, Tilshead, and Boles Barrow near Stonehenge, among others).

There are a number of instances of contact injuries at other sites – a woman buried in the Culdrum megalithic tomb in Kent had massive wounds to her head caused by a stone axe, and there were signs that her ear may have been cut off as a trophy. Healed and unhealed skull fractures have been found at Crickley Hill, Belas Knap, West Tump in Gloucestershire, from Salisbury Plain, Scotland, and Yorkshire. A study of 350 Early Neolithic British skulls found that people had a one in twenty chance of suffering a skull fracture, and one in fifty died from these injuries.

Defensive wounds to the forearms have been noted at, for example, Barrow Hills in Oxfordshire and Wayland's Smithy in Wiltshire. At Tulloch of Assery in Scotland one tomb contained a victim of an arrow, while another had within it a boy of about fourteen who had suffered damage caused by a blow to the skull. In Surrey, excavations at the causewayed enclosure at Yeoveney Lodge near Staines found skulls in the exterior ditch. One showed evidence of previously healed wounds, but he had suffered repeated violent blows to the head before he died and was decapitated. Various disarticulated human bones were also found in the ditches.

Modern survey methods have greatly increased the number of known enclosed sites across Europe – before 1970, only three sites were known to exist in southeast Bavaria, but now over 3,000 have been recognised in the region, mostly found through the use of aerial photographic surveys. There are many differences and regional variations, and only a very small number of these sites have been excavated, or, at least, excavated to modern standards. Some were undoubtedly ritual sites, while others may have been peaceful settlements using minor banks and ditches for practical purposes, to prevent animals or children straying. Still others may have been demarcated meeting places – for markets and fairs, perhaps. How many represent defences against aggression we simply do not know, but the evidence, though patchy, shows that violent attacks were possible, and even the most peaceful farmer might have felt the need to make at least a show of defensive ability.

Evidence of weapons

The range of weaponry to be found in the Neolithic of northern Europe suggests an increasing degree of both manufacturing and usage skills. There seems to have been a growth in the use of archery, with the finds of bows and many arrowheads of different forms. There are also many forms of stone tool, and evidence of spears and clubs.

Bows were found at two sites in the Somerset Levels, and although neither was complete, it could be estimated that one from Meare was 190cm long. They were both made from yew wood, and the Meare example had traces of leather bindings still attached; these were arranged to give a decorative finish to the bow, and also, probably, to give it more strength. An experimental reconstruction produced a bow that was similar in range and power to those

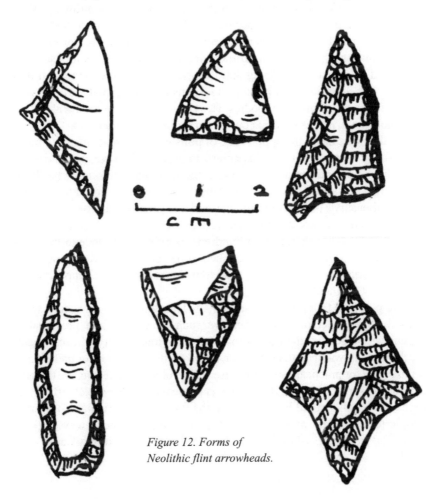

Figure 12. Forms of Neolithic flint arrowheads.

used by the medieval English archers at Agincourt in 1415. Lighter bows, one of hazel, have also been found – one near Glastonbury and one in Peeblesshire.

Different types of arrowhead were used *(Figure 12)* – a common form is the 'leaf-shaped' arrowhead, made of struck flint; one was found still attached to part of its shaft at Blackhillock Bog in Aberdeenshire. 'Tranchet' or 'transverse' arrowheads are triangular in form, with a wide straight edge, possibly used for bringing down birds in flight. These are excellent hunting arrows, and the leaf-shaped variety is more than capable of killing a deer (or a person) at a range of up to 100 metres, if shot from a bow similar to the one found at Meare.

Clubs have also been discovered in Britain – two in Cumbria and one in Somerset. The Cumbrian examples were accompanied by a throwing stick, or atlatl, made from antler, the use of which increases the speed and power of the throw. Antler picks, generally regarded as digging tools (for example in flint mines such as those at Grimes Graves in Norfolk) could also have been used as weapons. Stabbing and throwing spears were made, and it is possible that slingshots may have been responsible for some of the depressed skull injuries noted on many bodies. Heavy polished stone axes and drilled shaft-hole stone maces may be considered probable weapons too.

On the other hand, the appearance of polished stone tools may say more about social changes that were happening in the period. These axes and other forms have been rubbed against a polishing stone until the surface has been worn down to a satiny smooth shiny finish. These objects would have taken perhaps thousands of hours to produce, and it is clear that unusual stone was prized – exotic colours and patterns were chosen, and the raw materials for these objects were sourced from hundreds of miles away. Jadeite from the eastern Alps was used to make a polished stone axe found in Kent, and stone from Cumbria and Cornwall was used to make many other examples found in southeast England.

The practical function of these items is less than clear – it would seem unlikely that a person would acquire such an exotic, and presumably expensive, object and then use it to cut down a tree, when a cheaply made local flint tool would do the job better. Some of the stone used for these items is too brittle for practical use in any case. These objects, therefore, are thought to be status symbols, or symbols of power or wealth or other social difference. Perhaps a parallel could be drawn with the way in which rich and powerful people today collect masterpieces of art which are locked away in bank vaults, or more pairs of expensive shoes or handbags than they could ever need!

Neolithic warfare overview

Overall, there is a fair amount of evidence for conflict in the Neolithic period, from single deaths to large-scale attacks on settlements, as well as the evidence implied from the increasing number of fortified sites. Some examples may represent murder or hunting accidents, but it is clear that elsewhere there were organised assaults and raids, resulting in multiple deaths. Bodies may have been mutilated, and trophies collected. This looks like war, if only on a very small and localised scale. Tactics seem to have been developed – the design of defences shows an understanding of the nature of assaults and the best ways of countering them, creating baffle entrances and killing grounds. The practice of 'softening up' defences with the use of projectile barrages seems to have been understood and utilised, and fire was possibly also used as a weapon. There is, understandably, little archaeological evidence of the use of 'fire-arrows', but it is certainly a possibility.

Hand-to-hand combat with spears, maces and clubs seems to have occurred, and deliberate execution of prisoners also seems to have happened. None of the combats seen in the archaeological record are likely to have been of any long duration; the defended sites would not have been able to withstand a siege for very long, as many have no water source within them, and where conflict is visible, it looks like a single-action occurrence, though some sites possibly suffered repeated assaults. In these cases, there appears to have been time to rebuild between attacks.

The causes of such 'wars' are hard to establish – they may include envy over trade and wealth inequalities, reprisals for trespass and incursions, ethnic violence against or by incomers, local feuds, conflict as a rite-of-passage for young males in which they prove their manhood, and raiding for women or slaves (and revenge attacks related to this). The excavator of Hembury and Hambledon Hill points to cattle as being a possible factor in the rise of raiding and enclosure – the larger enclosures at Carn Brae, and Hambledon, and at Chez-Reine seem to have been designed for stock control, and he speculates that cattle raiding could have become 'the ultimate object of rapid warfare'. It must be remembered, though, that the examples of aggression are in a very small minority compared to most Neolithic sites. Most people, one hopes, would have led peaceful lives – but the high incidences of healed trauma, especially to skulls, suggest that danger was present at some times for many individuals.

A feature of the Neolithic period is the appearance of large 'communal' monuments in the landscape – henges, cursuses, stone alignments and stone circles, and large tombs of many types. Some of these structures must have taken hundreds, if not thousands, of people working together to construct over long periods of time – perhaps, in the case of the largest monuments, generations of families contributed towards the enlargement and maintenance of them. This suggests large-scale organisation of people – with, presumably, someone directing the operations. This in turn suggests the beginnings of political structures in society – people with the power to encourage others to do what they say. They may have been the elders of the community, or strong warriors, or (and many believe that this is the likeliest scenario) people who combined leadership with ritual power.

The alignment of monuments with events like the midsummer and midwinter solstices is well known; the creation of cursus monuments and the long lines of standing stones at sites like Kermario in Brittany suggest ritual processions. The fact that some of these monuments also contain carvings of axes, boats and possible body armour or shields, as noted in Chapter 2, is interesting. We can also note that some settlements seem notably richer in exotic trade goods than others – there are new levels of wealth and influence derived from trade contacts. Objects that symbolise status or wealth, without apparent practical functions, were made, such as the polished axes. We are dealing with societies that are beginning to display characteristics of chiefdoms or tribes, and their ability to cooperate in the building of monuments allows us to contemplate their ability to unite for larger-scale aggression too – the start of true warfare.

By the Later Neolithic, evidence for aggression becomes more rare. Only two Late Neolithic defensible enclosures are suggested for Britain – Mount Pleasant in Wessex where a large timber palisade was erected, dating to around 2200BC (this site will be further discussed below) and Meldon Bridge in Scotland, with a palisade that may have been part of a ceremonial landscape rather than true defences. There are fewer available bodies to study, as a change in the way the dead were treated begins to be evident, with the closure or abandonment of the older communal tomb monuments. Much else was about to change at this time; as new tools of copper and ornaments of gold began to appear, the Stone Ages came to an end.

Change in the Chalcolithic (Copper Age)

Between about 3500 and 1800BC major changes took place across northern Europe. Older forms of settlement, funerary practice and technology gave way to new ideas, styles and methods. These changes were accompanied by a range of artefacts sometimes known as the Beaker package *(Figure 2)*, which included finely made pots – some shaped like upturned bells, a new range of archery equipment, the use of buttons on clothing, and the use of metals, especially those that melt at relatively low temperatures – copper and gold.

The use of metals had appeared earlier in southeastern Europe – as early as the late sixth millennium BC copper was being smelted in the Balkans. Sites in that region contain many metal objects – in the cemetery at Varna, which is dated to between 4700 and 4200BC, 3,000 gold objects have been found, totalling about 6 kilogrammes in weight. These included arm rings, gold discs and shapes apparently sewn on to clothing or cloaks, gold mounts for rods, and even a gold penis sheath.

Copper and other metals were extracted from mines in southeastern Europe – some which have been investigated include Rudna Glava in Serbia and Ai Bunar in Bulgaria. Sophisticated methods of metal extraction were employed, such as fire setting and water management. Metal extraction spread across Europe to sites such as Pioch-Farrus 4, at Cabrières in France, Mount Gabriel in Ireland, the Great Orme near Llandudno in Wales, Mitterberg in Austria and other sites in Iberia and Corsica.

Europe's earliest known metal user was found in the melting ice of a glacier on the border between Italy and Austria. Nicknamed Ötzi by the press, this man died around 3300BC, and he has proved to be very important. His date of death suggests that he should belong to the Neolithic period, but he was found to be in possession of a copper axe hafted onto a yew handle – making him in effect a Chalcolithic individual.

His axe is 99.7 per cent pure copper; tests of his hair showed metal compounds, suggesting he had actually been involved in smelting the metal himself. Ötzi had other weapons with him – a flint knife with an ashwood handle, and a quiver containing fourteen arrows, two with flint arrowheads and the rest unfinished. Tools for making and mending arrows were in his pouch. He had also been making a yew bow.

Studies into his body revealed that he had died violently – an arrowhead had penetrated his shoulder, probably piercing a major blood vessel, causing him to bleed to death. His killer had attempted to retrieve the arrow, pulling out the shaft but leaving the head behind. Ötzi had also suffered cuts and bruises on his upper body and a blow to his head.

Unconfirmed DNA tests on his arrows found material from other people – it seems he had used one arrow to shoot two different individuals and recovered it on both occasions – and there was also DNA from other people on his knife and his coat. It has been speculated that Ötzi was one of a group of people, probably from a valley to the south of the Alps in Italy, who went to the mountains either to raid, or to search for metal ores. They had come across another armed party, and there was a skirmish, in which several people were injured by weapons, and Ötzi himself died. Possibly others died too, but their bodies did not fall where the ice could preserve them for us to study. The lucky discovery of Ötzi's remains has shed new light on this period of transition between the Stone Ages and the new era of metal users, and caused a major reassessment of the dates for change in this period.

Metal objects found their way north ahead of the technology for making them – the oldest metal objects found in France were found in the Paris Basin, a region without any metal ore sources. Sheet-metal copper beads were found in a grave dating to 3517–3357BC (radiocarbon dating); other copper objects found dating from a little later in the Paris region include flat axes, daggers, points perhaps from arrows or a spear, awls and more beads. A tanged dagger was found at Aremberg in the Nord-Pas-de-Calais. It must have been a matter of great prestige to be able to obtain these exciting new objects.

The objects were found in the latest Neolithic archaeological levels or in assemblages of material associated with Beaker styles. The origin of Beaker culture material seems to be in Portugal around 2900BC and from there it spread, often by sea, around Europe, and down rivers such as the Seine and the Rhine between 2700–2500BC, bringing not only the metal objects, but eventually the knowledge of how to make them.

Along with the metal objects came a new burial rite in the Lower Rhine area and elsewhere – a single inhumation with a Beaker pot and sometimes other grave goods, often including a stone battle-axe. In Britain, many of these graves were covered by forms of round barrow mound.

Around 2400BC, copper production began at Ross Island in Ireland – chemical and isotope analyses show that not only were sites like this supplying copper across Ireland, but also exporting it to Britain, where some 66 per cent of artefacts found have similar chemical signatures. By about 2100BC copper was being mined at Bryn Copa, Cwmystwyth, in Wales (the first mine site to have evidence of a drainage system of hollowed logs), where a gold disc artefact has also been found in a burial. Whole new classes of specialists were born – the miners and the metalsmiths.

Work at the Great Orme mine has discovered many tunnels and shafts dating to this period, along with the stone and bone tools that were used to extract the metal ore – antler picks, shovels made from the shoulder blades of cattle, and stone hammers to crush the ore. Whole families must have worked in the mine – some shafts are too narrow for adult humans, and must have been dug out by children, working by the light of small fat lamps far underground, and scrambling up and down simple notched tree-trunk ladders and ropes. The profits from the mining must have made the dangers and effort seem worthwhile for these families, who probably did not understand that the copper ores were also toxic.

The smiths, the men who could turn the stone into shiny tools and weapons, must have seemed like magicians. It is possible that these masters of their craft were often itinerant, moving from community to community, setting up their simple hearths and furnaces, and from stone and fire creating a new world. From that time on, smiths have had an otherworldly connection in the minds of many people, and have even become gods, such as Thor with his smith's hammer, or Vulcan, the Roman god of fire and metal.

Originally, many antiquarians believed that these new technologies and customs were brought into northern Europe by a whole new group of people, the so-called Beaker folk, but more modern studies can find no real differences between many of the artefacts and skeletons of the people using these innovations and those of the original inhabitants, and so the preferred explanation now is that it was an invasion of ideas, rather than of people. Very recently, however, new research in France and the Mediterranean does seem to suggest a movement of people at this time, albeit piecemeal rather than in a deliberate migration or invasion, and as they moved, so the new ideas came with them. Perhaps the answer is that both things happened – some new people migrated into northern areas, but the knowledge of the new technology raced ahead of them and was adopted by the indigenous peoples.

Copper used for tools and weapons on its own tends to be brittle and blunts easily; it also tends to bubble when cast, creating weaknesses in the artefact. If, however, about 10 per cent of tin or another metal is mixed with the copper, a far stronger substance is created, which we call bronze. Tin bronze is the best and strongest alloy, but tin is not widely available in Europe – it is restricted as an accessible ore to the Atlantic fringe (Cornwall, Galicia and Ireland), so in other parts of Europe other metals were used, notably arsenic. With the discovery that alloying copper with another metal produced a harder substance, easier to cast, which retained a better edge, the Bronze Age proper began.

Chapter 4

The Coming of Metal

The beginning of farming, of more or less permanent houses and settlements, and of more advanced technological activities such as making pottery, had great social consequences. By the time metals began to be processed and used in the making of tools and weapons, there was a need for a more complicated political side to daily life – the means of choosing leaders, the defining of what those leaders were expected to do, and the ways in which leaders could impose their decisions and will on to everyone else. We can imagine the village 'big man' would have co-opted some strong support, both in arguments and meetings, and in the physical control of his followers. So for the first time, there is a possibility of a new class of people. In addition to the hunters, the gatherers, the farmers and the craftsmen, there are now the warriors. Of course, these may have been farmers or craftsmen themselves, most of the time. But when trouble arose, there was a small core of trained fighters to depend upon – and they had special weapons and equipment for the job. For the first time, then, in this period, armour was developed, and weapons designed specifically for use against fellow humans.

Violence in the Early Bronze Age – evidence from burials
The Early Bronze Age from about 2700BC saw the development of metal technologies, and the emergence of new kinds of societies. It was a period of massive agricultural expansion across Europe, with the foundation of numerous villages and farmsteads. People were by now leading a much more settled life, building more permanent homes, and creating more fields. The landscape of Europe was being tamed rapidly in many areas. But a tamed landscape could also mean more competition and more violence.

A number of Early Bronze Age sites have produced evidence for violence. In Zealand, a male body was found accompanied by a dagger and eleven flint arrowheads, possibly originally in a quiver, plus one more embedded in the throat of the victim, and it seems clear how he died. At Wassenaar in the south of the Netherlands near The Hague, twelve people were buried together around 1700BC. The site is a small coastal dune, in which was dug a large pit. The dead were laid side by side, alternating head to foot, east to west, and they were buried before rigor mortis had set in. There were two very small children, two adolescents, two young women, two young men and four older men in the group. A flint arrowhead was found in the ribs of one of the younger men, and three of the older men had injuries on the jaw, the skull and the upper arm.

This is a rare find in the Netherlands – most evidence there suggests this was a peaceful period, with small farming settlements and no signs that some people were more powerful or wealthy than others, although some farms were a little larger than average. Horses were being introduced into the area, and there are some weapons hoards, but no other evidence for warfare. This family had died violently, but had been buried carefully, though quickly. Was it their neighbours who cared for their bodies? And who attacked them? We will never know.

A copper knife was found in the spine of a person at Pas-de-Jouliés cave in Trèves, France, and another with a burial at Baumes-Chaudes, Lozère, demonstrating that these new metal tools quickly found a violent use. Arrowheads have also been found among the remains of a number of people in some late Neolithic/early Chalcolithic communal tombs in France. At the tomb at Fourneaux many of the bodies, with scattered arrowheads among the bones, had been deposited within a very short space of time, and then the tomb was possibly abandoned. Of course, such a scenario does not mean warfare was involved – there might have been a plague or other local disaster, and the arrowheads were simply part of the equipment carried by the dead.

At Stora Vikers, Gotland, a cremation grave was found to include bone points, which may have been inside the body when it was placed on the funeral pyre. Another site with possible Early Bronze Age conflict evidence was found at Sund in Norway. A pit contained about twenty-two people along with some animal bones. Seven of the adults in the grave show signs of injury caused by bronze weapons – but not arrows. Four had older, healed injuries, suggesting that conflict was not unusual and that they had experienced fighting at an earlier date. Half of the dead were children. At nearby Toldnes there is a large cemetery site, and studies of the bodies there as well as those at Sund suggest that, at the time, the population was facing a great deal of distress from starvation, malnutrition, intestinal parasites leading to weakness and disease, and of course the threat of violence.

There may have been a class of specialised warriors here in Scandinavia in this period, according to analysis of weapons and bone osteology. People who train with weapons from an early age tend to show changes in their bones where particular muscles have been developed more strongly; it is also often the case that the warrior class in a society tends to have a better diet than the farmers and peasants, and this too can be recognised by studying the chemistry of the bones. Apart from these sites, however, the Bronze Age in

Scandinavia is notably lacking in evidence of traumatic injury, although poor survival of bone in the ground probably skews the picture.

Bone does not survive for any length of time in soils which are acidic and free-draining, or when burial is shallow and insects and bacteria can attack the remains. In some conditions, a human body can completely disappear in less than a year, according to a Home Office pathologist. Archaeologists have to rely on discoveries made in neutral or alkaline soils, or in special places that are undisturbed, such as caves and bogs, and these are relatively rare finds, especially as most modern archaeology is concentrated on sites where building developments are planned – not usually in bogs and caves!

In the Czech Republic, cannibalism may have been practised at the site of Velim, rather than (or as well as) warfare. Bones – single, partly articulated or as part of whole skeletons – were found thrown into a ditch along with general rubbish. The ditches were opened and filled several times, and cut marks were observed on human bones, similar to those on animal carcases. This may have been a ritual site; it is possible the victims were acquired through warfare, but the evidence is not direct.

In Britain, as well as the Amesbury Archer mentioned earlier, other skeletal remains suggest conflict. Near the Archer a second burial has been discovered – the so-called 'Stonehenge Archer', who was wearing an archery bracer (a stone or leather cuff to protect the wrist from the recoil of the bowstring) on his left arm; there were also three barbed-and-tanged flint arrowheads in the grave, and examination showed that this young man had been shot at close range by several assailants, but whether this was due to conflict or a form of execution is unclear.

More examples of death by arrow come from Barrow Hills in Oxfordshire and Fordington Farm in Dorset. One of the individuals at Barrow Hills also had a possible break to an arm caused by an attempt to defend himself. A man buried at Chilbolton in Hampshire had similar injuries, and was buried alongside another arrow victim. These defensive wounds are known as 'parry fractures' and have also been seen at Pyecombe in Sussex and elsewhere, and there are head wounds, perhaps caused by a slingshot, in a burial inserted into a pre-existing tomb at Barnack, Cambridgeshire. Also at Pyecombe was the body of a woman with an axe wound to her head, which had begun to heal at the time of her death. These examples all come from barrows or other contexts associated with the Chalcolithic or Early Bronze Age period, and some were buried with Beaker pottery and related goods, allowing us to give them an approximate date.

The problems of burial evidence in the Bronze Age
The situation regarding evidence from graves in this period is complicated.

The shift towards Beaker-period artefacts and ideas included a major change in burial customs. From this time onwards for up to 1,000 years, burials (both inhumations and cremations) are found under barrow mounds, each apparently built to serve as the tomb of a single individual, in contrast to the collections of remains of numerous people found in the Neolithic tombs. The burials were often accompanied by grave goods – pottery, tools and weapons, ornaments, and food remains (and possibly containers of alcoholic drinks). It is suggested that at this time, individual people emerged as holders of status (and possibly wealth) and were singled out for special treatment after death. The impression is of a change from a communal social ethos to an hierarchical one.

In the early part of the period, a number of different forms of barrow were built, named after their shapes – bell, bowl, disc, saucer and pond *(Figure 13)*. Some researchers believe it possible that the different forms of barrow were seen as appropriate for different genders and ages, so that most bell barrows apparently contain adult male burials as the first occupant, while most disc barrows contain adult females, and the saucer forms contained adolescents. Unfortunately, earlier antiquaries and enthusiasts regarded barrow digging as a form of entertainment, and the vast majority of surviving barrows of all forms were attacked with garden spades and pickaxes long before modern archaeological science came into being. Many barrows in the landscape today can be seen to have a tell-tale dip on top – evidence of the unrecorded or gung-ho assaults made by these early enthusiasts. (One gentleman recorded how he and his gardener had opened a dozen barrows in one day). These diggers were after the pots, metal objects and occasional gold ornaments in the graves, and frequently threw away the bones without any attempt to record them. No plans were usually made of the excavations, and of course most were done before the advent of photography. As a result, any attempt to clarify the matter of barrow form related to the age and sex of the first burial within them is necessarily speculative.

However, if the impression of age and gender divisions is true, then we must be looking at a society where status can be inherited rather than earned, as the younger people and children could not reasonably be expected to have gained respect through leadership or martial successes. After the initial burial, the barrow mounds were often used for further interments – perhaps more family members, or people who desired to be buried close to a revered leader or ancestor. As the number of known barrows is relatively small, and even allowing for all those that have disappeared under the plough or building developments, it is clear that they were built for only a small fraction of the population, presumably the elite. What happened to the vast majority of the ordinary dead is unknown, and so we do not have any information about their lives or manner of death.

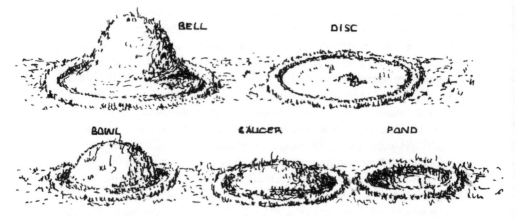

Figure 13. Forms of Early Bronze Age barrow mounds.

As time went on, the various forms of barrow mostly disappeared in favour of a more simple 'bowl' type, without any visible distinctions. Some barrow mounds seem never to have had any burials at all, and it has been speculated that these represent 'cenotaph' monuments – possibly raised to commemorate an individual or group who died away from home and whose bodies could not be recovered. It is conceivable that such people may have been involved in a distant battle, as is the case with modern cenotaphs; examples of such barrows have been found at Hove in Sussex and in Surrey, and one might imagine, too, that Silbury Hill in Wiltshire, then the largest man-made mound in Europe, might have served a similar function. Further into the Bronze Age, flat-grave cemeteries appear, cremation becomes more common, and eventually barrow-building begins to die out. By the Later Bronze Age, graves of all kinds are very rare finds.

All this makes it hard to find evidence for warfare – not enough bodies survive, and not enough surviving remains are in a good enough condition to offer much information, especially if they have been cremated. Nevertheless, prehistoric cremations can sometimes yield useful information despite the burning of the body; it was not usually possible to make a fire hot enough to turn a body completely to ash, as happens in a modern crematorium. After the funeral pyre had gone out, the ash and charcoal would be sifted to recover the fragments of burned bones remaining, which were then gathered and placed in the grave, often in a pottery jar or urn. Sometimes enough of these remain sufficiently intact to at least give information about the age and gender of the individual.

Another feature of this period is that gender becomes more marked in the way bodies were treated after death in several parts of Europe – males and females were buried with different equipment and goods, and sometimes in different ways. Often, the burials are 'crouched' – that is, laid on their sides, with the legs drawn up as if asleep, and it is common to find that the men have been consistently laid lying on one side and the women on the other, although which side, right or left, depends on the region. Male burials are far more often equipped with weapons, and it has been suggested that this era marks the point at which male status as warrior first becomes marked in European society.

This is confirmed by Early Bronze Age stone carvings that clearly show gender differences, and signify the differences between men and women by the depiction of weaponry with men and jewellery with women. Thus warrior status seems to have been clearly important at this time, which further suggests that combat was part of the ethos of daily life, however rarely it might actually have occurred. The status of women, on the other hand, seems to have been more confined to the domestic sphere, and they may have become less powerful in areas such as decision-making between groups – another factor which might indicate an increase in aggressive responses!

Settlements in the Early and Middle Bronze Age

The Bronze Age saw the increasing development of defended or defensible sites in some parts of Europe. Most notable are the defended settlements of southwest Iberia which, although outside the remit of this discussion, can be briefly described. Stone-walled forts were constructed, some with complex defences, such as Los Millares in Almeria. Here, an outer, bastioned wall defended a hilltop, itself defended by a second stone wall. Narrow, complex entrances with 'guard chambers' controlled access through both of these walls, with a barbican protecting the outer entrance. At the highest point of the hill, around a second summit, a further stone wall was constructed, with a bastion tower and another narrow, oblique entrance. Smaller forts were constructed on the surrounding hills. These sites are all dated to the Chalcolithic period in a region where population density had been increasing, and resource competition was probably strong, but they seem to have been abandoned by the end of the period until reoccupied some time later in the Early Bronze Age.

Elsewhere in Europe, in a number of cases, people began to choose to build their settlements on higher ground, for example in the South Wurttemberg area of Germany, some of which became defended sites in the Later Bronze Age period, a time which we call 'Urnfield' after the practice of that time of burying the dead in cremation urns in flat cemeteries. Banked and ditched settlement enclosures are found in central Europe, Slovakia and Poland from the Early and Middle Bronze Ages.

The fortified hilltop settlement of Spišský Štvrtok in Slovakia dates to c.1700–1500BC and here stone walls encircled the central area of the settlement. At Fidvár, also in Slovakia, at the start of the Early Bronze Age, a ditch and rampart were built, enclosing about 0.3 hectares; this was later enlarged with a second ditch and rampart enclosing 3.6 hectares, and then a third ditch further out. The settlement contracted at the end of the Early Bronze Age and a new strong fortification was built around a smaller central area. At another site, Barca, a ditch and timber-framed rampart enclosed a village of densely packed houses.

These sites are notable for the material wealth of the artefacts found – gold, amber and bronze hoards of daggers, beads and pendants. It seems clear that in this part of Slovakia, the need for some sort of defence was well understood, and suggests that a history of raiding may have preceded the making of the palisades and banks. Possibly, it was the increased wealth of some settlements that would have motivated the possible attackers. Hilltop sites were also found along the Danube and in Transylvania. Further west, a Middle Bronze Age site was constructed high above the Rhine valley in Alsace, on the Hohlandsberg, and in Herault, there is a Chalcolithic and Early Bronze Age fortified enclosure at Le Lebous, overlooking the Mediterranean.

In the north, such sites are rare or non-existent, although there is some evidence that some Late Bronze Age settlements in Britain started life as hilltop villages in the Middle Bronze Age – these may include Rams Hill in Berkshire, where an enclosing ditch was an addition to a pre-existing site, and Mam Tor in Derbyshire was occupied from perhaps 1500BC, and although not fortified at this time, was sited in an elevated and defensible position.

Only two sites in Britain dating from the Early Bronze Age are considered to suggest they were constructed with defence in mind. Both are in Wessex; the first is Mount Pleasant, near Dorchester, which was originally built around 2400BC as a henge monument (a henge is a circular bank and ditch with a single entrance, with or without standing stones within it). Settings for timber posts and standing stones were excavated at Mount Pleasant and bear comparison to sites such as Durrington Walls and Avebury, although these latter sites were much larger and were possibly more to do with settlement and/or ritual practices. Then, around 2100BC, a ditch was constructed to support around 1,600 oak posts, 40cm in diameter and possibly standing around 6 metres above ground level around the Mount Pleasant site. Two narrow entrances gave access, one being framed by massive posts, 1.5 metres in diameter. This palisade of posts had been deliberately burned down, and burned stone in the interior suggests that the central stone circles had also been destroyed. There is some argument about whether this site enclosed a settlement, or a ritual, possibly funerary, centre; the low rise on which it is situated is not particularly defensible, but it may be that in either case it represented a symbol of one group that another group wished to obliterate with violence.

The second site is near the chambered tomb at West Kennet in Wiltshire – here two enclosures, surrounded originally with palisades, sit side by side on the south bank of the River Kennet. Timber posts up to eight metres tall were set in incomplete circles, possibly between 2600 and 2100BC, although the dates are uncertain. Again, they had been burned down, presumably deliberately. Neither enclosure is sited in a defensive location, being set low in the river valley. There is speculation that in both the Mount Pleasant and West Kennet cases, new Beaker-using groups came into conflict with groups using the older 'Grooved Ware' type of pottery – new ideas and beliefs versus older ones, and the newer culture was set on destroying the older one. An alternative explanation, however, may be that these groups were one and the same – the local people decided to adopt the new ideas (including metal use, new forms of arrowhead, and new forms of burial) and wanted to start with a clean sheet. They may have destroyed the older monuments themselves as outmoded, unwanted, and perhaps in their eyes, failed symbols. No other evidence of warfare comes from these sites.

Many settlements are known in the period in Scandinavia, but they seem to be small farms for the most part, without any evidence for defences.

In south Germany and Switzerland, pile-built houses were sited on the edge of lakes – again, not defended, but defensible. At the site of Siedlung Forschner on the Federsee, a series of different 'neighbourhoods' was found in one settlement, beginning around 1750BC and surviving into the late Middle Bronze Age. The houses were built on timber piles on the edge of the lake, the whole settlement being surrounded by strong wooden palisades and divided by fences.

In Hungary and Bulgaria, 'tell' settlements developed – villages built on artificial or partly natural mounds. They may have been placed on higher knolls above flood plains, simply to stay dry, but they were also more defensible in those locations.

In most cases, it is impossible to say whether the creation of these settlements was dictated by a need to protect the inhabitants, or as a form of status symbol, or to maximize resources, or as a reaction to local weather and water conditions. The evidence for warfare in this period is very thin, with the exception of evidence for weaponry, and some pictorial representations of warriors and weapons, until we get to the Late Bronze Age in around 1200BC.

Land organisation

The organisation of the land in the Middle Bronze Age tells us something about the way societies were operating during the period. Most northern European communities practised mixed agriculture, with stock farming being more important than growing crops in some areas, depending on the types of soil in the locality. Elsewhere, the arable farming became extensive, and communities began to lay out vast field systems – the so-called 'Celtic' fields. The new fields were laid out in huge blocks on a single axis ('co-axial'), sometimes covering many square kilometres, and not always aligned directly with the underlying shape of the landscape. They are found across much of Britain and in northern France, Germany and the Netherlands, and recent research from Denmark has suggested these field systems may have begun to be created as early as 2000BC.

Clearly this is a managed landscape, with a single architect or small group of leaders directing the work. It would have been a major task, involving many workers, to design the scheme, organise the workforce, dig the ditches and raise the banks of the field boundaries. The implication is that each set of 'co-axial' fields represents the claimed and owned territory of a single community; a territory that might need to be protected against trespass and raiding.

Again, we are looking at a hierarchical society – there are people in charge, whom the rest of the community follow and obey. Perhaps these leaders were also warriors, or were supported by a warrior elite, maintaining their control through their ability to protect the community against aggression. They may have been the owners of the various forms of fine weaponry that appeared at this time. The spread of these field systems is also something that is yet to be understood, but it is possible that they were begun by powerful groups, and then copied by others who either wanted to emulate them, or felt that it was necessary to firmly delineate their own territories in the face of the expansion of the most powerful communities.

Weapons and Armour in the Early and Middle Bronze Ages

Perhaps the most immediately noticeable thing about weaponry in the Chalcolithic and Early Bronze Ages is the amount of archery equipment that has been found. Archers' wrist bracers have been found in many graves. In fact, what is usually found is a possibly ornamental stone plate, sometimes with gold rivets, that would have been attached to a leather cuff that would have been strapped around the arm – the stone plates themselves are too small to be effective, and are better seen as a mark of wealth or status, or just pure decoration. Barbed-and-tanged arrowheads, often beautifully made and delicate, are also common finds for this period. There were fifteen of these buried with the Amesbury Archer – possibly originally arranged in a quiver. Some graves, like the ones at Amesbury and Stonehenge, and on Boscombe Down, also contained gold ornaments, suggesting that these bowmen enjoyed high status, but whether as hunters or as warriors is unknown.

No bows of the period have been found in Britain, but they may be indicated by small bow-shaped pendants found in a number of male graves, a study of the decoration of which has raised the possibility that the bows in use were relatively short composite weapons. Wearing the bow pendants might have been a form of social honour or status symbol, denoting that the wearer is a warrior or hunter to be respected.

Stone battle axes are also found *(Figure 14)*, with a drilled hole for hafting, and copper and flint daggers or knives are also known. These weapons may not have been used for combat, however, being more likely just a basic tool for every use from eating to craft working. Over time, these developed into new forms, and were also made in tin bronze. The daggers were generally riveted to their hafts, which seem to have been made of organic materials – bone, horn or wood – and the hafts do not survive. A probable wooden club was found in a grave in West Lothian, and it is to be expected that other wooden or bone weapons would have been in use.

Copper axes are among the signature artefacts of this period, soon to be followed by stronger bronze versions. These were originally flat cast axes, and the stone moulds have sometimes been discovered. The bronze axes became larger, and often acquired flanges and hints of stop-ridges – these were necessary to haft them more securely. A flat axe, when used to hit an object, had a good chance of absorbing the force backwards into the haft, splitting it, and perhaps resulting in the loss of the metal axehead itself as it flew off into the undergrowth. The flanges allowed the haft to be bound on more securely, and the stop-ridge absorbed some of the force of a blow before it could be passed back into the wood. Replica axes of this type have been made to be used to build a copy of a Bronze Age boat from Ferriby and have proved very practical as tools; they would have also been extremely effective as weapons *(Plate 5)*. Carvings of these axes appear on Late Neolithic and Chalcolithic tombs in France, and on one of the upright stones at Stonehenge.

It seems likely that ownership of metal tools was restricted in the early period to particularly important or wealthy individuals, as there are interesting examples of flint knives and daggers carefully carved to imitate their metal counterparts – presumably the alternative for those aspiring to, but not yet achieving, the necessary importance or wealth that would bring them the real thing. Another form of weapon was the halberd – like a heavy riveted dagger blade fixed at right angles to the haft, forming a pole-arm. These have been found in central Europe and Ireland, and miniature halberd-shaped pendants have been found in British graves, perhaps, like the bow pendants, a mark of status.

At Bush Barrow, near Stonehenge, a remarkable grave was explored in 1808. It contained a mature male skeleton, which had been buried with a wealth of objects. The man had gold plaques sewn on to his clothing, and fine tools and weapons, including a flanged bronze axe, a drilled stone mace head, and two daggers, one of copper, the other bronze. The bronze dagger was a third of a metre long, and the pommel had been decorated with a pattern of thousands of minute gold pins. Only in one other place are such exactly similar dagger pommels known, and that is Brittany, confirming cross-Channel contact between Wessex and northwest France at this early date. Breton-style arrowheads have also been found in Glamorgan. Depictions of Bronze Age bows are found on carved stone stelae from Le Petit Chasseur in Switzerland, in rock art from Italy, and rock carvings from Sweden, although finds of the actual weapons have not been made.

From Ireland comes evidence of shields – at Kilmahamogue, Co. Antrim, a mould or former for making a shield was discovered. The shields produced would have been of leather, stretched and steamed over the mould. The mould gave a radiocarbon date of 1950–1540BC. Organic shields of wood, wicker or leather would have been very effective protection against bronze weapons, as they would have absorbed the shock of a blow very well, but they do not survive in the ground.

Moving further into the Middle Bronze Age, we see more changes and developments in weaponry. The axe developed into the palstave – a narrow-bladed axe with a much more developed stop-ridge and side flanges, and metal body armour began to appear. It is more than probable that armour existed before this time, but being made of wood or leather, it has disappeared in the soil, and so we know very little about it.

The rapier and the sword are important innovations of this period – because for the very first time we are seeing weapons made for the *sole* purpose of killing other people, rather than hunting weapons being used aggressively. The early sword form in use in Northern Europe was the rapier – a thin, thrusting weapon. Rapiers, like daggers, were riveted on to their hilts, and so were liable to break away if used in a slashing manner. They seem therefore to have been less popular in close general combat than the thrusting spear; the spear also had a much longer haft, which had the advantage of keeping the enemy further away from oneself. For close-quarter fighting, the sword soon replaced the rapier, as a more practical weapon.

The first swords in northern Europe appeared in Germany and Scandinavia, and were simply larger versions of the rapier – long, thin thrusting weapons – but this seems to have been recognised as a very limiting

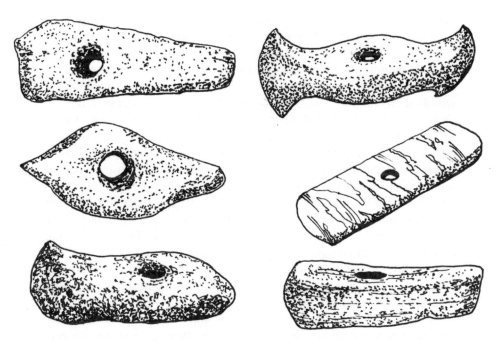

Figure 14. Forms of Early Bronze Age stone battle-axes.

factor in their use, and before long proper, broader swords with stronger hilts were developed. These swords allowed the user to slash and cut as well as thrust. The early swords had straight parallel sides, and were on average about 60cm long. Then they developed into shaped blade forms, particularly the 'leaf' or 'willow' shape – the sides curving down from a wide centre to a narrow point, and the blades developed from flat to sinuously shaped forms with a thicker central portion, making them much heavier in use and able to deliver a more powerful blow. Projections near the hilt were added, to deflect an enemy weapon that might have caused damage to the hand, and the grips improved. Grooves were added to the blade – these might have allowed blood to flow off the blade more easily, or may have been considered helpful when trying to withdraw the blade from an opponent's body, or may simply have been decorative *(Plate 6)*.

Elaborate pommels were added, though some developments seem actually to have impaired the use of the weapon (such as elaborate 'antenna' spirals attached at the top of the hilt), leading to the suggestion that some swords were made for display only. Patterns of re-sharpening on swords bear this out – some are heavily marked by repeated sharpening, while others seem never to have been sharpened at all. Swords with solid hilts, as opposed to flanged, tend to show very little evidence of wear from use, and may have been weapons worn for show by people of a certain social standing, rather than being made for warriors and actual use in fighting.

Most swords come from rich graves – it does not seem that the average person would own one. Ordinary cemeteries of the period rarely produce any swords at all, although a survey of 694 male graves with weapons in Early Bronze Age Denmark found that they were relatively numerous. There were 420 graves with a sword in them, three with a sword, dagger and spear, fourteen with sword and axe and twelve with a sword and a dagger. Just three graves were equipped only with a spear. Two graves held a sword, dagger and axe. Graves with just a dagger numbered 201, and those with just an axe sixteen, while six had a dagger and an axe. Archery equipment was more rare – only one grave with a sword also had a bow, one with a dagger had a bow as well, and only four had the bow as a sole weapon. The swords were arranged in the graves either hanging from a belt at the waist, or from a baldric hanging across the chest. In all, about 47 per cent of male Early Bronze Age Danish graves had swords – a much higher proportion than observed in other parts of Europe.

Great variation in the forms of swords appears across the continent, especially in Scandinavia, where by the Middle Bronze Age large numbers of weapons were being imported from central Europe and then copied locally. Whether these imports came by way of trade, brought by travelling swordsmiths, or carried by warriors is unknown. There are traces of sword hilts, scabbards, and sword belts in Norway, Denmark and Sweden, showing that later simple leather and metal fittings succeeded earlier, more elaborate carved wood scabbards and chapes (a metal fitting at the end of a scabbard that prevents the point of the sword cutting through it). The earlier equipment suggests an element of display in the design, while the later pieces appear much more functional. A study of the resharpening of Danish Bronze Age swords also shows a difference in the way they were used – those of the earlier part of the period were sharpened just at the end, implying they were used like rapiers, with a thrusting action like modern fencing, whilst those of the later Bronze Age have been sharpened all along their lengths, suggesting they were used in a form of fighting using cut and slash motions. Scandinavian swords were made using the 'lost wax' casting process, in which each new casting required a new wax model to be created. As a result, there is more variation in swords in the region than in other parts of Europe where reusable stone moulds were preferred.

Spears with socketed ends to fit on to a shaft appear at the end of the Early Bronze Age, and are thought to have replaced the dagger and rapier as thrusting weapons. There are many varieties of spear and spearhead, but they

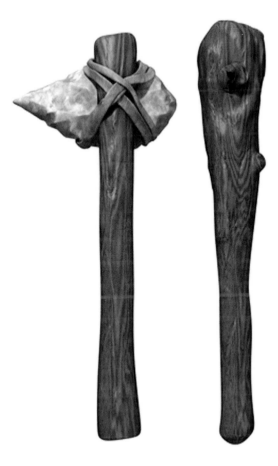

Plate 1. Simple primitive weapons.
(EduardHarkonen1/Dreamstime.com)

Plate 2. A passage grave in Brittany. (Peresanz/Dreamstime.com)

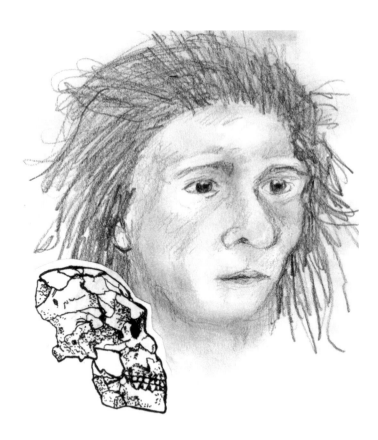

Plate 3. Skull and facial reconstruction of 'Pierrette'.

Plate 4. Swedish rock carving depicting armed warriors on a boat. (2012Photos.com)

Plate 5. Replica Bronze Age axes and other tools.
(Photo: author)

Plate 6. Replica of a Bronze Age sword. (Courtesy Neil Burridge, neil.bronzeagecraft.com)

Plate 7. Replica of the Nebra 'sky disc'. (Photo: author)

Plate 8. The Viksø helmets. (Courtesy: National Museum of Denmark)

Plate 9. The reconstructed entrance to the Biskupin lake settlement. (TomaszParys/Dreamstime.com)

Plate 10. The broch of Mousa.
(TE1/Dreamstime.com)

Plate 11. The reconstructed crannog at Loch Tay. (Don.simon1/Dreamstime.com)

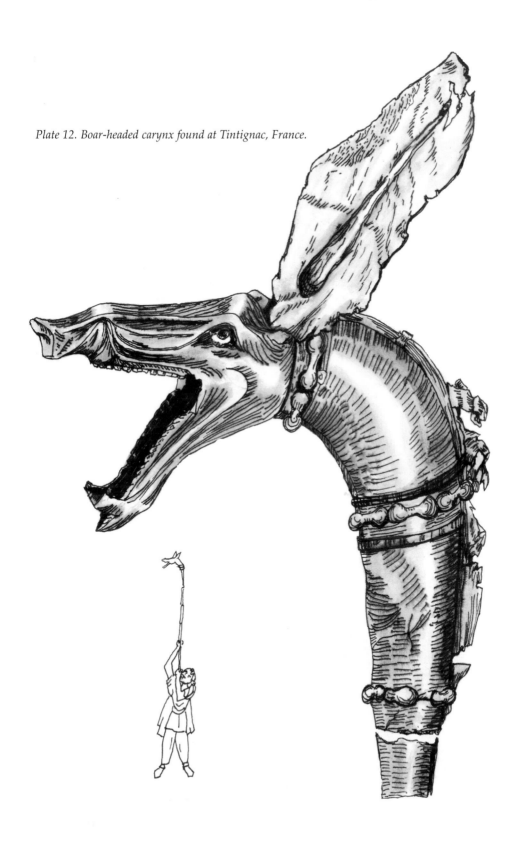

Plate 12. Boar-headed carynx found at Tintignac, France.

Plate 13. Model of a Roman ballista. (3drenderings1.Dreamstime.com)

Plate 14. Reconstruction of the Roman siege works at Alesia. (Anže Mulec/Dreamstime.com)

fall into two main categories – those for throwing and those for thrusting or stabbing. Throwing spears would be light with small heads (to minimize the loss of metal if the spear could not be recovered), and the heads are quite common finds. It seems likely that an exchange of thrown spears may have been the first stage of a battle in this period – a way of 'softening up' the enemy from a distance – in the same way that Tacitus describes the tactics of German warriors in the Roman period. The maximum effective distance for throwing a spear of this type would have been about 50–60 metres, and the usual distance was probably half that. Once the spears had been thrown, the two sides would then close in for hand-to-hand fighting with swords and the heavier spears.

Bronze shields have been found in Hungary, Poland, the Czech Republic, Scandinavia and northern Germany, but more than half those known come from the British Isles. None has so far been found in other parts of western Europe. They were generally hammered from a blank disc of tin bronze weighing about 1.5 or 2kg, to a thickness of between 0.3 and 1.3mm and a diameter of between 25 and 70cm or a similarly sized oval shape. The rims were rolled over for strength, and a bronze handle was riveted to the inside. Some were highly decorated.

Several different types appeared in various regions, one of the oldest in northern Europe being from Lommelev Mose in Denmark. This was a round shield with concentric ribs and groups of bosses ornamenting the face in a radiating pattern, and probably dates from the thirteenth century BC. Some Scandinavian forms are oval, with ribbed decoration. Several exclusively British types are found, some quite small and others large and particularly heavy. Organic shields of wood continued to be made and used, however, such as one from Cloonlara in Ireland of a similar date. Studies of some of the bronze shields show damage and repairs – one from the Thames has what appears to be a sword cut and a hole made by a spearhead. One of three shields from Yetholm in Scotland, probably Late Bronze Age in date, has a hole in the central boss made by a sharp object such as a sword.

Many people have doubted the effectiveness of these bronze shields, believing they were too thin to protect the user, but recent experiments replicating the types and thickness of metal used have shown that in fact they worked quite well. Experiments with wood and leather shields have also shown that they, too, could be effective. Nevertheless, some shields were probably display items, and the more decorated examples may well fall into this category. Highly polished, they would have conferred a degree of highly visible status on a Bronze Age leader. They may also have had a ritual function – the majority of shield finds come from watery locations – rivers, lakes and bogs, where they seem to have been deliberately thrown, as votive offerings, as part of funeral rites, or perhaps as thank-gifts to the gods for victories. As they would have been expensive pieces of kit, their choice as offering would have made the sacrifice all the more meaningful.

Some areas have large amounts of bronze weaponry in such wet deposits – notably the River Thames – 75 per cent of all bronze finds above Teddington are of weapons. There were spearheads, 82 per cent showing heavy use damage such as broken tips, chipped blades and crushing. Five Early Bronze Age daggers and forty-nine Middle Bronze Age dirks and rapiers have also been found, with 86 per cent showing use-wear of a similar type. A number have torn rivet holes, suggesting that they had been used in a slashing action (unsuccessfully?). Some of the dirks were fashioned from cut-down rapiers, a bit of Bronze Age recycling. Some 84 per cent of the swords also showed damage from actual use.

Their deposition in the river may have the same possible explanations as those offered for shields, above. Some of the weapons had been deliberately twisted or broken before they went into the water, perhaps ritually 'killing' them. This could have been an act of display, showing how rich the community was to be able to dispose of so much expensive metalwork, a disposal of weapons taken from enemies that were taboo to use, or they may have accompanied funeral rituals which possibly involved committing the dead (either as a body or as ashes) to the river along with their possessions – 'killing' the weapon may have allowed its spirit to voyage along with that of its owner into the next world. (It is interesting to note that most such deposits come from *east*-flowing rivers; we could compare modern Christian grave orientations which are placed so that the dead would face east on the Day of Resurrection, while these prehistoric funerals would have committed the dead to a river flowing towards the rising sun). The Thames would probably have formed a territorial boundary, and perhaps also a spiritual one – between land and water, life and death.

Body armour does not appear in Britain, although the famous Mold 'cape' – a sheet-gold covering for the shoulders and upper body found in Wales – is similar to a piece from Slovakia made out of bronze and probably intended as armour. There are examples of body armour such as cuirasses, helmets and greaves to protect the shins from Europe, however. Greaves of shaped sheet-bronze are found dating from the Late Middle Bronze Age at Cannes-Ecluse in France.

Duels and champions?
The rapiers, made for thrusting, along with the ornamentation seen on some scabbards from Scandinavia, and the general lack of evidence for any sort of large-scale fighting, had led to the suggestion that in the Early and Middle

Bronze Ages, disputes were settled by duels between champions rather than battles between larger numbers of combatants. This would have fitted in with the notion of heroic challenges and confrontations associated with the ancient Greek world in the minds of scholars trained in classical studies. Certainly, the rapier is not generally considered to be a mêlée weapon, being too thin and slight, and with a point action rather than a cutting or slashing one. The riveted hilts, too, would probably not have stood up to much punishment in such a general fight.

Does this impression stand up to scrutiny? Yes and no. The general lack of evidence for violence suggests either a particularly peaceful era, or one in which alternative means of settling disputes were normal. Yet violence certainly did happen, even if we only have evidence for a limited number of cases. Some rapiers do show damage to the rivets, in some instances with the blade having been torn away from the hilt, suggesting that an attempt had been made to use them less like a fencing weapon and more like a sword.

While arrowheads are found, archery seems to have been on the decline in many parts of Europe during this time, and may only have been retained for hunting purposes by the end of the period – but spears seem to have taken the place of the bow, and many and various types were being developed. The thrusting spear *is* a mêlée weapon, and this suggests that along with duels, larger-scale actions could have taken place, using light and heavy spears, halberds and clubs. Studies of weapons found in various deposits suggest that many of them show signs of damage from actual use, as do some of the bronze shields that have been recovered. The evidence becomes much stronger in the Late Bronze Age, when larger groups of such metalwork appear.

Evidence from settlements suggests that when violence between groups broke out, it tended to do so in the open field rather than within defensive works. Perhaps challenges were made and champions fought duels to decide the issue, or perhaps duels were fought before a more general engagement, for the glory of individual warriors and their bands; however, fights involving larger numbers of people armed with battle weapons rather than duelling weapons must have taken place, and the fitness of the weapons for such larger-scale encounters was steadily improved over the period by the various technological and stylistic changes that we see.

The evidence for so-called 'parade' or 'ceremonial' armour and weaponry seems relatively strong – elaborate scabbards, unsharpened swords and so on – so the notion of a rising elite is attractive. The men who organized the setting out of field systems, who controlled trade and production over increasing areas of land, presumably wanted to look like strong warriors, even if they did not expect actually to fight. And in some places, people were buried with all the accoutrements of a warrior. Could this just have been a symbol simply of social class or status, rather than military prowess? It is clear that we need to know much more about this period, the social and political forces that were developing, and the role of warfare within it.

The end of the Middle Bronze Age was marked by major changes across Europe and the Middle East, not least because of a major climatic turn for the worse. The reasons for and the timing of this change are the subject of much debate among archaeologists, and there are many theories. Major volcanic events have been blamed, like the explosion of the Thera volcano which ended the Minoan civilization, or other volcanic activity in the Indian Ocean, but none of these seems to fit the dates particularly well. One quite persuasive theory suggests that a meteorite may have struck the Atlantic Ocean just off the North African coast, sending up vast clouds of steam and dust particles into the atmosphere. Another suggests major tectonic plate movements causing widespread earthquakes and tsunamis. Whatever the cause, for a number of generations the peoples of Europe and the Middle East were faced with worsening conditions leading to famine and depopulation – and in some cases, probably, to war.

The Late Bronze Age – reactions to crisis
The Late Bronze Age is a period in which weaponry, defensive sites and other evidence for warfare seems to become much clearer. It was also a time of change and consolidation, when social and political boundaries became more evident. The stress caused by the climatic deterioration may well have been a causal factor in this, but there are other possible reasons too. Populations continued to rise, and much of the available land in Europe was being intensively managed and controlled. Wealthy, powerful, even 'princely' elites are visible in the archaeological record, and massive trading, production and settlement centres appeared.

There also seems to have been a rise in the readiness for war – an increase in weapons production and iconography, new forms of defence sometimes imported from the Mediterranean, and relocation of settlements with an eye to defence all occurred.

Fortified or defended villages appear in northern Europe and hilltop settlements became more common. Sometimes settlements were arranged within sight of each other, perhaps for mutual support. All across Europe, fortifications were being erected, in a number of different forms. Massive efforts were expended to create some of these – thousands of man-hours, thousands of trees cut down, hundreds of thousands of cubic metres of soil shifted. People clearly saw a need for protection right across the continent.

The hillforts of the Iron Age are increasingly providing evidence that they were first built in the Late Bronze Age. In Ireland, a number of sites have produced pottery and other artefacts of Late Bronze Age date – Dun Aonghasa on the Aran Islands, for example, although it is thought possible that this extraordinary clifftop enclosure might have served a ritual purpose *(Figure 15)*. In Sweden too, sites have proved to have origins in this period, including Predikstolen near Uppsala, and in Germany reinforced ramparts of timber and stone were being constructed at the Schafberg near Lobau and elsewhere. In Wales, the Breiddin hillfort was constructed on the site of an earlier settlement somewhere between 1000 and 800BC, with houses, storage buildings and smithying contained within the large rampart. Other hillforts in Britain are producing similar evidence.

There are a number of defended hilltop sites that are more securely dated to the Late Bronze Age and have been called 'elite residences'. These include Mam Tor in Derbyshire, Springfield Lyons in Essex, Marshalls Hill and Rams Hill in Berkshire and a number of others, which now have carbon-14 dates giving them a Late Bronze Age identity. At Rams Hill, a box rampart was constructed – a timber frame, faced with posts back and front and filled with earth, with a possible walkway and breastwork on top. A large ditch ran in front of the rampart, separated from it by a short flat berm. Mam Tor was surrounded by a rampart of dumped earth and rock. A box rampart was built

Figure 15. The defended cliff-top site of Dun Aonghasa.

at Dinorben in Wales in the ninth century BC. Over a spread of earlier occupation debris, the rampart consisted of rubble and clay, reinforced with timber 'rafts' behind a palisade with posts set in a trench, and a lower post wall on the inner side, providing a flat 'fighting platform' behind the raised parapet of the outer wall. At Castell Odo in North Wales, a wooden palisade was being constructed when the settlement was burned, possibly during an attack.

In southern England, a form of enclosure called a 'ring-work' is found relatively often, although examples appear in other parts of the country and in Ireland. One such was at the site of Queen Mary's Hospital at Carshalton in Surrey, where a very large V-shaped enclosure ditch was dug, three and a half metres wide and two metres deep, which contained Late Bronze Age material.

Several sites in Scotland have also produced Late Bronze Age dates – Trapain Law, Eildon Hill North and Edinburgh Castle have revealed evidence of occupation, though not of defences.

In France and southern Germany, a number of large forts also began at this time, and a few of these have been excavated in some detail, such as the Heuneberg, Kyberg and Château-sur-Salins. A number of sites are known between the River Main and the River Danube, including some forts set on promontories overlooking the river valleys. The sites that have been studied have produced evidence of occupation from the Middle Bronze Age onwards in many cases. In France, the same picture emerges at sites like Citu and Châtelet-d'Etaules (the latter with a timber box-rampart), and the Hohlandsberg in Alsace, which was surrounded by a dry stone wall.

Sites that were not on hills also began to acquire defences. Even small farmsteads such as Loft's Farm in Essex or Paddock Hill in East Yorkshire were surrounded by substantial ditches and ramparts. Spurs and promontories were also utilised, and protected by cross dykes. In Poland and northern Germany, villages within large palisades also have their origins in the Late Bronze Age. At Altes Schloss, streets three metres wide and probably constructed from wooden planking were lined with rows of timber houses, about thirty in total, as well as storage pits and a well. A clear street ran all around the inside of the enclosing palisade. There are other similar sites in the region of north-east Germany and Poland, many of which clearly survived well into the Iron Age.

The Middle Thames Valley – a case study
Discussion of many of these sites, and those in Europe, centres around the way in which they are arranged across the landscape, suggesting that territories had been formed and the landscape divided up among the builders

of these forts and settlements. This territoriality can be traced in a number of case studies; one in particular looks at the Middle Thames Valley. Work on tracing the field systems of the area seems to show that the farmed land occurred in relatively discrete blocks; this region is particularly rich in depositions of Late Bronze Age metalwork, particularly in the river itself, and has been the subject of a large number of important excavations, as well as the source of many more isolated finds of artefacts. Large-scale gravel extraction, and a great deal of new building works for industry, housing and Heathrow Airport, have given archaeologists the opportunity to investigate many sites, and it is possible now to stand back a little and look at the larger picture that a combination of these researches is beginning to give.

What emerges is that whilst there were no large single towns or villages at this time, there are several agglomerations of smaller settlements which are sited very close to each other – around the confluence of the Thames and Kennet rivers near Reading, around Windsor and Eton, and around Heathrow and Staines *(Figure 16)*. Some of these farmsteads were sited less than half a kilometre from each other. Other examples can be discerned in the Lower Thames area as well, for example around Mucking in Essex. Middle Bronze Age settlements and cemeteries have been found on the upper river terraces, especially to the south and west of the valley, but these were apparently abandoned in favour of a move into the valley bottom in the Late Bronze Age.

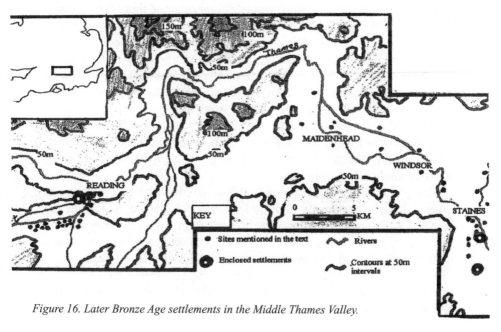

Figure 16. Later Bronze Age settlements in the Middle Thames Valley.

Farmsteads and small hamlets were built on the gravel islands, some only just above the water level, and presumably these became actual islands during the winters or in periods of heavy rainfall, as the rivers spread across the floodplain. This was not, on the face of it, a particularly comfortable or healthy living environment. There is very little evidence of arable farming except for the growing of flax, but plenty for stock farming – droveways, waterholes and so on. These agglomerations grew surprisingly large – a very conservative estimate, based on the number of houses so far discovered, for the population of the Kennet–Reading group suggests around 400 people were living there – and probably a great many more houses might be found were more sites to be excavated. Similar figures are found for the Staines–Perry Oaks–Heathrow group. We tend to think of settlements at this period as consisting of just one or two extended families, so these numbers are significant. This is also an area where a very large number of bronze weapons have been found – swords, spearheads, axes and shields – some in the rivers and some in hoards.

In between these large settlement groups, there seems to be unoccupied land where, despite much investigation, settlements and artefacts are rare. Presumably this land was used – for grazing, perhaps, but not actually lived on. To the west of the area, the valley is crossed by a major (undated) earthwork, called the Grim's Ditch. This seems to have been some sort of cut-off point – pottery found to the west of the dyke is generally different from pottery found to the east of it. The impression is of a frontier, although we cannot be sure the earthwork was in existence at the time. If the Grim's Ditch is, as some have suggested, from the Dark Ages, it is still possible that it marked a territorial boundary that was much older. A number of enclosed sites are recorded east of Grim's Ditch such as Mayfield Farm, Thorpe Lea and Perry Oaks, as well as the 'elite' site at Marshall's Hill, and at Runnymede Bridge there was a large site with what appears to have been a defensive or controlled riverside palisade structure.

Why did people abandon their earlier homes, cemeteries and farms to move down into a damp, often misty, river bottom, and start to crowd their settlements together? There are a number of possible explanations, any or all of which might be possible.

Firstly – trade. Artefacts found in this area, particularly at Runnymede Bridge, demonstrate major trade links down the Thames to continental Europe. Finds here included artefacts from the Rhine valley, Switzerland and the Eastern Alps. It is possible that the communities of the river were controlling trade, and perhaps gaining much of their wealth from extracting tolls from traders and profits from customers further away.

Secondly – climate change. If the worsening climatic conditions meant that grain was not ripening in the fields, stock farming would have become a viable alternative here, as it was in Wessex, where long 'ranch boundaries' were constructed over the earlier field systems. The river valley, with its rich meadows, was and is still prime dairy country, the decline in milk production in the area only really occurring after the Second World War as more land was taken for building development. Dairy and beef farming might have become a more reliable source of food in the poor weather conditions.

Thirdly – aggression. The enclosures, the presence of outlying defended settlements such as Thorpe Lea to the southwest, and the amount of weaponry present suggest that people were prepared for defence. The siting of the settlements in the valley floor may have meant that they were hard to access for much of the year, and their closeness to each other would have allowed audible warning signals to be sounded. This is especially true of the Kennet–Reading group of sites, where the shape of the valley allows sound to travel extraordinarily well (although nowadays, the roar of the motorway, the railway and the aircraft overhead make this hard to appreciate).

If defence was the main reason for these settlement sitings, who were they defending against? Possibly each other – that would serve to explain the apparent 'no-go' areas between them. And possibly against their neighbours to the west and or south. Beyond the Grim's Ditch, the land rises to the edge of the Berkshire Downs, and here, on the eastward-facing spurs, we find a number of promontory defensive sites also dating, where the date is known, to the Late Bronze Age. It is notable that the Thames-side settlements tend to face southwest, and the stronger sites such as Thorpe Lea are sited in that general direction or with viewsheds towards the west.

People living on the abandoned Middle Bronze Age terrace sites would not have been able to see anyone coming from the south or west due to the rising land behind them. Did the people begin to feel too vulnerable to surprise attacks from those directions? Were the westerly neighbours jealous of the trade wealth coming into the valley? Were they likely to mount raids from south or west on the villages? None of the Thames-side sites is obviously protected on their north or eastern sides – clearly no problems were anticipated from that direction.

We have very little skeletal evidence from these sites, and no clear evidence for war, but in the absence of other good reasons for these shifts in settlement locations and their gathering together in close, possibly protective, proximity, we might be allowed to suggest that warfare could have been a possibility here in this period, or at least that people were prepared to meet aggressive actions from outside the valley.

By the Early Iron Age period between 700 and 600BC, most of the Middle Thames settlements seem to have been abandoned, but we do not know why. The climate was improving, but the Thames valley is rich land, and it seems odd that it should not be utilised fully. Villages begin to appear south of the river, along the various tributaries, by the Middle Iron Age, perhaps in response to emerging political groupings. This is an area of the past which still requires a great deal more work to be properly understood.

Elsewhere in Britain and Europe, there is more evidence for the possibility of war – in the form of weapons and armour, and evidence from the bodies of the slain. There are also forms of pictorial material, which for the most part are not found in the earlier centuries of the Bronze Age.

Chapter 5

The Rise of War

The weather had turned awful – the summers were short and chilly, the winters long and wet. The crops rotted in the fields, and in the uplands, peat and bogs began to form over what were once fields and gardens. Eventually, decisions had to be made. In some places, the fields and crops were abandoned in favour of cattle and sheep runs; in others, whole settlements were left deserted and the inhabitants tried to move elsewhere. People went hungry unless they could adapt. Inevitably, some people turned to violence to get what they needed. In response, more and more villages began to build defences, and warriors became important. In some places, people moved together for protection, creating new centres within protective ramparts. New weapons and armour were developed, as the warriors sought to become more effective; old customs and rituals had to be abandoned. Perhaps people had lost faith, or perhaps the effort to maintain the older ways became too great compared to the effort to survive in this changed world. No one knew why the climate was so much worse than in their grandparents' day, nor did they know if better conditions would ever return. So they armed themselves and struggled on, seeking new contacts, new trade, and new ideas to help them survive.

Sites and trauma in the Late Bronze Age

Evidence for aggression in the Late Bronze Age can be found in skeletons. At Tormarton, in the Cotswolds, the bodies of several men were discovered during the digging of a gas pipeline. The oldest man, aged around thirty-five, had been stabbed in the back with a spear that had gone on to puncture his pelvis. The same had happened to one of the younger men – the bronze spearhead had been rammed so hard into his body that it had stuck into the bone; he had also been stabbed in the back and his spinal cord had been severed. He may have been finished off by a further spear blow to his head. The bodies had been thrown without ceremony into a ditch. Further investigations at the site found the partial remains of other men and a child in the V-shaped ditch, at least 70 metres long, that had then been quickly filled in with large blocks of stone, possibly from part of a rampart behind the ditch. It is possible that the ditch was a territorial marker, one that other individuals objected to, leading them to attack the builders.

This occurred at the very end of the Middle Bronze Age or start of the Late Bronze Age – around 1300 to 1000BC. Territorial divisions of ditches and banks are also evident on Dartmoor and elsewhere in the southwest from this period or earlier. On Dartmoor, a system of 'reaves' – stone and earthwork boundaries – divided up the farmlands into parcels relating to separate settlements and valleys. In a time of poor weather conditions, boundaries must have become very important, as people sought to delineate and protect the land they relied on for their survival. By the end of the Bronze Age, conditions had become so bad that peat was forming over the previous farmland on the western moors, making agriculture impossible, and the Dartmoor villages had to be abandoned.

Further skeletal evidence from Britain for violence in this period comes from Dorchester-on-Thames, where another spearhead was found snapped off in the pelvis of an individual of unknown gender. In County Armagh, at Drumman More Lake, some 200 years ago, a human skull was found with a socketed Late Bronze Age dagger embedded in it. There are a number of sites that suggest that a head cult, or head hunting, might have been practised at this time, something which the Romans assert went on later in the Iron Age in France. Skulls have been found in the River Thames, many of them from young men, and disarticulated skulls have been found at Billingborough in Lincolnshire that had been made into cups – the top of the cranium had been sawn off – and the same may be true in Leicestershire near the River Soar, where cut marks suggested the individual had been decapitated and the skull left with animal bones including a horse skull at a 'burnt mound' site.

'Burnt mound' is the name given to enigmatic heaps of burned stone, often found near rivers or other water sources, which have been variously identified at ritual sites, sites for funeral pyres, saunas, cooking places or even (in southern Ireland) as Bronze Age microbreweries!

In 'Sculptor's Cave', on the Moray Firth, a group of human cervical vertebrae that date to the Late Bronze Age have been found in a cavern used right up into the later Dark Ages. Some of the decapitated people here were children, and the suggestion has been made that their skulls were displayed at the cave's entrance and on its walls in some form of ritual 'temple'.

Further trauma is recorded in Europe – at Over Vindinge an older man had a spearhead embedded in his body, but had apparently survived for some time afterwards. Another spearhead was stuck into the spine of a person found in a cave known as the Grotte du Pas de Joulie Trèves near Aveyron, and there is an individual with the tip of a flint arrowhead embedded in bone that probably dates from the Bronze Age at Hogeloon in the Netherlands. In general, however, there is very little weapons trauma recorded in Europe, partly due to the widespread practice of cremation at this time, which makes identification difficult.

At Tollense in Northern Germany, however, evidence of a massacre has appeared. A great many human and animal (mainly horse) bones have been found over time in the area, and in 2008 a major excavation programme was begun. Previous finds had included human bones with evidence of weapons trauma, arrowheads and spearheads, and a wooden club, which had turned up over a number of years in this area. The new excavations found even more – another two wooden clubs, one of which resembles a baseball bat and was made of ash, and another made of blackthorn which has a mallet shape *(Figure 17)*. These were found within a metre of so of each other.

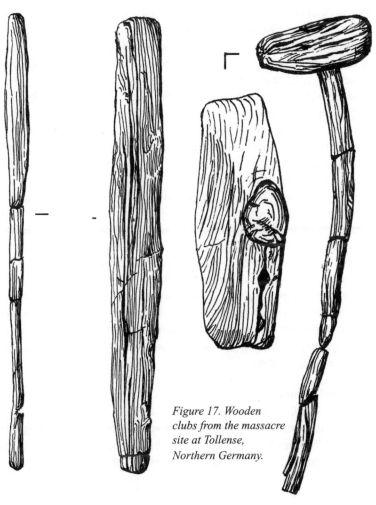

Figure 17. Wooden clubs from the massacre site at Tollense, Northern Germany.

More flint arrowheads were also discovered, and the bones of about 100 people have been excavated so far. Most of the bones belonged to young men between the ages of twenty and forty, but there were also the remains of some children and young women. A number of the remains showed evidence of traumatic injuries – blows to the skull, and arrow and spear wounds. Some people had healed, or partially healed, trauma that had occurred earlier, sometimes only a day or two before they died, sometimes weeks before. One person had a broken leg, perhaps caused by a fall from a horse. It was possible to establish that a large number of the injuries observed had happened very shortly before death.

The bones had been scattered over a distance of some 1.5 kilometres by the flood waters of the river. The area of the discovery had been open woodland at the time these people died, but close enough to farmland where cereal crops and flax were growing for the pollen from these crops to have spread. The local inhabitants owned a relatively large amount of imported bronze objects, and built burial mounds for their dead. Several Late Bronze Age settlements are known in the area, and like the people in Britain, they may have been suffering as a result of the climate change.

The events at Tollense are thought by the excavators to have taken place over a period of several weeks around 1230BC. The violence that had occurred had involved longer-range attack with bows, and close combat with spears and clubs, and some of the fighting may also have involved horses. There was no evidence of axes or swords, and the excavators are clear that this was not a dueling form of warfare.

We do not know who was doing the killing, and who was being killed, but it seems likely that the victims were migrants. It was possible to establish that some of them had eaten millet, a crop not often found in north Germany in this period, and there were also finds of bronze pins that are of a type usually found 400 kilometres to the southeast of Tollense.

Perhaps the local farmers decided that these incomers represented a threat to their own livelihoods, already stressed by the change in weather patterns, and they reacted to their presence violently. They were not prepared to accept incursions into their territory by outsiders and so went on the attack, slaughtering many of the migrants and driving the survivors out over a period of a few weeks or months.

Weapons and Armour
Defensive armour becomes a more common find during this period. Shields are often found in the Late Bronze Age in some areas – some ninety have been found in Europe as a whole, more than half from the British Isles. There is a variety of materials and forms – wooden and leather shields which are

known from Ireland, along with heavy cast-bronze shields and thinner bronze shields that possibly were backed by organic formers. The Yetholm type of shield dates from between 1200 and 800BC, and most of the known examples come from the British Isles, with one exception found in Denmark. Three of the twenty-two known surviving examples were found in a peat bog called Yetholm in Scotland, mentioned in Chapter 4.

They are circular, with a decoration of concentric rings of small bosses and rings and a central domed boss. Similar shields are shown in rock carvings from Sweden. They are made of a bronze alloy of copper and 11–14 per cent tin, and are generally about 0.6mm thick, with a folded strengthened rim. The decorative bosses were made by hammering from the back of the shield. The largest example was found in Ayrshire, with twenty-nine rings and twenty-nine circular arrangements of bosses, while the smallest, which was found near Molesey in the River Thames, had just eleven sets of rings and bosses. This shield measured 63.8cm in diameter, and the metal is 0.5mm thick, weighing 1.484kg. A riveted grip was fixed behind the central boss, and there are two holes in the body of the shield which are thought to be places to attach a strap so that the shield could be carried on the warrior's back when not in use. A late example, with a diameter of 72cm and dated to around 700BC, was found in a bog at Lough Gur in Co. Antrim.

There is no indication that these shields were reinforced with wood or any other material. It has been said that these shields would have been useless in combat, being too thin to withstand a blow. However, this belief is partly based on an experimental reconstruction made largely of copper, which was indeed easily destroyed; but tin bronze is not copper – other experiments have suggested that in fact these shields could have functioned adequately. The handles are quite small, and again this is said to make them awkward to use, but no proper experimentation has confirmed this opinion.

An example of this type of shield was found at South Cadbury in Somerset, where it had been placed in a ditch in the mid-tenth century BC. This shield had been deliberately stabbed with a wooden stake, a 'ritual killing' of the object. It is unusual to find a shield in a 'dry' context; most shield finds have been made in watery places – pools, bogs and rivers, suggesting they had a great deal of value as ritual offerings as well as status symbols for the living. The making of these shields would have been a costly and time-consuming process, with up to 200 repeated sessions of annealing, quenching and hammering, to prevent the metal becoming too brittle.

The original blank is unlikely to have been any larger than 19cm across. Each hammering session would have stretched the metal by just one or two millimetres, involving hours of work and large amounts of fuel for the annealing fire. This would therefore not have been a piece of equipment available to everybody, but must have been reserved for just the richest and most powerful warriors.

The Nipperweise form of shield is represented in Britain by an example from the River Thames near Long Wittenham in Oxfordshire. It was made of sheet-bronze, and has concentric raised ridges and a central round boss. Wear on the reverse of this shield proves that the user was right-handed, and carried the shield in his left hand. It had two loops on the rear to attach a suspension strap. Actual weapons damage has been seen on the shield. Two or three diamond-shaped holes are visible, thought to have been made by spearheads, and other such holes had previously been hammered closed, suggesting the shield had been used in a number of fights. One other English Nipperweise shield is known, as well as four from Germany and a single example from Poland.

A rare leather shield was found in a peat bog at Clonbrin in Co. Longford and may date from the thirteenth century BC. It was found in nearly perfect condition, having been preserved by the tanning action of the peat. It had been made of vegetable-tanned hide (probably ox hide), and had seen some action. The boss was protected with a double cap, sewn on to strengthen and protect the hand. Experimental trials with an exact replica showed how very well shields of this type could perform – neither sword nor spear succeeded in piercing the shield fatally.

Wooden shields have been found in Germany, the one from Mehrstetten carrying a decoration of bronze studs set in a cross shape, as well as a number of bronze examples. No shields have yet been found in France, although representations of them have been found in rock carvings. A stone stela from Substantion in Hérault shows a warrior surrounded by what seem to be chariot wheels, a spearhead, and a notched shield. Shields with a notched top are known from other places and periods – the point of the notch is apparently to allow the warrior to see past the shield more easily.

The depiction of shields in Swedish rock carvings also suggests a ritual as well as a military use for them. Large deposits of bronze shields have been found in Scandinavia, such as the seventeen that were placed in a lake not far from Stockholm during the Nordic Bronze Age between 1500BC and 500BC. In some rock carvings, the shields appeared to be held by dancers, often aboard ships, and it has been suggested that the round shields doubled up as a symbol for the sun *(Figure 18)*. Similar shield-shaped carvings have been found in Britain – for example in Northumberland – and groups of 'rosettes' and concentric circles may have a similar symbolic meaning. Sun or wheel symbols are very common in art across northern Europe at this time, as well as a symbol resembling a small duck or goose, called the waterbird symbol.

Figure 18. Shields in Scandinavian rock art.

A solar chariot was found at Trundholm in Denmark. It is a six-wheeled bronze model wagon which carries a model bronze horse, and a large bronze disc, 25cm in diameter, gilded on one side, and decorated with concentric circles and zigzag borders. The gilded side probably represents the sun, and the ungilded side might have been intended to represent the moon. Another recent circular find from Saxony-Anhalt is the Nebra 'sky disc', a 30cm round bronze disc on which have been inlaid a series of gold symbols – a probable sun and a moon, groups of gold discs possibly representing star constellations, and arcs marking the angle between the solstices *(Plate 7)*. At the bottom is another gold plaque thought to represent a sky boat. The tin and the gold used in this artefact, which may date from as early as 1600BC, were both found on analysis to have come from Cornwall.

This, and the waterbird symbols, suggest that water transport as well as wheeled transport were important to communities at this time in a ritual sense but also, surely, in a very practical way. A series of recent finds of Bronze Age boats demonstrates that in this period, river and ocean travel were common. As well as the well-known example from Dover, boats have been found at Ferriby on the Humber, Caldicot in south Wales and Brigg in Lincolnshire, and the remains of wrecks have been discovered by underwater archaeology at Langdon Bay and Salcombe. A possible port existed at Mount Batten in Devon. There is also evidence for an increase in the use of horses for riding as well as possibly for traction, at least for the wagons of the upper classes. This may have implications for warfare, a topic that will be returned to later.

Most of the Swedish rock carvings that show shields depict warriors with helmets (some horned) and swords or axes, and generally show combat between two or three people at most. Some have thought that this confirms the impression of Bronze Age 'champion duels' rather than larger-scale combats, but we must be very wary of making such an assumption. The artist may have been using the pair of warriors to symbolise a battle in a more general sense, a kind of shorthand for a battle scene that would have been appreciated as such by his audience. On the other hand, the rock art may depict legendary combats between gods or ancient heroes, a story-telling device rather than an account of real life.

Other forms of personal armour are also known. Helmets of a whole variety of designs have been discovered or are represented in art. They have the same general geographical distribution as shields, and are also usually found in watery contexts. Perhaps the most famous are the horned helmets from Viksø in Denmark, which have been dated to 1000–900BC. The two bronze helmets were made by cold hammering two sheets each of bronze, which were then riveted together. A cross-shaped piece with a raised crest and a hooked beak was added to the crown, the crest being grooved to hold perhaps feathers or a mane of hair along the main front to back line, with two further fittings for similar decoration on either side of it. Two large bosses surmounted by crescents on the front form bulging eyes and eyebrows. Further smaller bosses add decoration over the surface of the piece. Two large horns are riveted to the top of each helmet, curving like the horns of an ox or aurochs, with knobbed finials on the ends *(Plate 8)*.

Such helmets are depicted in art – in the rock carvings and on small bronze figurines such as those from Grevensvænge, which depict kneeling figures holding axes, as does a razor from Vestrup in Denmark. Horned helmets in rock carvings like those from Sotetorp in Bohuslän are also worn by men holding axes and wearing swords, and sitting in a boat. They are holding round objects in their hands – perhaps shields, or sun symbols. The Viksø helmets also carry small designs on either side that resemble boats, with a waterbird symbol on the prow of each. These may be solar ships, like the depiction on the Nebra sky disc. Thus these helmets contain all the symbolism of this period – the sun boat, the power of the ox, the waterbird, the mane of the horse which pulls the sun ship on the Trundholm 'sun chariot', and the beaked owl or hawk of war.

The helmets remind us how difficult it is to separate pragmatic military usage from ritual and religion in prehistoric times. How easy it would have been to wear such helmets into battle is another issue. They would seem heavy and unwieldy objects, and may have been more ceremonial than practical, although they may also have been designed to affect the morale of both supporters and enemies, adding extra height and ferocious appearance to the wearer.

Other types of helmet appear in Germany and France *(Figure 19)*. Conical and bell-shaped helmets have been found at several sites including Beitzch

Figure 19. Some European Bronze Age helmets.

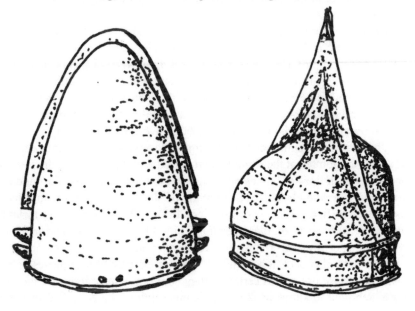

and Sehlstorf, and crested helmets occur at Lesum and other places, while simple cap helmets have been found at Mainz, Thonsberg and Wonsheim in Germany, and in France crested helmets have been unearthed at, among other places, Auxonne, Paris and Armancourt, and cap-type helmets at Mantes. At Bernières d'Ailly, a hoard of nine helmets placed together in groups of three was found.

Only one of these helmets has damage that might have been caused by battle – the cap helmet from Wonsheim, which has marks possibly caused by blows. Most of the known helmets are of relatively thin metal, and many have small holes that may have allowed the attachment of a lining of thick cloth or other protection for the head. A single find of a cap made of thick layers of stitched cloth was found in the oak coffin of a man discovered at Muldbjerg in Denmark, and this might also have served as a kind of helmet or head protection, or been the cap worn under a metal helmet. A Late Bronze Age helmet from Hungary has damage caused by blows, and it is probable that the inside of this helmet was lined with leather and textile attached via rivet holes around the base. The helmet is much too big for any normal head – it could only fit if it was well padded.

Large complex spiral armrings found in Central Europe have been assumed to be male jewellery; they are often found alongside swords. There are two types – those with inward spiralling rings to be worn on the wrist, and one, much larger type with flatter rings for the upper arm. It is suggested that these were in fact forms of armour, the one protecting the hand and the other the elbow.

Greaves, some richly decorated, to protect the legs, are known from Kloštar Ivanić in Croatia but also from Germany and France (at Cannes-Ecluse for example). Bronze cuirasses (breastplates) have also been found – in fragments at Albstadt-Pfeffingen in Germany, and complete examples from Saint Germain du Plain and Marmesse in the Haute Marne in France, nine being found placed one inside the other at the latter site (see Figure 23 for a contemporary statue showing a cuirass being worn by a warrior).

The Marmesse cuirasses have been dated to the eighth or ninth century BC; these are jointed at the shoulder and closed with hooks. The cuirasses are decorated with lines of bosses outlining the contours of the body around the arms and over the chest. They are made of sheet bronze, and would have looked magnificent in their original condition, although how comfortable they were to wear is another question. They, like the greaves and helmets, were almost certainly worn on top of leather or padded linings or gambesons.

There are also occasional finds of smaller circular bronze pieces called phalerae whose use is less certain – they commonly have loops on the rear for attachment to straps or fabric. In Roman times, objects called phalerae were worn on breastplates as military decorations, but these prehistoric examples may have been worn on the chest as a form of protection, could have taken the place of a shield boss or, more likely, were part of horse harness. The four attaching loops often found would suggest that the object could have been mounted on the chest of a horse as a form of shield for the animal. They are generally much smaller than the shields themselves – about 20–23cm in diameter. The tombstone of a Roman soldier called Vonatrix, found in Bonn, shows a number of these phalerae mounted on leather harness straps around the chest and body of the horse, where they form both decoration and a certain measure of protection, and there is no reason to suppose they could not have been used in a similar fashion a thousand years earlier. Indeed, horses shown on the Gundestrup cauldron, which will be mentioned in more detail later, seem to be wearing harness with round attachments on the withers and chest that might well be phalerae *(Figure 22)*.

Swords developed in many different forms in the Late Bronze Age. This was the era in which the true sword came into its own, with its origins in the Early and Middle Bronze Age rapiers and dirks, but now becoming a stronger and more versatile weapon. It is probable that the sword was, like the helmets and bronze shields, reserved for people of a certain status in Late Bronze Age society – swords were expensive articles which took careful and lengthy construction. That they were used in combat seems clear, however; a study of Irish swords has shown that 90 per cent have damage consistent with fighting, and swords from the Thames have similar amounts of use-wear damage.

Swords of this period range in length from 50 to 90cm and blades were produced with different shapes implying new kinds of fighting. A widely distributed form in Britain and in Europe is the Rosnoën sword, with its rectangular tang, small or absent shoulders and straight blade. Dating from 1350–1200BC, it is believed that this form of sword was imported into Britain from northwestern France, where large numbers have been found. Ballintober swords are another early form used between 1300–1150BC; these are a British form which are found particularly in the Thames valley, although they also occur in Ireland and France. They have similar hilts to the Rosnoën swords, but with larger, pointed, shoulders. They have leaf-shaped blades that are ridged.

Leaf-shaped blades are fairly common; the Hemigkofen form came into use between 1200–1100BC and had a high-flanged hilt and large rivet holes on the shoulders and hilt. The Erbenheim form is slightly later (1150–1050BC) and is longer, with a narrow leaf shape and large shoulders. Swords with solid cast hilts are less common in Britain (three of the four known being found in Cumbria) and these also have heavy, straight blades and tapering shoulders.

107

The Cumbrian swords may have been a local hybrid form of the Riegsee-type sword, combining continental sword forms with local dirk and rapier types.

A later form is the Wilburton sword, dating to around 1000–900BC, with a number of local variants. The hilts of these swords flare out and the blades are again leaf-shaped. The Rixheim swords appear around 1000BC; these have narrow blades, and are thought to be a development from the Rosnoën forms. Swords of the Ewart Park phase, 950–800BC, are found across Britain, but once again particularly in the Thames valley. The blade is narrow at the shoulders, then widens out midway into a curved bulge, and this form appears to be a British development. By the eighth century BC, the 'carp's tongue' shape appeared – a wide parallel blade which narrows into a thrusting tip about three-quarters of the way down – and this possibly also originated in northwestern France. The blades have a midrib with grooves on either side, and the hilts are often finished in a T-shape.

Gündlingen swords have a more westerly distribution in Britain, and date to 800–600BC. They are like the Ewart Park forms with wide hilts and short broad shoulders, and long narrow blades with grooves. The hilts were probably finished with bone or wooden plates and pommels *(Figure 20)*.

Figure 20. Some Late Bronze Age sword forms (top–bottom): Middle Bronze Age rapier, Wilburton sword, Hemigkofen sword, Carp's Tongue sword, Gundlingen sword.

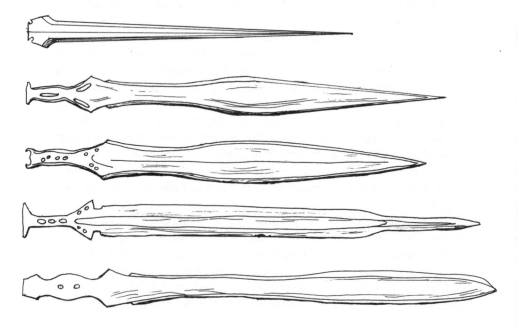

The casting technology that created these swords was highly advanced and skilful. This was truly 'cutting edge' technology! The swords were cast at the maximum possible length, some over 24 inches long, and were finished extremely finely. Later swords have an alloy mixture of 8–9 per cent tin and 1–3 per cent lead, the lead possibly being used to make the cast flow more smoothly. They were cast through the handle, a very difficult process when the hilts were designed to be thin and small. Early rapiers were cast from stone moulds, as were spearheads, but by the Late Bronze Age two-layer clay moulds were used, and the fragments of these are sometimes found. It is suggested that the two parts of the mould were covered in a layer of clay to hold them together during the casting. This was a very tricky process, requiring much experience and knowledge; each casting destroys the mould, unlike the reusable stone moulds.

The sword then had to be finished – the 'flashing', or stray fringe of metal along the edges, must be cleaned off, as well as the metal from the pouring point. Neil Burridge, an expert in bronze casting, has pointed out that Bronze Age swords are almost never symmetrical – each one is slightly different, and most have some minor misalignment. The blade is then ground and polished, with the tip being finished properly. The edges must then be forged – the outer three millimetres or so hammered down to a thin sharp finish. After that the handles must be made and riveted on. The whole process takes many hours of painstaking work.

Fragments of a Wilburton period sword mould found at Sigwells in Somerset were able to be refitted to a sword in Taunton Museum that had itself been found 25 miles to the north in the nineteenth century! The Sigwells find also included mould fragments for casting a socketed spear and a socketed axe. Other mould fragments have been found in Britain and Ireland, notably at the Rathgall hillfort, County Wicklow, where some 400 mould fragments for swords, spearheads and axes have been excavated. Sword moulds have also been found in Germany and Northern Italy.

An innovation in the Late Bronze Age was the introduction of the ricasso, a modification below the hilt – this is a length of unsharpened blade, the purpose of which is unclear. It might have allowed the user to extend his hand grip, or even use two hands on the hilt, to give greater force or direction control to the blow.

These swords could be used either as slashing or thrusting weapons, and were more effective and stronger than the preceding rapiers. Later swords tend towards the slashing function, suggesting a change in ways of fighting by the end of the Bronze Age. Their points were blunter and rounded. It has been noted that often the hilts of these swords became bent as a result of slashing actions, even leading to the hilt breaking off. This suggests frequent use of the weapons. In Denmark, swords with curving single-edged blades have been found, that could not have been used in a thrusting manner at all. Only three of these have been discovered, two at Rørby in Zealand, one of which carries an incised picture of a ship, the earliest known depiction of such a vessel in Denmark.

Another form of sword that has its origin in the Bronze Age is known as Naue II, a form whose use lasted well into the Iron Age, and was later copied in iron. These swords vary between 50 and 85cm long, and usually have straight sides narrowing to a point, allowing them to be used for both thrusting and slashing. They are found at first in Central Europe, Scandinavia and Britain, but later spread into the Eastern Mediterranean and Levant.

A unique find was made near Groatsetter or Grotsetter on Orkney. It is based on the Ewart Park type of sword, 70cm in length – but carved from yew wood. No yews have ever grown on Orkney, so the sword, or the wood, was imported from further south. Carbon dating puts this object at 900–815BC. It had clearly been highly valued – there were signs of careful polishing and decorative carving near the hilt. It had been well used – the blade was in excellent condition, but the hilt was quite worn and had lost its pommel. The fact that no damage seems to have occurred to the blade suggests that this weapon was not used in anger, so could it have been used for practice, or as a pattern for making bronze copies?

Neither of these explanations holds water – practice sessions would have surely damaged the blade sometimes, and there are no known exact copies of this sword in existence in bronze (and such copies would have been extremely heavy and difficult to use). So it may have been either a status or a ritual symbol – marking the importance of an individual who did not have access to sufficient bronze on Orkney to have a real version – or simply been an object of religious significance because of its form rather than its function.

There are many other sword types, some very local and some widespread in their distribution, that combine features such as flanged hilts, grooves, shoulders and so on in different ways – this is a very specialised area of research, and the list given above is only sufficient to give a flavour of the variety that was available at different times in the Late Bronze Age. The distribution of swords across northern Europe shows some regional differences; they are most common (in terms of numbers found to area) in Ireland, Denmark and north Germany, relatively less common in Britain and in France. Swords with a full metal hilt are most common in Denmark and north Germany, but are rare in Britain and absent in Ireland, where the hilts were of organic materials (wood or bone). Scabbards and chapes (metal pieces attached to the base of a scabbard to stop the sword from piercing the bottom) are also found. Some of the scabbard plates are highly decorated, especially from southern and eastern Europe.

The sword appears to have been a status weapon, not available to the average fighter, because of the expensive and lengthy process of manufacture. More common is the spear, and here there are a bewildering number of variant shapes and sizes. Some spears were designed for throwing, and might also therefore be called javelins or lances, while others are heavier and were apparently used like a pole-arm, for close-quarter thrusting, more like an assegai. Spears can, of course, be used as hunting weapons, but the sheer number of these weapons and their associations would suggest that combat was a primary reason for their manufacture. A study of spearheads discovered in the Thames found that 82 per cent of them had some sort of use damage – notches, broken tips – that probably occurred in actual fighting. One or two examples also seem to have been of a 'ceremonial' rather than purely functional type, such as the 70cm-long spearhead found in the River Wandle near Croydon in Surrey.

At the start of the Late Bronze Age, many spearheads found in Britain are leaf-shaped, with peg-holes to secure them to their shafts. Both hollow and solid cast forms were made. The base of the spearhead is socketed, and the blades typically have a central spine, with or without parallel grooves running down to the tip. Some spearheads have side or basal loops to secure the hafting or pierced sections at the base of the blade, and some have complex stepped profiles. Spearheads with barbs appeared in the Late Bronze Age in southern Britain, although some of these seem to have been too thin to be used effectively, and may have been a ceremonial form.

The shafts very rarely survive at all, and not to their original length, so it is impossible to be sure how long they were. However, the Tormarton skeletons mentioned earlier show how devastating a weapon the spear could be. Arrows are extremely rare finds by the Late Bronze Age, and it seems that archery had gone out of fashion, perhaps replaced by the spear, in all its forms.

Martial music and art
One additional type of find is associated with warfare in this period – the lur. A lur is a cast bronze S-shaped curving trumpet; most have been found in Denmark (thirty-nine so far) but they are also present in Sweden, northern Germany and Norway. Danish lurs are usually found in pairs in bog deposits, such as the three pairs found at Brudevælte Mose in North Zealand. Each horn has a small mouthpiece, and a body between one and a half and two or more metres long, tapering outwards towards the bell end that is mounted with a circular flat plate decorated with large bosses. It is possible that reeds

were used in the mouthpiece to alter the tone. The Brudevælte Mose lurs have been dated to 800–700BC, and are still playable. Some specialists believe that these were war horns, although others think that their tone was too muted for such a purpose. War horns certainly appear in the following Iron Age, however, so these may be ancestors of the type.

The Late Bronze Age is also a period when iconographic depictions of warriors become more common across Europe. In Scandinavia, rock carvings depict many aspects of normal and ritual life, as well as symbols whose meaning is unknown. There are circular indentations called cup-marks, spirals, circles, wheels, boats, ploughs, wagons, nets and traps, animals, people and weapons. The more than 1,500 examples of rock art of Northern Bohuslän have been dated to 1800–500BC. Similar rock carvings have been found in Norway, Denmark and in other parts of Sweden. The carvings depict axes, swords, spears, clubs and bows, as well as horned helmets and shields. The thickened legs of some figures have been considered by some to represent the wearing of greaves. Some warriors thus armed are depicted in ships, while others stand alone or in groups of two or three. A more complex scene was found at Tegneby which appears to show a number of armed warriors on horseback, carrying spears and rectangular shields (?) in a confrontational situation *(Figure 21)*. Many articles have been written about the apparently ritual nature of such carvings, doubting that they illustrate real warfare. However, the details strongly suggest that the people of Bronze Age Scandinavia knew and used such weapons and armour in conflicts aboard ships, on horseback or face to face. The carvings may have been made as

Figure 21. Rock carving from Tegneby depicting a battle.

part of a ritual, but the familiarity of the content tells us that battles were a feature of life.

Britain lacks such representational rock art, although there may be a case for reinterpreting some of the circular and labyrinth forms found in Northumberland and elsewhere – could lines of concentric circles be symbols for shields, and therefore conflict?

Rock art has also been found in the Alps and Iberia. A particular Alpine form from northern Italy and Switzerland is the statue-menhir, but there are also carvings of axes, halberds, spears, shields and swords at sites at Valcamonica and Valtellina, dateable to the Bronze Age because of the distinctive shapes of the weapons. One statue-menhir from Sion-Petit Chasseur in Switzerland appears to be wearing a padded corselet and a baldric or sword harness slung across the body. There may also be an indication of a helmet. Most other martial rock art of the period comes from Mediterranean lands, particularly Iberia, where 'warrior stelae' are found, containing depictions of axes and daggers.

In East Yorkshire, a discovery made in 1836 by labourers cleaning a ditch at Roos Carr found a number of carved wooden figures made of yew, 35–41cm high with quartzite eyes, a curving boat, shields and other items 'too much decayed to remove'. A number of the objects were eventually given to a museum in Hull, one being somewhat delayed in being donated as one of the people viewing the discovery had apparently given the 'ancient doll' to his daughter to play with!

A reconstruction was attempted in the nineteenth century, glueing some of the figures into the boat, and attaching arms, shields and paddles wherever they seemed to be appropriate. This has now been reversed, and the heavy glues and varnishes used by the Victorian conservators have been removed. Details of differences between the five figures in existence suggest that there were originally two boats with crews of four figures. Pieces originally thought to be arms have now been identified as penises and reattached in the proper place. The pieces have been dated to the Late Bronze Age or Early Iron Age. Nine other surviving similar carvings are known from Britain and Ireland, only one being clearly female. The presence with the Roos Carr figures of the shields, and holes in the (real) arms that may have been to insert spears, strongly suggests that these figures represent armed ship-borne raiding parties, reminiscent of some of the Scandinavian scenes.

Forms of war in the Late Bronze Age
The Scandinavian rock carvings *(Plate 4)*, the weapons and armour, the Roos Carr figures, the siting of settlements in relation to rivers and hills – all these suggest the types of warfare that may have happened. Sea-borne raiders

certainly seem a strong possibility, roaming the coasts of the North and Baltic seas, landing at isolated villages and plundering them. Such activities were certainly not restricted to the Viking period – there are even tales of such raiders in the eastern Mediterranean in the Later Bronze Age. The Egyptians and others recorded the raids of the Sea Peoples, as they called them, a confederacy of piratical raiders from the Aegean and possibly Sardinia, Libya and Italy, around 1200BC. (Intriguingly, these raiders are often depicted with round shields and horned helmets. However, most people believe that they came from islands in the western Mediterranean, not from farther north!)

Nevertheless, there is no reason to suppose that similar actions were not taking place in the North – boatloads of armed warriors from Scandinavia and elsewhere roaming the seas in search of either booty or new lands to settle. The rock carvings suggest that, on average, each boat contained between twelve and twenty-four crew, and a helmsman.

Drawings on metalwork such as razors offer similar images of double-ended boats with curving stems and sterns, and a reinforced keelplank for beaching. In the period before the construction of docks and wharves, the only way to bring a ship to shore would have been to run it up on to a beach, and then float it off again at high tide. Rocky or gravelly shores would have quickly worn through the bottom of the boat if it was not provided with a reinforced keel. It is interesting to wonder whether the Roos Carr figures represent similar British activity, or rather figures of the feared raiders who were threatening the shores of the northwest of Britain itself. But there are also the images of the solar boats to consider, and so we can also have several possible explanations for the images that may relate to religious stories or mythology.

Ocean and river-going boats existed in the Late Bronze Age, and a number have been discovered, such as the boats from Ferriby, Must Farm near Peterborough and Dover in Britain, and the slightly later Nordic Bronze Age boat from Hjortspring. That the Dover Boat was sea-going has been proved by the presence of marine worm damage in some of the timbers – worms that do not live in fresh water. These boats are large – perhaps up to 50 metres long in some cases – and evidence from food waste heaps shows that they were often used in deep water, as the large amounts of fish remains found at settlement sites include those from species not usually found near the coasts.

The Tegneby rock carving also suggests the use of horses in battle. Some people have maintained that without proper stirrups, it is not possible to fight from horseback with spears or swords, but this is simply not the case. Saddle design is what is important, not necessarily the stirrups. A padded and contoured cloth or leather saddle can perfectly well support a rider securely enough to allow him to throw a spear or wield a sword, but unfortunately, of course, such organic items do not survive burial in the soil, and so we do not have evidence of their structures and capabilities. But we should remember that the Late Roman heavy cavalry were notably effective warriors – and they did not have stirrups either.

The phalerae discs found in the Late Bronze Age would support the possibility of the use of horses in battle. Some of the longer Bronze Age swords might have been designed for use from horseback, to slash downwards at a foe, especially those weighted towards the bottom of the blade. Horses and horse gear appear across Europe with much more frequency in the Late Bronze Age, including in ritual contexts such as the Trundholm sun chariot, and in depositions of horse skulls, and in votive offerings of horse decorations in lakes and bogs. Most horses would have been relatively small animals at this time – the size of native British Dartmoor or Exmoor ponies – but there is some evidence to suggest that larger breeds were being introduced in southern Europe by the end of the period.

It is possible, then, that this is the era that saw the first introduction of cavalry and cavalry fighting styles in Northern Europe. There are also numerous depictions of wagons (sometimes recorded as 'chariots') in rock art, and it is not completely beyond the bounds of possibility that these could also have been used in war, horses and wagons extending the range of warriors to a far greater extent than in previous periods. The change from arable to stock farming as a response to the climatic downturn would probably also have required mounted 'cowboys' to control the herds, and perhaps would have resulted in mounted cattle raids as well.

The increased mobility of the period also saw a massive extension of trade networks across Europe, and the rise of certain groups in control of trade hubs and routes who built themselves 'elite' settlements and erected defensive palisades and walls for protection. The presence of wealth can lead to the presence of those who wish to get their own hands on the goods, and thus the threatened wealthy folk became involved in the development of defences and defensive warrior bands, who in turn might be tempted to relieve other wealthy groups of their possessions – a rising spiral of aggression which, coupled with the effects of the worsened climate conditions and subsistence stress, made warfare more and more likely.

New forms of weapons were created for a different kind of warfare. While a rapier can be used in a fencing match, the slashing sword invokes a more general kind of combat, as do the heavy thrusting spears. War bands may still have been quite small – but even in the post-Roman Dark Ages, the concept of an army was limited to just thirty or so men. Along with warrior status came a new social order – chieftains who would attract followers on the merit of their fighting prowess and the wealth they could gather. Martial display became important, with the manufacture of impressive display armour, designed for its appearance rather than its usability. A new ethos had arrived, one that would strengthen in the Iron Age and survive well into the first millennium AD – the age of the warrior aristocracy.

Thus, as the Bronze Age drew to a close, there was a rise in the power of chieftains in Europe – those who controlled the trade routes from the north down into the Mediterranean in particular. There were two major trade avenues – the amber route and the tin route. The amber route led from the Baltic Sea down through Central Europe to the Danube, and across the eastern Alps to Greece and the Levant. The tin route ran from Britain and Ireland either by sea or through the river networks down to the south of France to Greek trading colonies and Etruria. Along these routes, large hillforts appeared from at least the seventh or sixth century BC onwards. The early Late Bronze Age/Early Iron Age sites are often known as 'Fürstensitze' – princely centres with evidence of trade, manufacture and settlement. Each one seems to have controlled a more extended territory around it, containing farming and other settlements that were probably dependent on the centre in some way. The sites stretch from Burgundy to Bavaria and beyond.

Current thinking does not place aristocratic elites necessarily within these centres, as no particularly rich finds tend to be made within them, but the aristocracy probably lived nearby; the Fürstensitze were central places for emerging tribal identities, market and ritual centres, production sites and much more. Many sites are accompanied by extremely rich graves sited not far away, some with four-wheeled wagons, exotic trade goods, gold and even silk and coral. Along with the trade goods came ideas and knowledge exchanged between the Mediterranean world and the north – ideas that affected architecture, art, politics and society.

In the Late Hallstatt period at the very end of the Bronze Age, the Fürstensitze developed as trading and organisational hubs for chieftains of great wealth. They mainly flourished between the eighth and fifth centuries BC – the earliest part of the Iron Age. In the sixth century BC, the Mediterranean trade became an important part of the power structure of these places – sites like Mont Lassois in France and the Heuneberg in Germany grew in size and strength. Mediterranean imports appear – particularly pottery and bronze equipment for drinking and serving wine, and of course the containers of the imported wine themselves. Wine became the 'must have' drink for northern aristocrats and, as we shall see, also became central to the onset of war with the Romans later in the period.

One site of this period which is particularly interesting is the Heuneberg in southern Germany. This began as a defended site in the Middle Bronze Age, with a ditch and bank and a wooden palisade. Then it was abandoned for some time until, in around 700BC, a new settlement began on the site. The central plateau of the hill covers an area of two hectares and initially was surrounded by an earth and timber wall. Around 600BC a new wall, perhaps in total six metres high, was erected – on a foundation of limestone a mudbrick wall was built, possibly with a roofed walkway on top, and faced with lime plaster that was apparently renewed regularly. Bastion towers were built along two sides of the wall, projecting outwards. There were two narrow entrances opposite each other, each massively built – the west gate led to small suburban settlements and measured eight metres high and twelve metres across, finished with ashlar masonry, and the east gate went down a steep road to the River Danube, where there may have been a timber wharf.

No other mudbrick construction is known in northern Europe, and it seems that the people of the Heuneberg had learned about such building methods from their Greek trading partners. This wall surrounded a sizeable and quite densely-packed settlement of large timber and wattle-and-daub houses with regular streets, as well as metalworking and other craft workshops. One house in the southeast corner was very large – 14 x 30 metres, perhaps the home of the chief, or a communal hall. The wall lasted for about seventy years before being replaced with a more local style of construction. This citadel was surrounded by 100 hectares of further land within the walls and defences on the western side, away from the river, within which were further hamlets. The outer area is thought to have held a population of between 5,000 and 10,000 people.

Rich graves surrounded the Heuneberg, under barrows. The Hohmichele barrow held a main chamber made of oak over the graves of a man and a woman, but it had been robbed not long after it was made. All that remained were glass beads, pieces of amber and gold threads from a fine fabric. Another grave in the mound had not been robbed, and also held a man and a woman with jewellery including thousands of glass beads, and embroidered cloth. There was a four-wheeled wagon and harness for two horses, bronze feasting vessels, an iron knife, and a quiver with fifty-one iron-tipped arrows. The woman's body had been laid on the wagon, and the man was lying on the floor, leading to speculation that the most important person in this grave was the woman.

Further rich female graves have also been found nearby. Another grave in the area held the body of a two-year-old child with Etruscan jewellery imported from north Italy. Clearly, there was a very rich and powerful class of society present. The population of the Heuneberg was too large to have survived on local produce, so it is presumed that the centre controlled a much wider area.

The mudbrick wall seems to have been destroyed with some violence, and was then replaced with a more conventional hillfort rampart structure. This was itself destroyed, at least partly by fire, in the fifth century BC. The site was then largely, although not entirely, abandoned. Many theories have been suggested for why this happened – competition from other hillforts, climate change, and changes in the Mediterranean world which led to a loss of trade are all possibilities. Perhaps a combination of events created the conditions in which the centre could no longer survive at its former level of wealth and influence.

Several other Fürstensitze have been excavated – the Glauberg, in Hesse, also began at the end of the Bronze Age but was rebuilt and fortified in the sixth or fifth century BC. A massive bank and ditch was created, cutting off a large spur of a hill, and further walls were added to surround the centre. Drystone and *murus gallicus* techniques were used. A *murus gallicus* is a stone wall laced with bracing and supporting timbers throughout. An annexe was added to surround a spring and a water reservoir, creating a fortification 650 metres long, of around eight and a half hectares. Two complex gates led into the enclosure.

South of the defences was a burial ground with a very large barrow mound. It held the graves of two warriors with swords and other weapons. A further mound was later discovered, also over a warrior burial. A stone statue was unearthed, that had fallen to the base of the mound, which shows a male figure wearing a so-called 'leaf crown' or headdress, and carrying weapons. It has been dated to the fifth century BC. The man is wearing trousers and a tunic which appears to be padded or covered with protective plaques. He has an oval shield and a sword which hangs from his right hip. He is wearing a torc neckring with pendants just like one found within the grave, as well as arm and finger rings. Fragments of three other statues have also been found.

At Hirschlanden, not far from Stuttgart, another statue has been found, probably sixth century BC in date. This also shows a warrior, this time nude except for a conical hat and a belt in which a dagger has been stuck, and he too is wearing a torc. The hat is very similar to a birch-bark hat found in the grave of a chieftain at Hochdorf in Baden-Württemberg.

The Hochdorf chieftain died at around the age of forty. He was six feet two inches tall, and had been buried with massive wealth, including the nine-foot-long bronze couch on which he was laid. The couch was mounted on wheeled castors in the form of unicycling people. He also had a torc and other jewellery, a gold-plated dagger, gold-plated shoes, a razor, nail clipper and comb, and arrows and fishhooks. In the grave was a vast cauldron which had held 400 litres of strong mead, as well as a four-wheeled wagon, sets of bronze feasting dishes and nine drinking horns, which had been hung from the walls of the burial chamber.

Mont Lassois in France is a steep hill with a flat top, also associated with rich graves. It was also begun in the fifth or sixth century BC, at a junction of the River Seine and a major route. Massive banks and ditches surrounded the site, which enclosed a planned settlement of houses, workshops and storage buildings. One large building (35 x 21 metres) lay at the centre of the site; there was a porch at the front and an apsed wall at the back, like a type of Greek feasting building. Mont Lassois has also produced many finds from Mediterranean trading – Greek vases, amphorae which had contained wine, and bronze vessels.

The most notable grave in the area, however, was female – at Vix. The deceased lady was aged around thirty-five years old, and had been richly dressed with several necklaces and brooches. This grave also contained a wagon, a 480g gold torc, and numerous bracelets, as well as imported feasting and drinking vessels. The most famous item in the grave was the *krater*, a Greek wine-mixing vessel, 1.63 metres high, weighing over 200kg and with a capacity of 1,000 litres. Clearly she was a woman of some power as well as wealth, and while no weapons were found in her grave, she may well have possessed her own band of warriors, or been a strong figure among the leadership of the warrior aristocracy. Further rich graves in the area include both male and female burials, rich goods and wagons. Fragments of stone statues have also been discovered.

These sites (and many more across central Europe not described here) all share common features – wealth, trade goods and special burials. They seem to indicate the presence of a controlling aristocracy, separate from and dominant over the rest of the local population. The massive defences of these princely seats demonstrate their interest in the protection of the great wealth brought by contact with the cultures of the Mediterranean.

Chapter 6

Warfare in Iron Age Northern Europe

It was no longer a world of small family or village communities. Now, you belonged to a much larger group – a tribe, with its own territory and identity. Aristocracies ruled the tribes, supported by the work and tribute of the craftsmen and peasants, and they announced their importance with fine jewellery and armour, and with decorated wagons and chariots. Some were buried in great monuments full of treasures. Each tribe began to make for itself important centres of trade and production, carefully sited to control the roads and rivers down which the merchants travelled. And each group of aristocrats used the wealth of the trade to gather supporters and warriors around them, and to make alliances with their most powerful neighbours. As well as new types of goods, new ideas and new ways of seeing the world they travelled the trade routes, many of them from the south, from the peoples whose lands encircled the Mediterranean Sea. The southerners were urban people, for whom cities were the mark of civilisation; they saw the Northern Europeans as barbarians. But they were barbarians with much that the south wanted and needed.

Europe in the Iron Age
In this period, new identities emerged. The Late Bronze Age Hallstatt cultures gave way to a new set of artefacts and artistic representations which are found in pottery, jewellery, weapons and much more – a style called La Tène. This style is named after a lakeside site in Switzerland, where it was first recognised, but in fact the origins of La Tène culture appear to come from further north in Germany and eastern France. The Greeks named this culture 'Keltoi', although in reality, there were many regional and local variations. We usually just speak about 'Celts' in the north European Iron Age, but this is to ignore the Germanic peoples, the Gauls, the indigenous peoples of Iberia and Scandinavia, and the peoples of the British Isles. None of these groups were 'ethnic Celts', but all adopted, at least to some extent, elements of 'Celtic' culture, while also retaining local styles.

The one thing that does seem to be common among many of the peoples of the North is language. It is probable that local languages survived and were used, but perhaps the Celtic language group formed a type of 'lingua franca' used between traders and travellers, and words from those languages entered the local dialects. The evidence for this is largely based on Roman and Greek accounts, on personal and tribal names recorded by the Mediterranean observers, and on place-names.

Place-names tend to be particularly long-lived and are a useful source of information for archaeologists. While most have been altered over the centuries, as each new group of people moved across the continent and brought their own words with them, some have remained buried in our modern language, and we can trace them back to their origins. Some examples might include 'briga' – a high place, still found in Bregenz in Austria, Briançon in France, and Bredon in England, or 'windo' – white – in Windisch in Switzerland, Wien (Vienna) in Austria, Vendeuvre in France and the Roman fort of Vindolanda in England, and 'hal' – salt, found in Halle in Germany and Hale in Cheshire, as well as Hallstatt itself.

Despite the use of a common language, the various tribes and societies were often very different from each other in other ways; it would be a mistake to assume that all Celtic-speakers were the same. Developments in various parts of northern Europe were often locally distinct and more based on older, local patterns than on any general (and mythical) Celtic model.

By the Late Hallstatt period, bronze was becoming scarce. The more easily worked deposits of copper seem to have been running out, and it is clear that people began to be very aware of the need for recycling. They were burying broken or damaged items in hoards to await melting down and recasting into new tools and weapons, or trading in scrap bronze, as occurred between Britain and Brittany; evidence for this trade has been found in the cargoes of wrecks off the British coast. But a replacement metal was needed, and it was found in the form of iron.

Iron is much more widely available across Europe as a natural resource, although more difficult to work and requiring more labour and fuel to produce. It first appeared in eastern Europe about 1000BC, and its use spread slowly across the continent. The new metal was not adopted as quickly as one might think – largely because wrought iron is not significantly more useful than bronze. It is brittle, liable to rust and less attractive to look at. But it is easily found, and can be used alone, instead of having to combine two metals for an alloy, as is necessary with bronze. In fact, the only alloy of iron in antiquity was with charcoal, to form steel.

Steel is occasionally found later in the period, but its main use was as an addition to the edges of iron swords, to give a sharper cutting surface. So iron items from the early period are scarce, and even allowing for the fact that much will have rusted away, it seems that it was not generally used for many purposes for some time. Early iron artefacts tend to be bracelets, pins and other decorative items rather than tools and weapons.

Settlements

Besides the great Late Bronze Age/Early Iron Age centres discussed in the last chapter, other types of settlement appeared, many with defensive capabilities. At Biskupin settlement in Poland *(Plate 9)* a village some two hectares in size was created on an island in a lake. About 100 timber houses were built in a rectangular grid of eleven three-metre-wide streets. The two-room houses all had similar layouts and size, about eight by ten metres. Around the houses was a strong wooden palisade on a timber and earth rampart more than 450 metres long. Dendrochronological (tree-ring) dating puts the beginnings of this settlement at between 747 and 722BC. At one point the defences were renewed. Like the princely centres mentioned in the last chapter, this site remained in use until the fifth century BC, and then, like them, was also abandoned. Lake villages were also built in Britain a little later (from 300BC) at Glastonbury and Meare, in Somerset. Swiss and Austrian lakes saw similar settlements, constructed on piles, some with palisades around them.

Settlements in western and northern Britain and Ireland were built in several defensive styles in the Iron Age. Some different forms are unique to the British Isles – brochs and duns in particular. Duns are settlements enclosed by dry stone walls, while brochs are circular, tower-like structures. Early brochs on Orkney have been dated to 600BC, while most have dates from about 400BC onwards. Some were very large – the surviving Broch of Mousa, Shetland, is 13 metres high *(Plate 10)*. A broch is made of dry stone walls up to three metres thick, with an internal diameter of between five and fifteen metres. The walls are doubled, and in some surviving examples a winding stair led up to the roof between them, lit by vertical openings in the inside wall. Stone ledges supported internal floor levels climbing the inside of the structure. Entrance was via a narrow passage, some of which had blocking bars and guard cells, into the ground floor space, where there were further cells built into the walls.

At one time it was believed that the brochs were open to the sky, but it is now thought that they had roofs. Some brochs had further defensive ditches and ramparts around them, such as Kilphedir in Sutherland, and some were surrounded by a stone and turf wall within which were contiguous stone houses, as at Gurness on Orkney. Many brochs are sited on coasts, near landing places, on islands or at the entrances to sea passages, while others appear to be sited to oversee the small areas of good arable land in the region, such as Dun Carloway broch, Lewis. (It is confusing that some brochs are known as duns, but they can be distinguished from proper duns by their form).

Duns appeared around the seventh century BC; their walls were timber-laced and, in some cases, fire had been deliberately set to burn the timber and melt (vitrify) the face of the stone wall (as also occurred at some hillforts) to make them harder to climb by an attacker. Dun Aonghasa, one of a number of forts on the Aran Islands, sits precariously on the edge of an 87-metre-high cliff; there are four concentric dry stone walls, up to four metres thick. The third line of wall is also surrounded by a chevaux-de-frise – a wide (up to 38 metres) field of stones each up to 1.75 metres tall, planted at angles in the ground to make access even more difficult.

The surviving structure is incomplete, a part having fallen into the sea at some time in the past, but what remains is a six hectare enclosure, with a view of up to 75 miles of coastline. The earliest activity on the site was around 1000BC when the enclosure was begun. Until 500BC a thriving community lived in the dun in a range of timber houses, and remains of their feasts, jewellery and weapons have been found. Then the fort was abandoned as a settlement, but the further walls and chevaux-de-frise were built, so it must have continued to have an important function.

It seems clear that these types of settlement, with their heavy defences, were built to answer sea-borne threats. Many have excellent views of the routes along which raiding ships could approach, and would have perhaps provided a deterrent, and at least short-term protection, to the local inhabitants, who could take refuge inside the walls or towers. Of course, there is also the possibility that the brochs and duns were themselves the strongholds of such raiders, and provided secure places in which to store the booty they brought back from piratical attacks both on each other and on undefended settlements. Many of these sites are close enough to reasonably suitable landing beaches to make this possible.

In other parts of the north and Ireland (and at least one example in Wales), crannogs were built. These are artificial or semi-artificial islands, made up of dumps of stone, timber and earth in lakes, reached by a causeway of stone or timber. Construction techniques and size vary enormously. Round timber houses were built on platforms or piles on the islands, and housed perhaps just a single extended family, protected from raiders by the surrounding waters. A reconstructed crannog and house has been built at Loch Tay in Scotland *(Plate 11)*, where it is possible to visit and gain an impression of what life would have been like for these lake dwellers.

Wales and Ireland also saw the construction of raths or 'ringforts' – circular enclosures of stone or earth banks – in the period 800–400BC. They are also found in the West Country, although here they are called 'rounds'.

Many of these continued in use into the Middle Ages, and their origins and functions are sometimes very obscure. They may be 'mini' hillforts or strongly defended farmsteads.

Enclosed homesteads, surrounded by minimal defences of ditch and bank, perhaps surmounted by a hedge or fence, are a feature of much of the rest of Britain and Brittany in the Iron Age. These defences are not strong and could never have stood up to any large-scale assaults, but they might have given a measure of protection, at least psychologically, to the inhabitants. Despite this, there are also areas of open, undefended settlements, such as in East Anglia.

In the west, northeast and central south of England, along the coasts of Britain, Ireland and Western France, and further inland in parts of France, Belgium, the Netherlands, Germany, Poland, Austria and further afield in Iberia, the main defensive structure of the Iron Age was the hillfort. As mentioned in the previous chapter, the practice of building defensible settlements on hilltops began in the Late Bronze Age, if not before. By the Iron Age, much larger enclosures began to appear in numbers across much of Europe.

There is a vast amount of academic debate about these monuments – originally seen as military structures, they have subsequently been considered as ritual centres, elite centres, markets, production sites, status symbols, symbols of tribal identity and any combination of these things. The truth is probably that whatever the original purpose of building a hillfort, all the other facets of its meaning came into play over time, in the same way that Norman castles were also dwellings, power symbols, held courts and gaols, treasuries, and so on, and over time became stately homes and symbols of gracious living, ancestry and status. What cannot be denied is that military tactical and strategic thinking went into the design and modifications to hillforts during the Iron Age (and indeed later, as many were refortified during the Dark Ages and the Medieval period).

The term hillfort is in itself misleading – many are not on hills at all, or only on a spur or a promontory of a hill or cliff. There are flat ground hillforts, island hillforts, slope hillforts and cliff hillforts. The defining features are circuits of large ramparts and walls (of stone, earth and timber), large ditches, and a limited number of entrances, sometimes very complex. Some hillforts have a single circuit of wall and ditch (univallate), some have two circuits (bivallate) and some have three or more circuits or partial circuits (multivallate). Construction of walls varies from region to region and period to period. Few hillforts escaped later changes and modifications, especially to entrances, and some acquired extra enclosed annexes. Some have been found to have supported very large settlements, while others seem to be virtually empty. No two are exactly alike, although very few hillforts across Europe have been excavated in much detail, and there is still a lot to discover.

The ramparts of the earliest hillforts seem to have been mostly of dumped earth or stone, revetted by large timber posts often arranged in a box-like formation, behind a short berm of flat ground and a deep V-shaped ditch. Such ramparts would have tended to collapse over time, as the timber rotted and the ditch silted up. The ramparts might then be rebuilt as a larger dumped bank, with a timber revetment and palisade on the outer side and a walkway along the top, perhaps with an additional timber breastwork.

If these also slumped, they were often replaced with a 'glacis'-style rampart – a dumped earth wall, possibly with a timber or stone breastwork along the top, but without the berm – the outer slope of the rampart continued in an unbroken line down into the flanking ditch, creating a longer, steeper slope. This form can be seen in massive examples at Maiden Castle in Dorset, with a slope of 25 metres at some points, making them very difficult to assault. The building of multiple ramparts could have been a defence against enemy slingshot or even burning brands attached to spears, creating a wide, steep range of protection too great to be traversed by such missiles.

A later modification was to create a much wider, though shallower, ditch in front of the rampart – the so-called 'Fécamp' style after a site in Normandy. Such ditches may incorporate a chevaux-de-frise of stone, or could possibly have contained sharpened stakes set at angles or cut thorn hedges. It seems likely that these ditches were intended to counter horse-borne attacks – an Iron Age horse or pony could scramble up the side of a glacis slope, especially if it had slumped, but would have been unable to jump across the wider, obstacle-strewn Fécamp defence, suggesting that the use of cavalry forces had become more common later in the Iron Age for this kind of attack.

Early hillforts tend to have two entrances – often one on the east and one on the west side, but in many instances one of these, usually the west one, was blocked at a later date. There does not appear to have been a strategic reason for the siting of the gates, and there may have been a ritual significance, the openings facing the rising and setting sun; the decision to close the western gates may have been defensive, in order to minimise the weak points of the circuit while the retention of the eastern gate suggests that whatever the level of threat, custom and belief overcame military necessity.

New designs incorporated into hillforts over time included the slanting of the ramparts and ditches inwards to the entrances, creating a funnel effect, thus forcing any attackers into a crowded killing ground, or creating doubled entrances with gates and possibly towers defending them, guard chambers, and longer corridors (up to 45 metres) between double gates, like a castle barbican. Some corridors were stone-lined – a protection against fire?

Another addition was the building of 'hornworks' – further curving banks and ditches outside the entrances, creating a confusing maze for attackers to negotiate and providing extra platforms from which defenders could launch spears and slingshots. Usually, as well as funnelling attackers into smaller areas where their weapons would be less effective, these hornworks force the enemy to have to turn to their left, exposing their unshielded right sides to the defenders. (All the evidence seems to suggest that people in the past were divided into right-handed and left-handed proportions very similar to people today).

Clearly, good strategic thinking was going on. Whatever other functions the hillfort may have had, its defences were well-considered. A number of those writers who do not believe in the military design of hillforts have pointed out that the interiors of some can be visible from neighbouring hills, thus exposing the defenders to danger. This would indeed be a major drawback, but for one fact – during the Iron Age, archery becomes, apparently, very rare in many parts of the continent, and even where it is found, the distances would generally preclude an archery attack from neighbouring slopes.

The only other ballistic weapons available were the sling and the throwing spear, both relatively short-range weapons – at least until the arrival of the Romans with their catapults and ballistae. So it would not have mattered a great deal if the interiors were visible – the primary problem for an assailing force would still have been how to overrun the walls and entrances. The length of the walls would have been too great, in most instances, to be completely defensible; this suggests that both attacking and defending forces were generally low in numbers, and that interior defence was quite mobile, with warriors being quickly directed to counter attempts to breach the walls as and where they occurred.

Attacks on hillforts

So, did hillforts see warfare? Almost certainly. Evidence from a number of sites includes destruction levels, burned gates and houses, and the bodies of the dead. In some places, where there were several early hillforts, some go out of use over time until only one remains, dominant and often further developed. Did the builders of the other hillforts make alliances with those of the dominant one, or were they forced out? Evidence for attack has been found at several excavated sites – at Danebury in Hampshire, for example, huge caches of slingshot were found near the eastern entrance (the western one having been blocked up), and a similar cache was found at Maiden Castle.

At Crickley Hill in Gloucestershire, the first Iron Age hillfort that succeeded the earlier Neolithic site seems to have been attacked and the houses and gates burned. A new, much stronger entrance was then built with a stone barbican curving out from the main wall. The barbican was entered by a narrow oblique gate, and this then led to a massive offset gate into the main fort, with strong bastions on either side, and a fighting platform which ran all around the structure.

Twice in its history the gates of the hillfort of Danebury in Hampshire were burned down, and at the late period Bredon Hill fort in Worcestershire, the remains of about fifty people were found in the entranceway, presumably evidence of a forgotten battle.

More evidence for violence at a British hillfort has recently come to light at Fin Cop in the Peak District. This hilltop was occupied in the Late Bronze Age, but the defensive ramparts were first begun in the Iron Age. A four-metre-wide stone wall was built, carefully constructed and faced with limestone blocks. There was an external rock-cut ditch, so that the combined height of the wall and ditch would have been between three and four metres. However, it became clear during excavation that the ditch had not been finished – blocks of stone had been cut out, but not yet removed from the bottom. This phase has been radio-carbon-dated to between 440–390BC. Another section of the rampart and ditch was also found to be unfinished. In the ditches were more blocks of dressed stone, clearly thrown down from the wall as the defences were levelled.

Underneath these blocks, the excavators found the articulated skeletons of many people, including that of an adolescent who seems to have been thrown in still alive. The stone wall was then pushed down on top of the bodies. Much still remains to be investigated of the 400-metre circuit, but everywhere a trench has been dug, bodies have been found, suggesting that many people, perhaps even hundreds, died here. So far, nine bodies have been examined in detail – two of these were adult women, one an adult of undetermined gender and the rest were children, including four babies, a toddler and a young teenager. No wounds were visible on the skeletons, but all showed that these people had suffered a number of times from malnutrition and dietary deficiencies.

This can be determined by X-ray examination of the bones and teeth – each time a growing body experiences a period of disease or malnutrition, growth slows down or halts, leaving a slightly denser layer of bone. Once the person gets better, or gets more food, growth starts again, with less dense new bone being created. The same happens in tooth enamel. The X-rays show these sections of lighter and denser bones as shadows called Harris lines, or in teeth, enamel hypoplasia. It is possible to establish how many times the growing body had suffered stress, and even the approximate age at which these stresses occurred.

It was evident that the time between the building of the wall and its destruction was very short. It suggests that the hillfort was being hastily constructed in the face of a threat, but there was not enough time to complete the defences before it was attacked. The lack of male bodies suggests that either the men were killed elsewhere, had left the site for some unknown purpose, or had been taken as slaves.

A nearby hillfort, Ball Cross, has a similar sequence of levels, again suggesting that the walls were destroyed in a single event, but this latter site is on acid geology, where no bones survive. Close to Fin Cop, under the hillfort, is a cave, in which the skeleton of a teenage boy was found, and it is speculated that this lad went to the cave to hide, and, perhaps already wounded, died there alone, although as yet his remains have not been securely dated, so we cannot be sure his death was directly related to the attack on the hillfort.

Several other sites in Britain have also produced human remains with possible evidence of violent death – some skeletons placed in disused storage pits at Danebury hillfort had weapons damage visible on their bones. One man had suffered blows to the head, and a spear thrust through his forehead, and another had been hit in the face with a sword, although this did not kill him. A human femur with sword cuts showing on the bone was also found. Isolated human skulls were also discovered at Danebury, and those found at Bredon Hill may have been set up in the entranceway of the hillfort as trophies, as may also have occurred at South Cadbury hillfort in Somerset.

Other bodies have occasionally been found with spear or sword injuries, although as the number of Iron Age burials that have survived is very small indeed, there is not enough evidence for warfare from this type of deposit. Bog bodies may also represent violent episodes, as may spears found in bodies at the cemeteries around Wetwang Slack in Yorkshire. We need to be careful with these last cases, though, as these practices may have nothing to do with aggression – the removal of skulls from the dead may also have been a funerary ritual, a way of allowing the soul to go free, and 'killing' dead bodies with spears and arrows is a long-lived tradition in Britain and Europe, perhaps to ensure that there would be no subsequent haunting by the spirit of the deceased. Bog bodies may have been people killed as ritual sacrifices, or execution victims, rather than captured prisoners of war.

Oppida

Early Iron Age hillforts also appeared in eastern France and parts of Germany, but this type of site proliferated in the Later Iron Age; they spread across much of the continent, often associated with trade routes or important sources of minerals, such as Stradonice in the Czech Republic (near deposits of iron ore), and Staré Hradisko not far away on the amber trade route from the Baltic. Many of these sites developed from the second century BC into what the Romans called *oppida* – proto-towns – which combined residential settlement, production sites, market places and administrative centres for a territory. About 170 have been identified, some on older hillfort sites, and others on new sites.

Mont Beuvray (Bibracte) in France initially covered 200 hectares, later reduced to 135 hectares, and was surrounded by two walls, the inner one five kilometres long and built in *murus gallicus* style. It has been estimated that the building of this wall would have needed more than 10,000 cubic metres of wood and 30 tons of iron nails. The second wall was even longer, and is estimated to have stood between four and five metres high. Unlike the hillforts, some *oppida* had many entrances – fifteen at Mont Beuvray, with the Rebout Gate being monumental in size (20 metres wide and 20 metres deep). *Oppida* in Bohemia and Bavaria were generally much larger than those found in northern and western France or in Britain. Construction varied – the *murus gallicus* was common in the west, stone walls in central Europe and earth and timber in the east. In Britain, earth and timber are used in the south, and stone in the west, reflecting the availability of local materials.

The *oppidum* of Manching in Bavaria enclosed 380 hectares, and had seven kilometres of surrounding wall in *murus gallicus* style. The interior, with its large timber, wattle and daub houses, was divided into quarters for particular activities – one area for weavers, one for metalworking, and others for working bone, stone, amber, and making glass and pottery, which was being produced in an almost mass-produced way. Manching was at a crossroads for trade routes and developed from an undefended village settlement into a major centre.

The Later Iron Age demonstrates an increasingly formal organisation of tribal and territorial identities, of borders and centres. The *oppida* seem to have clearly belonged to distinct tribal groups, with political structures, which controlled the surrounding areas and economies, an identity which was advertised on the local coinages that began to appear. *Oppida* in Europe were an early form of urbanisation, and in southern France (and Spain) they were influenced by Greek and Etruscan trade settlements and contacts. These southern sites tended to acquire the features of towns to a far more developed extent than those to the north, which retained a more scattered, organic, growth and organisation.

An example is the site of Aulnat in the Auvergne that originally showed only local trade connections, but by the later Iron Age was beginning to adopt new technologies and burial practices. Other low-lying settlements in the area, which had been involved in trade and production, then became abandoned, and the Aulnat site appears dominant. By the third century BC, imported Mediterranean fine wares appeared, along with gold coinage, possibly originally brought back by mercenaries who had fought with the Greeks and Macedonians. In a short time, lower value 'potin' coins were being made, and wine amphorae were being imported. By 120–100BC the hilltop site was abandoned, within a single generation, and a new settlement was built with defences, near the river, apparently to facilitate trade. This too was soon abandoned in favour of a new town built on Mediterranean lines, which was eventually defeated and taken by the legions of Julius Caesar. By 10BC this town became the origin of the modern city of Clermont-Ferrand.

There is a pattern of low-lying open settlements, which are abandoned, and the founding of *oppida*, densely occupied and then themselves abandoned, through the last centuries BC in the Auvergne region. Elsewhere in France, different patterns emerge. In the Aisne valley, in the north around Reims, most Iron Age settlements were on the valley terraces, including the *oppidum* of Villeneuve St Germain and the site at Guignicourt. These both had bank and ditch defences, and they surrounded settlements with houses in fenced enclosures and streets laid out in an organised pattern, as well as workshops for iron working and other crafts, and both sites made their own coinage. Later in the period, Villeneuve St Germain was abandoned in favour of the hilltop site of Pommiers, which had Fécamp-style defences.

Similar sequences are known in other areas of central and north France, southern Germany and Switzerland. In other areas, though, the pattern of settlement seems to have been more stable; the problem with sites such as Paris, Reims, and Bourges is that modern towns overlie the same sites, and therefore archaeological investigation is much more restricted.

There are other places where small farmsteads were the only form of settlement throughout the period, with no large *oppida* appearing, as in the Champagne region and much of Brittany. According to Roman accounts, each tribe might have several *oppida*, some being of more importance than others, that functioned as local capitals. They were built to defend the inhabitants and their wealth, but also sited to make sure that sources of wealth were accessible, and rarely offer much evidence for actual warfare except for the armour and weaponry often found within them. They seem to have been headquarters sites, often with ritual centres as well as production workshops and housing.

In Germany, the *oppida* continued until around 20BC, when they seem to have been abandoned in favour of a dispersed rural settlement pattern, presumably because the Roman occupation of Gaul and alpine areas had reduced trade to an extent where these large centres could no longer function economically.

The Gaulish *oppida* maintained their defences in the last centuries BC because the trade with Greece and later Rome destabilised the political landscape, a subject which will be further discussed in the next chapter.

Oppida in the north and west were far less developed in general. The Camp d'Artus in Brittany enclosed 35 hectares within 2.6km of stone walls – much smaller than many of the southern French *oppida*. The enclosure was divided into two, the smaller (four hectare) part possibly forming an elite or ceremonial centre in which was a large round structure. The outer walls stood 3.5 metres high and were up to 12 metres thick. The local tribe, the Osimes, used horses, possibly for armed raids, and made their own coinage. Not enough excavation on the site has taken place to establish whether it was also a production centre, but it is estimated that the site could have held a population of around 1,000 people. So far, no traces of the organised planning, streets and so on, found in the south have been discovered at the Camp d'Artus. It was probably typical of such sites in northern France, Belgium and southern Britain, with the exception of the late British 'territorial' *oppida* which will be discussed later.

Weapons and armour of the Iron Age

Some remarkable pieces of Iron Age armour and weaponry have survived, especially pieces that might be described as 'ceremonial' or 'status' artefacts. However, there are also many more prosaic, everyday weapons, such as the caches of slingshots mentioned above – 11,000 at Danebury and over 20,000 at Maiden Castle. The slings themselves were probably made of leather or wool, and have not survived. Experimental work has proved that most of the pebbles used as shot could have been launched with a range of between 90 and 100 metres at a velocity sufficient to cause injury to an attacker.

A massed group of slingers well sited on the raised hornworks around the entrance to a hillfort could have caused a very great deal of damage to would-be attackers. It is probable that most boys (and probably some girls) would have learned to use a sling early in life, especially in the farming communities, to ward off danger to their flocks and herds, or to scare birds away from newly sown crops, and such practices continued in rural life well into the 20th century in some areas, when it was still the role of children to oversee the fields and pastures.

Daggers and swords with elaborate decoration have been found, some from the Thames, such as the dagger from Mortlake dating from the Early Iron Age. This piece had been imported from continental Europe. Unlike European examples, British scabbards for daggers have twin supporting loops on the back, to attach them to a belt (continental examples tend to have a single loop).

Long swords of the Gündlingen type appeared in Britain in the early eighth century BC, and some are associated with winged chapes. It is thought possible that the wings would have allowed a rider to steady the scabbard with a foot to enable him to draw the sword more easily while mounted. Another way to wear a sword was to have it slung across the back – some small carved chalk figures from Yorkshire depict warriors wearing their swords in this fashion. Long iron La Tène swords began to be used in the late fifth or early fourth century, at first designed mainly for thrusting, but later shaped as slashing weapons. A particularly fine example of a sword in its scabbard was the beautifully decorated one found at Kirkburn, also in Yorkshire, dating from the third century BC.

The swords were made in one of two ways – once the basic shape had been forged from a bar of iron, the edges were hardened by cold hammering, or the sword was constructed by joining strips of iron with different carbon content under heat – in effect, steel edged. This made a flexible and fairly strong weapon. They had parallel straight sides and a rounded tip, although some still carried a longitudinal rib like earlier bronze swords. British swords tended to be a little shorter and thinner than continental ones, and Irish ones were noticeably shorter. Three main groups of swords are found – long swords between 65 and 70cm in length and between 5 and 6cm at their broadest point, medium-length swords of between 60 and 64cm, and short swords, generally later, around 50cm long and 3 or 4cm across.

In France, the long swords of the fourth century BC are also often associated with large spearheads, and it has been suggested that a warrior's panoply would have included both weapons. They had a tendency to bend in use, and Roman writers noted that in battle, Celtic warriors often had to withdraw from the fight for a few moments to straighten their weapons!

There is much debate on how the swords were used. In Europe in the earlier part of the period, chariot warfare seems to have been common, and it is believed that the long sword with its rounded tip would have allowed the warrior to slash at his enemies as the chariot drove through them. Alternatively, these weapons could have been used by riders like those shown on the Gundestrup cauldron. The thinner, shorter swords might have been infantry weapons, more useful for face-to-face combat. Hilts had to be strong, particularly if the sword was used in a slashing manner, and they were often highly decorated, with castings, inlays and engraving. One form of hilt was shaped like a human figure, the grip being the body within the outstretched arms and legs, and the head forming the pommel. The scabbards were usually of iron plates, or bronze, and were often decorated with engravings.

Many different types of spearhead were made in the Iron Age, and like those of the Bronze Age they were divided into lighter throwing spears and heavier thrusting weapons. They had sockets for the shafts, and early spear and lance forms were copies of the earlier bronze models. Broad short heads or very long narrow heads are found, usually with a central rib. Some British coins seem to show horsemen carrying light spears or lances, and the possibility of cavalry fighting with both sword and lance is strong.

War trumpets have also been found – these are called carynxes, and are depicted on the famous Gundestrup silver cauldron from Denmark, which shows an army arrayed for battle, among other plates depicting Celtic gods and goddesses. The cauldron shows both infantry and cavalry, the former armed with spears and sub-rectangular shields, followed by a single individual with a sword or mace and three carynx blowers, the latter with swords or lances *(Figure 22)*. There is also a hound depicted – a dog of war?

Figure 22. The 'army' depicted on the Gundestrup cauldron.

Examples of carynxes have been found in Britain and France. The example from Deskford in Scotland had a head shaped like a beast (possibly a dragon), with an open maw, within which was an articulated 'tongue' that would have vibrated when the horn was blown. The horn was carried upright, the body of the instrument being anywhere from one to two metres long, with the head mounted on the top and facing forward. A magnificent example has been found at Tintignac in France, the head in the shape of that of a boar remaining almost complete *(Plate 12)*. Boars are the most common shapes among the seven carynxes found at the Tintignac sanctuary site, but at least one other had the head of a serpent. They stood as high as a man, and have traces of enamel and coral decoration in some cases.

133

Such horns could have been used to give signals during a battle, but also were probably designed to instil fear and a loss of morale among the enemy, as described by the Roman writer Polybius, when he wrote about a battle against Celts fought in 225BC at Telamon in Italy: '[the Romans] were terrified by … the dreadful din, for there were innumerable hornblowers and trumpeters and … the whole army were shouting their war-cries at the same time'.

Iron Age armour

The classical writers tell us that sometimes the Celts fought naked, but one suspects that this would not have been a normal practice in the north European climate! Instead, there is plenty of evidence for much more practical items to wear in battle. An innovation from north of the Alps in the Iron Age was the introduction of chainmail. Small surviving segments have been found at Kirkburn, at Lexden near Colchester, St Albans and elsewhere. A first century BC statue from Vachères in France depicts a warrior with a chainmail tunic – he also carries a sword and a shield, and wears a torc as a mark of his status. Chainmail seems to have replaced the more solid cuirass, perhaps indicating a need for more mobility on the battlefield.

There is some indication that scale armour might also have been worn, based on the interpretation of stone statue figures found at the southern French sanctuary site of Roquepertuse, but cuirasses appear to be depicted on Early Iron Age statuary from the Glauberg *oppidum* in Germany and the (?) fourth-century warrior statue from Grézan, Gard, France *(Figure 23)*. The Romans adopted chainmail once they learned about it from the northerners.

Shields have been found in a number of sites – among the most famous in Britain are the Battersea shield from London, the Witham shield, the Chertsey shield and the Wandsworth shield boss. These are all bronze shields or shield facings, with intricate repoussé decoration and in some examples inlays of glass and coral. Those that survive are nearly all oval in shape.

Figure 23. Warrior statue showing a cuirass, Grezan, Gard, France.

There is, too, some evidence for more ordinary wood and leather shields, also oval. The shields of northern Europe tended to be long and flat, unlike the shorter, rounded Mediterranean forms. 'Celtic' shields usually had a round boss or an umbo in a thinner elongated shape, providing a secure handgrip for the user. More elaborate forms combined a ribbed umbo and boss in one, sometimes turning the arrangement into a decorative feature.

Helmets are more rare finds. The Waterloo helmet, from the Thames, is the most complete of the British finds – made of sheet-bronze, it has two conical horns, and swirling repoussé decoration. A number of different shapes of helmet are found in Europe – some tall with fittings for a crest on the apex, and some hemispherical, like the iron helmet fitted with repoussé bronze decorative plaques discovered recently at Tintignac. One extraordinary French helmet found at the same site is shaped like a swan or similar bird, the tail extending behind, and the neck and head swooping back vertically towards it *(Figure 24)*. Another from this remarkable site is a simple hemisphere mounted with a trio of large hoops set in a vertical triangle that more than triples the height of the helmet. These examples probably date from the fourth or third century BC.

A bronze statuette of a female goddess, possibly Brigantia or Brigid, in the Museum of Brittany at Rennes, is wearing a helmet whose basic shape is not unlike that of a Second World War German helmet, surmounted by a

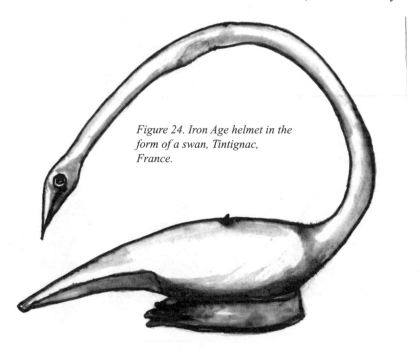

Figure 24. Iron Age helmet in the form of a swan, Tintignac, France.

goose or swan with outstretched head and wings, and an immensely long bronze crest that extends horizontally forward beyond the face of the wearer, and descends at the back all the way down to below the shoulders. These would appear to be examples of 'parade' armour, as they seem remarkably impractical for actual fighting.

Applied decoration was added to many of the finest helmets, again with glass or coral inserts. The Agris helmet, from near Angoulême, is spectacular. It has an iron base, over which were laid bronze attachments covered in gold leaf, riveted on with silver. Bands of foliate decoration cover the helmet and the one surviving cheek-piece.

However, it seems clear that items like this were not in general use, perhaps being reserved for the wealthiest or most important warriors, and it can be supposed that armour of organic materials was used by most fighters – leather or padded tunics and caps. More typical of the period are the so-called 'jockey cap' helmets, based on originals from Northern Italy, which began to appear in the fourth century BC *(Figure 25)*. They are bowl-shaped

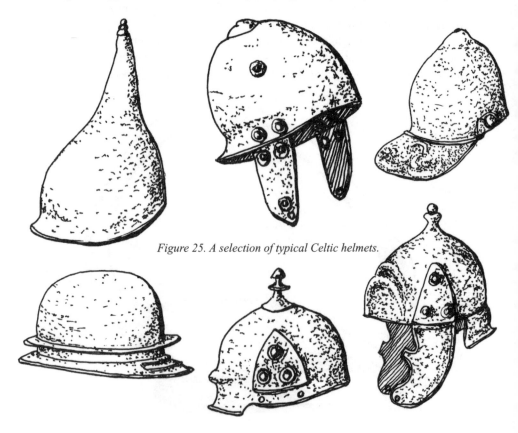

Figure 25. A selection of typical Celtic helmets.

with hinged cheek-pieces and a wide neckguard. Most have a fitting on the top to take a crest of some sort, such as the bronze boars found in Hounslow, Middlesex. The boar is a frequent symbol on weaponry of this period, as an animal renowned for its strength and fierceness.

As we have noted, the more special finds may not have been intended for practical use, but for display and for ceremony. Celtic chieftains probably desired a highly visible statement of their importance and power, and achieved this through spectacular armour and weapons – but this does not mean they could not have been used in anger. The rich examples that have survived have done so in some cases precisely because they were special, and so were placed in tombs or in votive deposits. The bulk of the more ordinary armour and weapons were probably not treated with so much care and attention, and so have failed to survive into the archaeological record – but as archaeologists like to say, absence of evidence is not evidence of absence! It is likely that there were far greater numbers of less extraordinary swords, helmets, shields and so on in general circulation at the time.

Armies and chariots
A remarkable find from Denmark illustrates the armour and weapons of a north European army in 300–400BC. The find was made in a bog at Hjortspring Mose; a clinker-built wooden boat, 21 metres long, had been deposited along with the accoutrements of its crew. It could have carried twenty-four men. There were the remains of a number of chainmail tunics, 169 iron spearheads (sixty-five from heavy spears, sixty-four from lances and a few 'special' forms), eleven swords, four with ash scabbards, and parts from more than fifty shields. It has been estimated that this deposit represents an invading army of about 100 men, each armed with two or three spears and a shield. They would have come in four boats, and each boat had twenty rowers, two helmsmen and a captain, the officers being armed with a sword, shield and chainmail tunic.

The deposit may represent a thankful offering to the gods by the people of Als for the defeat of these invaders. One of the most important aspects of this find is the revelation of an organised army in northern Europe at this time, a phenomenon that is usually only associated with the Mediterranean world.

The use of chariots in warfare was long-established in Asia Minor and the Mediterranean, but chariots in northern Europe were not generally the same, or even used in the same way. Chariots and chariot fittings, however, were another opportunity for display, and many examples of terret rings, horse bits, harness mounts and other fittings survive, intricately cast and brightly enamelled. In a number of areas, chariots, and sometimes the horses that pulled them, were interred with wealthy leaders in their tombs. The Marne region of northern France and the Arras cultural area of Yorkshire are particularly noted for chariot burials.

The horses that pulled these vehicles were small, sturdy animals, similar to modern Dartmoor ponies, between eleven and thirteen hands high, and were harnessed in pairs. There is some evidence that stud farms existed in Late Iron Age Britain to breed suitable cavalry and chariot horses. Further research into this possibility, through isotope analysis of horse teeth, is continuing.

Two-wheeled chariots are depicted in Scandinavian rock art from about 1000BC, shown with two horses, spoked wheels and a single driver. Average sizes for north European chariots are roughly two by four metres. The wheels, usually about 90cm in diameter, had single-piece iron tyres and iron hub fittings, the rest of the vehicle being made from lightweight woods and wicker or woven leather panels, with free-hanging axles for suspension.

Chariots were common in Europe until about 100BC, although they continued in use for much longer in Britain. They gave an attacking force the advantage of speed and mobility on the battlefield. At the battle of Telamon in 225BC, the Gauls had 20,000 cavalry and chariots, according to Polybius. These chariots held a driver and a warrior; the driver would bring the chariot within range and the warrior would throw lances at the enemy, and then dismount to fight on foot. The driver could then drive back to the warrior to pick him up if he was too severely beset.

Julius Caesar's only major encounters with chariots were in Britain, where he notes that chariots were very effective against cavalry. He also suggests that the chariot drivers were sitting, an arrangement which worked well on a reconstruction of a chariot from Wetwang Slack made for the BBC in 2001. This reconstruction, carefully made with advice from the British Museum, proved a stable vehicle, with a tight turning circle, and trials with various poses (throwing spears from the platform, jumping on and off while carrying sword and shield) worked extremely well.

Cavalry and mercenaries, and contacts with Greece and Rome

The horses used as cavalry mounts may well have been a little larger than the chariot ponies. The skills of Gaulish and Celtic cavalry soldiers were well appreciated by the Greeks and Romans, who were themselves late in developing mounted forces. 'Barbarian' cavalry fighters were recruited as mercenaries in the armies of Greece, Etruria, Rome and the Carthaginians. They had a major role as skirmishers.

Celtic cavalry is recorded as fighting with Hannibal in the Second Punic War, and Celtic mercenaries were recruited by Cleopatra VII of Egypt and

Herod the Great of Judea, and a whole group of Gaulish mercenaries established a kingdom in Galatia, near modern Ankara in Turkey, in the third century BC *(Figure 26)*.

Earlier, in the fourth century, the Greek writer and soldier Xenophon described Celtic mercenary cavalry in action against soldiers from the city of Thebes. He tells us that they charged the Thebans, throwing their lances, then wheeling away to make further charges, sometimes dismounting to rest themselves and their horses between attacks. If attacked, they would retreat rapidly, then at a safer distance turn and shower their pursuers with thrown lances. In doing this, they were able to draw the Theban army forward or push it back at will.

We hear that in 259BC, Celtic troops in Egypt mutinied against Ptolemy II. They were defeated, and left to starve to death on an island in the Nile, but a few years later Ptolemy recruited new Celtic mercenaries because of their usefulness. At the battle of Raphia, a combined army of Egyptian troops and 4,000 Celtic cavalry fought the Syrians. In this battle, one of the major uses of this cavalry was to pursue fleeing foot soldiers and cut them down. The only drawback of these troops was said to be their extreme susceptibility to superstition – one army having been unmanned by the appearance of an eclipse and refusing to fight at all, as they were sure this was to be an omen of defeat.

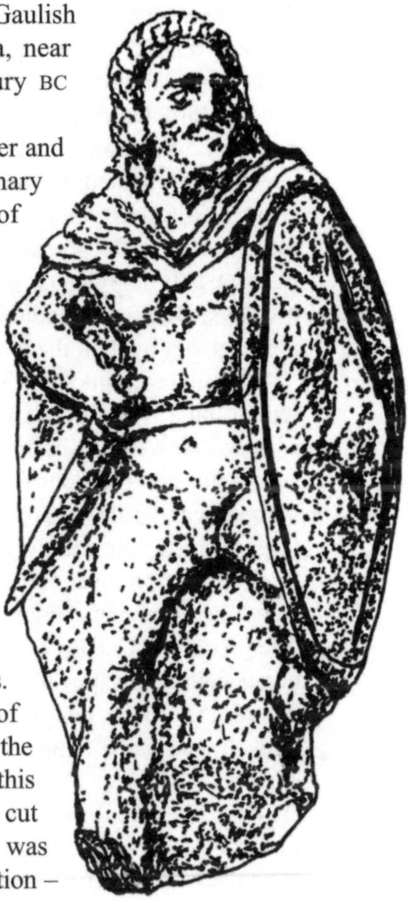

Figure 26. Statuette of a Celtic mercenary from Egypt.

Certainly by this time the Greeks and Romans were well aware of the martial qualities of the northern Europeans. In the early part of the first millennium BC, Germanic peoples had started to move westwards; in the fourth century BC further waves of migration followed, heading both south and east. Some moved into northern Italy, and raided southwards, attacking Rome itself in 390BC, forcing the Romans to pay them a large ransom. Groups of Celts settled in northern Italy, which became known as Cisalpine Gaul, from where they continued to threaten the growing Roman state until defeated at the battle of Telamon in 225BC.

Some groups moved into the Iberian peninsula, and during the fourth century BC groups of Gauls entered the Balkans, defeating local tribes; in

279BC they invaded Greece. According to Greek accounts, a great Celtic army of about 85,000 warriors was assembled in 280BC. This army split into three divisions, one moving against the Thracians, one against the Macedonians, and the third, under a leader called Brennus, advanced against the Paeonians, north of Macedon. Each division had some successes and losses, but eventually retreated. Brennus wanted another campaign, and raised another army, said to have included 152,000 infantry and 24,400 cavalry, although these numbers are probably greatly exaggerated. A Greek alliance met the Celts at Thermopylae on the east coast of the Greek mainland and held the invaders; Brennus eventually managed to find a way round the bottleneck of the pass, but by then the Greeks had escaped in ships.

Brennus continued towards Delphi, where he was defeated and forced to retreat, later dying of his wounds, or according to the Greeks, committing suicide. However, another story suggests that the raid on Delphi was successful and that loot from the shrine was eventually taken to the Celts' home town of Tolosa, modern Toulouse, and deposited as offerings in sacred lakes, from where the Romans later stole it in 105BC. According to Strabo, this amounted to over 50,000 bars of gold and 10,000 bars of silver, each bar weighing 15 pounds. Another account suggests a rather more modest hoard. The proconsul Caepio was ordered to send the bullion back to Rome, but it mysteriously disappeared on the way, apparently stolen by a band of marauders. Many people at the time were convinced that it was Caepio himself who had arranged for the raid. After that, the treasure was said to be cursed.

By 192BC the Romans gained control of the Cisalpine region, but by this time the Celts were well established in northern Italy and continued to live there under Roman rule. Germanic tribes moved into Bohemia and the eastern Alps. These included a tribe called the Cimbri, possibly originally from Jutland, and they defeated a Roman army in Noricum in 113BC; the Cimbri were joined by another tribe, the Teutoni, and they began to raid across the area north of the Alps and Italy. An attempt was made to invade Italy in 102BC, which was repelled by Roman armies that year and the next. Other tribes had also been pushed westwards across the Rhine, adding to the dislocation of polities across the region, a process which was still continuing when Julius Caesar began his conquest of Gaul in 58BC.

Skeletons and trauma in the Late Iron Age North
These and earlier people-movements and their effects may be related to the discoveries made in northeastern France at sites such as Gournay-sur-Aronde and Ribemont-sur-Ancre. These are the sites of Iron Age sanctuaries. Gournay began in the fourth century BC and was destroyed at the end of the

first century BC. It was a square enclosure surrounded by a palisade and ditch. In another ditch next to this sanctuary were discovered 2,000 iron weapons and pieces of armour, which had originally been displayed as more than 300 separate sets of equipment – sword, scabbard, shield, baldric, and lance, possibly erected on a platform or suspended on poles in the inner precinct, for perhaps a hundred years, until the supports and organic material rotted away. It is thought probable that this was a display of war trophies by the Bellovaci, a Belgic tribe moving into the area.

At Ribemont-sur-Ancre near Amiens, an even more macabre display was found. In the inner precinct, six cubic blocks formed metre-and-a-half square ossuaries, walled by human bones, on which further human bones had been crushed and burned. Other bones were scattered thickly across the area. Over 1,000 individuals are represented at the site. None of the bodies had a head, and the heads were not found at the site.

In the centre was a platform on which a further 500 headless bodies, complete with their armour and weapons, had been attached to poles for display. These bodies all belonged to men aged between fifteen and forty.

Many hundreds of weapons and pieces of armour were also found at the site, which has been dated to 280–260BC. Pollen evidence suggests that the corpses were assembled after a late summer battle. It is possible that the heads were taken away as trophies, or possibly deposited in the nearby river. One theory is that this site represents a war memorial, commemorating a victory after a battle between local tribes and migrating Belgic or Germanic warriors, possibly the Ambiani tribe. Such a visible symbol would possibly have served as a deterrent to other would-be invaders, or conversely as a symbol of dominance by conquerors.

The removal of the heads seems to have been a fairly common practice. One Roman writer described how the decapitated heads would be strung from the necks of the Gallic horses, or those of the most important enemies would be embalmed and kept in their homes as trophies. For the Celtic peoples, the head was the residence of the soul and the source of spiritual power. Cults of the head are recorded in southern France, at sanctuaries at Roquepertuse and Entremont, where shrines with carved stone heads and portal niches for real skulls were set up.

There may just be some other indications of the fate of prisoners of war in Late Iron Age contexts. At a number of sites there are some 'atypical' burials which could represent the unhappy end of some prisoners. The hillfort at Danebury in Hampshire contains a number of human burials in disused grain storage pits, some of which are crammed into very small spaces or appear tightly scrunched up as if they had been tied before burial. Some bodies had been weighed down with blocks of chalk or flint. These were the bodies of young men, and some had evidence of traumatic injuries of the type that might be sustained in fighting. There were no grave goods with these bodies, which had been disposed of in a way that was totally unlike the normal (and invisible) funerary rites of the period. A similar burial at the South Cadbury hillfort in Somerset was of a young man who had been placed, tightly bound, upside down in the pit. At Acy-Romance (Ardennes), a number of bodies had been placed in a sitting position around the edges of an open space possibly used for rituals with three set in a line facing east; the excavators believed that these twenty or so young men had been crammed into small wooden boxes (whether before or after death is unknown) and the boxes had then been lowered into pits until all the flesh had dried. The remains were then dug up and re-interred in the sitting positions. Another French site, Fesques in Seine-Maritime, produced further 'sitting' bodies among twenty-six recovered sets of remains. Analysis of the foot and ankle bones of these men suggested that they had been suspended by their feet at some time prior to death. At Hamn near Kville in Sweden, there is a Bronze Age rock carving which appears to show, among scenes of warriors and boats, a group of armless people hanging by their feet from a horizontal bar or pole. They could possibly be interpreted as prisoners of war; although this must be pure speculation, the suspension of bodies, the placing of bodies upside-down, and the unusual burials might be evidence of how victorious groups expressed their contempt for defeated enemies.

Beyond the sphere of Roman and Greek influence, other wars seem to have been fought. Evidence for one has recently appeared in Denmark, in a bog at Alken Enge. Here, finds including human bones hacked and damaged by axes, clubs and spears have come to light, along with weapons including a finely preserved iron axe. The bones represent hundreds of warriors who died around the start of the first millennium AD. The site covers a very large area, the boundaries of which are still not yet confirmed. Alken Enge was apparently used as a place of sacrifice over a long period in the Iron Age, and the press have been referring to the warrior burials as sacrifices, although they may equally well represent a mass war grave. The site is still being excavated, a process that may take many more seasons of work before the full story emerges.

A study of skeletal remains from Dorset, especially Maiden Castle and Poundbury Camp, found a number of skulls with trauma resulting from weapons use, particularly, possibly, slingshots, as well as sharp projectiles. Young adult females were represented amongst the injured, although the majority of those suffering trauma were young males. The examples of trauma in Dorset came almost exclusively from individuals buried at hillforts, and it has been suggested that the distribution of many of the wounds over the skulls might indicate that barrages of slingshots were employed, while direct facial hits would suggest that some slingers had more experience or skill. Some individuals had healed injuries, leading to the conclusion that violent episodes had occurred on a number of occasions.

The skulls studied came from the very end of the Iron Age, perhaps at the time of the Roman Conquest, and it is impossible to say whether the injuries were sustained in inter-tribal conflict, or in battle with the Roman forces commanded by the future emperor Vespasian, who was in charge of the conquest of Dorset and the West Country. There are also cranial fractures and injuries identified in Iron Age contexts at Cadbury Castle hillfort in Somerset, Danebury in Hampshire, and in cemetery populations in East Yorkshire. But burials are relatively rare in Iron Age Britain, and the examples that we have to study are the exceptional cases rather than the normal.

In Central Europe at this time, cremation was a preferred rite over a wide area, and thus few traces remain from which weapons injury can be identified. Inhumation burials occurred more rarely, for example in northeast France and in Belgium, and more commonly in southern Germany (but still few in number). Scattered bones have been found at several excavated sites, including examples with weapons trauma, at Manching, for example, along with broken weapons, but this evidence is not seen in formal burials.

Inhumation burials are found in the French Alps, and mixed cremation and inhumation practices went on in parts of central France. In northern Germany, cremation was generally preferred. Overall, this leaves the archaeologist with an unsatisfactory situation with regard to skeletal evidence for war in the late Iron Age, despite the other indications of conflict.

Chapter 7

The Roman Perspective

In the last centuries before the birth of Christ, the peoples of northern and southern Europe came to know more and more about each other. Traders crossed the Alpine passes, or ran barges up the river systems, calling at the great tribal hillforts to exchange Mediterranean pottery, metal goods, oil and wine for leather and farm produce, metals and amber, furs and grain. Northerners went south to serve in the armies of Greece and Egypt, and to learn about building methods, commerce, coinage and politics. Ideas were traded as well as goods. But perhaps the Northerners were too naïve, or too honest, to understand that by making contact with one of the Mediterranean peoples, they were opening the door to exploitation, invasion and conquest. How could they know that the oh-so-friendly handshakes of the merchants would be followed by the iron fist of the world's first professional armies? They had managed to deal with Greeks, Etruscans, and Phoenicians to mutual benefit; when they came to realise that the Romans were different, it was already too late for many. First contacts with Rome marked the beginning of the end for much of northern European tradition, art, history and belief.

Coming into contact with history
At the end of the Iron Age, the peoples of Northern Europe were increasingly connected to those of the Mediterranean world, who began to record their knowledge and impressions of the barbarians with whom they were trading and fighting. The Celts, Gauls and Germans did not use writing – their history was oral – so the only historical records we have are from the Mediterranean point of view. There are early Greek accounts of the peoples north of the Alps: Hecataeus mentions a Celtic city called Nyrax and uses the term Hyperboreans to describe these people, Hellanicus of Lesbos says they were a just and righteous people, and Herodotus, also in the fifth century BC, tells us that the River Danube lay in the territory of the Celts, and that the Celts live 'beyond the Pillars of Hercules' (usually thought to be Gibraltar) near the Cynesians who are the most westerly of the peoples of Europe.

Contact began even earlier than this, certainly from 600BC when the Greeks established trading colonies in southern France and Spain, at Marseilles, Nice and other locations. In the fourth century the geographer

Pytheas tells us that the British Isles lie north of the lands of the Celts, and in the second century BC Pausanias says that the Gauls were originally called Celts, and lived in a remote land on the edge of a tidal ocean, in which is the island of Britain. He also hints at knowledge of Scandinavia when he speaks of the most remote Celts called Kabares who are very tall and 'live on the edges of the ice desert'. Aristotle believed that Celts lived 'beyond Spain' and were very warlike. Ephorus, around 350BC, described them as being friendly, while Plato says they were drunken and aggressive, and tended towards barbaric acts.

We owe much of our knowledge to Strabo, who died in 24AD. A great traveller, he collected much more informative detail about the excellent agriculture and large houses of the Celts, and their social customs. He thought the women were good mothers, but that the men were quick to get into arguments, and were warlike but generous and naïve. They were, he says, keen to learn and acquire Greek and Roman culture. He admired their cavalry, which by his time had been co-opted into the Roman army. He noted that there were great social divisions between the nobles and peasants. Diodorus Siculus confirms many of Strabo's comments, and adds that the Celts were very fond of gold.

A much later writer, Ammianus Marcellinus, in the later fourth century AD, comments on the height of the Gauls, their good looks and arrogance. He notes that they were very clean, but he was clearly rather frightened by Gallic women, who were likely to enter a fight on behalf of their husbands and do a lot of damage!

Polybius has been mentioned earlier – his account of the battle of Telamon in 225AD is very detailed. He mentions the trousers and cloaks of most of the warriors and their gold torcs, but also that some warriors thought it more efficient to fight naked – although he points out that this did not work – their bodies were easier to hit with missiles when unprotected by clothes and armour. He also mentions the use of noise in Celtic battles – the shouting of war cries, the trumpets and horns – which unnerved the Roman army. The Roman writer Livy also notes the use of noise, including beating of weapons against shields, and leaping, screaming into the air, and other accounts add the noise of the hundreds of chariot wheels bearing spear-wielding warriors.

Polybius believed, however, that the Celts could not sustain a battle; they fought very well when fresh, but quickly lost heart if the first assault failed or was halted. On the other hand, they reserved their violence for their armed opponents, and did not attack the farms and villages on their routes. Strabo says that the Celts were, as a race, 'war-mad'. They would call out taunts and issue individual challenges when two forces drew up for battle. Their leaders wore brightly coloured clothing, and were resplendent with gold and enamel jewellery (a source of interest for Roman soldiers keen to acquire booty).

The height of the average Gaul or Celt was greater than that of the Greeks and Romans, and their light-coloured skins and hair set them apart as a different race in Mediterranean eyes. The Romans initially thought the huge Gaulish warriors they encountered were more than human. Diodorus Siculus, a Sicilian Greek writing at the time of Julius Caesar, says that they deliberately exaggerated their appearance – with big moustaches, and long hair which they covered with limewater to create a sort of punk rock crest.

The classical writers did recognise some regional differences between these peoples – the Gauls had fair or red hair, the British were taller than the Gauls but their hair was darker, and the Germans were taller again, with red hair, and were more savage. Strabo tells us that it was a disgrace for a warrior to become fat, and such a man could be fined, although other writers say they over-indulged with food and wine and were liable to become fat and flabby. The women were as big and strong as the men. Strabo says the Gauls were simple people, with high spirits, but boastful and liable to fall to pieces when they lost a fight.

Trousers were something of a novelty for the Romans, although they quickly came to appreciate their usefulness on horseback, and it was not long before the Roman cavalry adopted this barbarian garment.

The question of alcohol is an important one. Wine was the most important trade item imported into barbarian Europe, along with Mediterranean feasting vessels. The appetite of the northern tribes for the drink became almost a matter of legend. Before contact with the south, the peoples of the north had not been strangers to alcohol – they had been making beer and honey drinks for many centuries. Strong mead was the drink favoured by the upper classes, but the new drink supplanted mead and suddenly the tribal aristocracies could not get enough of it. Wine and the ability to entertain followers to great feasts was a central part of northern politics.

A leader who could provide lavish food and drink was displaying his wealth and power, and could attract the best warriors and the greatest loyalty. Being able to provide exotic drink in imported vessels was a sign of the importance and influence of the chief. To the horror of the Greeks and Romans, the northerners drank their wine neat (instead of watering it down as was the southern custom). And they drank a lot of it. One of the things the Romans most wanted from the north was a supply of slaves, and it was said that a slave could be purchased for a single amphora of wine.

The size of the trade is staggering. Hundreds of thousands of amphora sherds of a type called Dressel 1 have been found in Southern France dating from the late second to the late first century BC. Two major centres – Tolosa

(Toulouse) and Cabillonum (Chalon-sur-Saône) – were both actually built on amphora sherds. It became the habit from the first century BC to ship wine up the French rivers in amphorae to a river port such as Toulouse or Lyon, and then transfer it into barrels, some with a capacity of +1,000 litres, for onward shipping by barge into northern Gaul and beyond. Special wine barges were created for this trade – basically, 'ro-ros', so that the barrels could be easily loaded and unloaded.

The result of the desire for the luxury imports from the south led to tribal chiefs waging war on each other to acquire slaves to trade to the Romans, destabilising the country and paving the way for conquest. Tribal territories

Figure 27. Tribes of Pre-Roman Gaul.

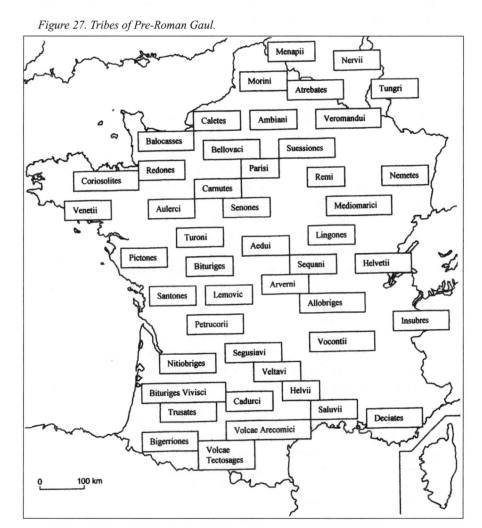

probably became more defined as a result, creating more recognisable borders and identities *(Figure 27)*. The Nervii tribe of Gallia Belgica (modern-day northwest France and Belgium), who were noted for their ferocity in battle, and the Germans too, believed wine weakened men, and they were aware of the dangers of the trade; in response, the Nervii closed their borders to Roman traders.

Roman contact with the Celts and Gauls had begun, as discussed earlier, in the fourth century BC, with Brennus at the Battle of Clusium. The Roman army that met Brennus and his tribesmen was not at all like the army of Julius Caesar 300 years later. It was not yet a professional army, but a militia formed from citizens of a certain status, and resembled a Greek hoplite force. The army was raised annually, and the men served for a year at a time, led by the two consuls elected to lead the Senate for that year. Not all politicians were good generals. Below the consuls came the twenty-four *tribuni militares*, each legion having six of these officers who were experienced soldiers. The entire force was arranged on the basis of social class, with a small core of *equites* (mounted nobles) and five classes of other citizens.

The centre of their battle line was made up of the more heavily armed upper-class soldiers, with less well armed and trained conscripted forces on the flanks. Each soldier had to provide his own equipment, meaning that the poorer men were often ill-prepared for battle. The Celts led by Brennus were able to rout the Roman flanks, and surround and kill the central force. The survivors fled back to Rome and barricaded themselves in. They were able to hold off a Celtic assault on the stronghold of the Capitoline Hill, but the tribesmen looted the rest of the city. The Celts were, however, weakened by the outbreak of an epidemic, and eventually a peace treaty was negotiated, with the Romans agreeing to pay 1,000 pounds of gold if the Celts would go away.

At this point a Roman relief army arrived, and further fighting broke out in the streets of the city, but neither side could gain an advantage in these crowded conditions, and so both retreated outside the city limits, and a battle took place the next day. The Gallic army was routed, according to the Roman accounts. Another version suggests that part of Brennus' army was British.

From this time on, the Gaulish or Celtic warrior became something of a bogeyman in the minds of the Romans, the only enemy ever to raid Rome itself.

As a result of this incident, the Romans began building a wall around their city – the Servian Wall. They also began a major restructuring of the army. The Greek-style long phalanx spear was abandoned, and more standardisation of weapons and armour was introduced. The composition of the army itself was altered, as the loss of so many upper-class citizens to Brennus at Clusium was seen to be unsustainable.

Three types of troops were created – the *hastate* – young soldiers with body armour and a rectangular shield, with a sword and javelins, supported by skirmishers, the *principes* – experienced soldiers, equipped like the *hastate*, who formed the main battle line, and the *triarii*, heavily-armed veteran troops who fought in the hoplite fashion – in large formations. Further troops of younger or less dependable men (*velites*) were attached to each legion, which then numbered about 4,800 in total.

In a typical battle formation, the front line consisted of *principes* armed with sword and *pilum* (a light throwing spear), behind their *scuti* (large curved hide shields); behind these came the *hastate*, with lighter smaller shields, and to the flanks the *velites* with just a *pilum*. The *triarii* with their heavier armour formed the reserve.

Over the next hundred years or so, lessons were learned – notably as a result of the campaigns of Lucius Cornelius Scipio (Scipio Africanus), whose actions against the Carthaginians were a great success. It became the practice to recruit auxiliary troops, particularly cavalry, to supplement the infantry army. The most important changes, however, took place as a result of the consulship of Gaius Marius in 108BC. Marius was a soldier, and had a successful career, but he was very aware that change was required, in particular in manning the army and supporting it. In order to qualify for army service up to this point, a citizen was required to own a certain amount of wealth, and to provide his own armour and weapons. This meant that the vast majority of the poor were exempt from military service, or were poorly equipped and untrained.

Marius arranged instead to pay these poorer citizens and to provide their kit, turning them into the world's first professional army. He divided up the legions into cohorts, to spread these new recruits among the veterans, and started the process in which a legion became self-sufficient, no matter where in the world it was sent. He encouraged recruits by offering retirement packages in the form of land grants, pensions and citizenship status. This army was permanent, and could be trained continuously; their equipment was standardised, and specialists – smiths, doctors, leather-workers, engineers, whatever was needed – were attached to each legion to ensure their ability to maintain efficiency in distant lands. More soldiers were recruited from the new provinces that Rome had gained after the Punic Wars – heavy infantry and cavalry and archers, serving in auxiliary units attached to the legions. Some of Marius' reforms were in place before his time, but he is regarded as the man who formalised the structure of the Roman army during its greatest periods of conquest and expansion.

The equipment of the Roman soldier by the time of Julius Caesar included a dagger and a short sword called a *gladius*, and the *pilum* or throwing lance about two metres long, with an iron shank designed to bend on impact, so that it could not be thrown back at the Romans, and if impacted into a shield would hamper the enemy. Different types of armour were in use in the late Republic and early Empire; mail shirts, copied from those of the Celts, were used, as was scale armour and from at least 9BC *lorica segmentata* – metal strips mounted on leather straps, forming a cuirass, with further strips protecting the shoulders and upper arms. Metal greaves protected the legs.

A rectangular curved shield, the *scutum*, gave personal protection and could also be used in formation as each man locked his shield with his neighbours, with those in the centre of the formation raising their shields to provide an overhead cover for the whole unit – the *testudo* or tortoise. Each soldier wore a metal helmet with cheek-pieces. They wore woollen tunics and neckcloths to prevent chafing by the armour, a sword belt, underpants and, if cavalry, trousers. They had oiled cloaks, and leather laced boots with iron hobnails on the soles. Around the waist was the *pteruges* – an apron of leather strips studded with metal to protect the groin.

Each soldier carried a pack containing a satchel, waterskin, food, cooking equipment and entrenching tools – shovels, picks or baskets – a total of about 27kg of kit. The amount of kit to be carried by each soldier earned them the nickname of 'Marius's mules'. Each tent group of eight men would also in theory have a real mule to carry a tent and other equipment, although these were not always available, or might be replaced by wagons. A marching Roman army also had ballistic weapons. The *ballista* was a form of large crossbow *(Plate 13)*, while the *onager* was a catapult weapon. Soldiers might also carry caltrops to strew in front of enemy cavalry. The caltrops, made of iron, each had four points arranged so that one always pointed upwards, and were strewn in a wide field in front of the ramparts and ditches where attackers or their horses would step on them.

The legions were divided into cohorts which were further subdivided into centuries of between sixty and 100 men, led by a professional non-commissioned officer structure under the legionary tribunes and legate.

The training of a legionary soldier included weapons drills, formation marching, swimming and physical training and combat training. The swords were used in stabbing movements from behind a shield wall – each soldier was protected by his neighbours, and the wall of shields would pin the enemy against an immovable barrier. Deployment in battle was still based on the three-line pattern, with light troops in the front and veterans to the rear. Gaps in the formation allowed flexibility.

The first act would often be the throwing of the spears by the front-line troops, who would then retreat through the gaps behind the other lines. The second line would then move in to fill the gaps and present an unbroken front.

They could then charge at the enemy, but if forced back, the third line would allow them through the gaps and then themselves form a new unbroken line. The retreating men could then rest and re-form. These formations could be modified as topography or situation required. Soldiers also practised forming square against cavalry, wedge formations for shock charges, scattered and circular formations and others.

The legion on the march was able to throw up a fortified camp every night, surrounded by a palisade and ditch, and laid out on a pre-conceived plan that allowed every man to know exactly where to find his unit, even in the dark. These camps provided strong staging posts as the legions advanced. More permanent fortresses were eventually built when a legion was permanently garrisoned in an area. The engineers attached to each legion were also trained in siege techniques – building trenches, siege towers, artillery positions for *ballistae* and *onagers*, and battering rams.

All this contrasted strongly with the ways in which the Gauls, Celts and Germans went into battle. Many Roman accounts stress that the Celtic first assault was the key. There was no organisation – the tribesmen attacked as a mob, brave and ferocious, and in that first moment, they could strike terror into the hearts of their enemies. In the early days of contact, they won a number of victories, such as Noreia and Arausio, as well as sacking Rome. The Romans learned from this, as we have seen. But so did the tribes. They were tough and quick to adopt other strategies. They began to employ the 'shield wall' and formations such as the wedge attack. They often had the advantage of numbers, were able to move quickly, and learned to use guerrilla tactics. They could also use the landscape to advantage, as was shown a little later by Arminius in the Teutoburger Forest. But they did not have the training and organisation of the Romans, and lacked the ability to supply and sustain lengthy campaigns. The Romans could resupply from bases by mobilising water transport as well as overland supply routes, utilising the string of forts that they built as staging areas, and by building roads for rapid movement. The tribal warriors wore less armour than the Romans and their weapons were sometimes inferior.

The use of chariots and cavalry was a strongpoint of early Celtic and Gallic warfare. The speed of their charge could halt and even force into retreat the Roman advance, but was countered by the Roman ability to re-form their lines, and to use ballistic missiles against them. But chariots were disappearing in continental Europe, in favour of cavalry, although they continued to be used in Britain *(Figure 28)*.

Caesar's campaigns
By the time of Julius Caesar's campaigns in France and Britain, there was a

Figure 28. Reconstruction drawing of a British war chariot (drawn by Karen Hill).

certain familiarity on both sides. Julius Caesar was born around 100BC and took the Roman path to political power through army service, gaining important rank, until in 59BC he became a Consul, in command of Cisalpine Gaul and Illyricum, and then adding Transalpine Gaul to his responsibilities. He had, therefore, a more or less free hand for his ambitions north of the Alps. By this time, southern Gaul had adopted many of the ways introduced by the Greek trading colonies – coinage, towns and even writing. Important tribes had fallen at least in part under the Mediterranean influence – the Helvetii, Aedui, Arverni, Biturges and Sequani among others.

North of this region, however, the old ways persisted among the tribes, albeit coloured by the desire to acquire Mediterranean luxury imports, especially wine. In 58BC, the Helvetii began a mass migration westwards. This worried the Allobroges, whose land they would have to cross, and Roman assistance was requested. In the event, a deal had been struck between the tribes before the Romans arrived, but Caesar saw this as a training opportunity for his troops, and attacked the Helvetii, driving them back across the border into what is now Switzerland, where, according to Caesar's account, they had twelve *oppida* and some 400 villages, comprising something over quarter of a million people, although this number is thought to be doubtfully high.

Much of Caesar's account seems to be designed as propaganda, stressing the superior military ability of his command and the savagery of his opponents, and has to be taken with a hefty pinch of salt! The Helvetii were tricked into waiting for negotiations, allowing the Romans to fortify their position and bring up more troops. As soon as the Romans were strong enough, Caesar refused the tribe permission to continue, forcing the Helvetii to turn north, crossing the lands of the Aedui, who also called on Roman help. The migration began to cross the River Saône, but the people were not all across when Caesar attacked, forcing them to retreat. The Roman soldiers built a bridge and threatened them again. The leader of the Helvetii, Divico, offered to move his people to settle wherever the Romans wanted, but he warned that if the Romans refused, a battle would follow.

The first skirmish was against Aedui cavalry, allied to the Romans, and the Helvetii won. They pushed forward with their migration while the Romans were waiting for their grain supplies to arrive. But Caesar's army quickly caught up with them near Mont Beuvray (the Aedui *oppidum* of Bibracte) and routed most of the warriors, forcing the tribe to retreat without their supplies and baggage. Three days later, after threats from Caesar, the Helvetii surrendered, agreeing to provide hostages and give up their weapons, although a large number of a tribe allied to the Helvetii attempted to escape. The tribe was then forced back to their original territory. According to Caesar's own estimates, only 30 per cent of the tribespeople survived to reach home.

Caesar's motives in this campaign have been much discussed, and it is suggested that he wanted an excuse to begin a larger campaign in Gaul that would strengthen his political position in Rome, and provide him with funds from captured booty, as well as turning the troops at his command into seasoned veterans. His reported successes ensured that his tour of office was extended, and supplies and troops continued to be made available to him. As soon as the Helvetii had been dealt with, Caesar turned his attentions to the Sequani, also ostensibly to aid the Aedui, and quickly defeated them too.

The Belgae of northeastern Gaul were next. Warfare against these tribes was not easy: they had a fierce reputation, and were politically strong, having formed alliances against Roman intervention. The Remi tribe, however, decided to betray their countrymen and side with Caesar. The allied tribes attacked an *oppidum* of the Remi, but Caesar came to defend it, and won a battle on the River Aisne. The tribes retreated and Caesar and his legions began to pick them off piecemeal. Caesar had a total of about 42,000 legionaries, and he claims that the opposition consisted of 75,000 warriors from the Atrebates, Veromandui, Aduataci and dominant Nervii tribes, although modern estimates suggest 25,000 would be a more likely number.

The tribes had moved their civilians to an area protected by marshes, and began to congregate on the far side of a river called Sabis (now the River Selle). Caesar learned that spies among the conquered Gauls travelling with his army had gone to the Belgae to report on his troops and dispositions. A plan to cut off the leading legion as soon as its baggage train appeared was developed, using barriers of cut thorn hedges to impede Caesar's advance. Forewarned, the order of march of the legions was changed so that six legions now led the army, with the baggage trains to the rear. The Romans began to set up a camp across the river from the Belgae, having sent some cavalry across the broad but shallow river to reconnoitre. The tribes then saw six legions arrive, not just the one they had hoped for, but they decided to go ahead with their plan, and as soon as they spotted the baggage train, they charged.

The legionaries were unprepared, and at first it seemed that the Belgae could not lose, but the well-trained Roman soldiers rallied quickly and crossed the river. They were able twice to push back the Atrebates on the left flank and the Viromandui in the centre with four legions, although they had not had time to form into their usual cohorts. While they were engaged in these fights, a column of Nervii took advantage of the gap to charge in to surround the two legions on the right flank, and the upper section of the camp. The Roman cavalry and skirmishers had been routed and were just managing to return when they met the Nervii advance; they turned tail and ran away again, and then the camp followers and baggage train handlers panicked. The auxiliary Roman cavalry, men from the Germanic Treveri tribe, decided that they would abandon Caesar and left the battlefield. Many Romans were now lying dead, including a large number of the centurions. The situation looked desperate, but was, according to his own account, saved by Caesar himself striding to the front of the line to give heart to his men.

Then the remaining legions finally caught up, and seeing the situation, their commander ordered his men to sweep round to attack the Nervii from behind. The tribesmen were now pinned, but they fought on as long as they were able, earning even Caesar's admiration. The elders of the tribe eventually came forward to surrender, because they had lost most of their fighting men and the majority of the tribal leaders. In his account, Caesar says that the tribe was utterly destroyed by this battle.

The Aduatuci had not arrived in time to take part in the battle, and hearing of the defeat, turned back, but they were defeated shortly afterwards and 53,000 of them were sold into slavery. The tribe virtually disappeared from history at this point. Other tribes in the area capitulated or were defeated in short order after the battle. The Nervii were not quite destroyed and did not give in completely – in 54BC they joined the Eburones led by Ambiorix, who had destroyed a legion and five cohorts, and they also sent men to join the confederacy to relieve the siege of Alesia in 52BC.

It was the speed of the Belgic attack which almost won them the battle, and the fact that they had caught the Romans unprepared. Their choice of a battle site was also important, as they forced the Romans on to difficult ground. But they were almost certainly outnumbered, and they lacked much cavalry. The Romans survived because of their superior training, and to some extent, sheer luck.

Caesar then sent legions to subdue the rest of northern France and Brittany, winning a naval battle against the Veneti when their sailed ships were becalmed in the Sea of Morbihan, and fell prey to Roman oared galleys. In 55BC Caesar made the first of his forays to Britain (although it is worth noting that there is absolutely no surviving archaeological evidence of Roman troops in Britain at this time). Britain was an obvious target – it was rich, exporting grain, metals, leather, slaves and other wealth to continental Europe. It also, according to Caesar, actively assisted Gaulish resistance, and welcomed refugees, especially from among the Belgae, who had already settled in Britain (either as invaders or migrants). The Roman town of Winchester became known as Venta Belgarum (the market-place of the Belgae). Scouts were sent to look for landing places for a Roman invasion, and merchants were questioned about the state of the country, although they gave little information away.

Some British groups became aware of the impending invasion and sent diplomatic parties to negotiate a surrender, probably aware of the devastation that had been suffered by their Gallic neighbours and wishing to avoid a repetition of the slaughter in Britain. Commius, leader of the Atrebates in Belgic Gaul, had become one of Caesar's allies, and he was sent to negotiate with as many tribes as he could to ensure an unopposed Roman landing. A fleet was assembled, consisting of transports for the legions, warships and cavalry transports. It was late summer, and it seems Caesar was in a hurry to complete his invasion before winter set in and the Channel became uncrossable. The Romans were rarely very happy at sea. As a result, the baggage trains and siege weapons were left behind.

The initial landing was attempted at Dover, but as the ships approached, the Romans could see large numbers of British warriors lining the top of the white cliffs, spears at the ready. They decided to sail on, possibly to Walmer, with British chariots and warriors tracking them along the coast. When the fleet finally anchored, it was unable to come very close in to the shallow shelving beach, so the reluctant troops were forced to jump into quite deep water while being attacked from the shore. Catapult fire from the ships eventually drove the defenders back sufficiently for the legions to reach the beach, but the cavalry transports were not yet in sight, and they were unable to drive the British off very far. A beachhead camp was constructed, and here Caesar met with various embassies and with Commius, who had been held prisoner ever since he had arrived in Britain. Hostages were given by the embassies, who agreed to disband their forces.

Things then turned bad for the Romans, as the weather became nasty. The cavalry transports could not land, and were forced back to Gaul, along with the supplies. One thing that Caesar had not bargained for was that the sea was tidal – the Mediterranean has only minimal tidal changes. Having beached his ships in Mediterranean fashion, Caesar was dismayed to find that they were inundated by the incoming tide or smashed against each other by the rough seas; many were wrecked or badly damaged.

The British quickly took advantage of the situation, preparing ambushes for the Romans who were forced inland to forage for food. Caesar had to commit legionaries to protect the foraging parties, and drive the British back. The weather continued to be stormy, allowing the British to regroup and attack the camp. The Romans managed to resist the attack with a force of cavalry that Commius had somehow raised locally, and those Britons keen to make an alliance with the Romans renewed their diplomatic efforts. But Caesar could see that his campaign was a failure, and he had as many of the ships repaired as possible and sailed back to Gaul. Most of the British reneged immediately on the agreements they had made with him. Nevertheless, he managed to 'spin' the expedition as a success to those back in Rome, on the grounds that no one before had managed to reach these distant islands.

Over the winter, he prepared a better-organised second expedition. A larger force was gathered, and augmented with traders and their ships recruited from amongst provincial Romans and Gauls, who presumably intended to share the profits of conquest. The same landing place was chosen, this time unopposed. Rather than become tied down on the beach again, Caesar immediately marched inland, possibly as far as Canterbury, meeting some British in a skirmish at a river crossing. The British retired to a forested stronghold (perhaps the hillfort of Bigbury).

It seems that the Romans were slow to learn about the British coastal conditions, however, as the very next day word reached Caesar that once again much of his fleet had been destroyed by storms and the tides. He was forced to return to the shore and set about the task of repair, and to send for replacement ships from Gaul. A fortified camp was built around the ships, of which no trace has ever been found.

Ten days later, Caesar was able to return to the river crossing, where he found a much larger British force waiting, under the leadership of Cassivellaunus of the Catuvellauni tribe, which had been pursuing an aggressive expansionist policy against other southern and eastern tribes for some time. A series of skirmishes ensued, with successes and losses on both sides; however, these persuaded Cassivellaunus that his warriors would not win a formal battle against the legions. He fell back on his chariot troops and embarked on a guerrilla campaign, slowing the Roman advance and harrying them at every opportunity.

By the time the legions reached the Thames, the only available crossing place (which may have been at Westminster, where a possible ford has been identified) had been defended with rows of sharpened stakes in the water, and an army had been assembled on the north bank. This did not stop the Romans for long, and they crossed to meet with an embassy from the Trinovantes of Essex. This tribe had not long before been the victims of the expansion of the Catuvellauni, and were inclined to aid Caesar against Cassivellaunus. Other tribes, perhaps similarly smarting under the pugnacious Catuvellauni, also joined the Roman axis, and led Caesar to a stronghold, possibly Wheathampstead, where Cassivellaunus was based. A peace treaty was negotiated – the Catuvellauni agreed to give hostages, pay a yearly tribute, and cease their aggression against their neighbours. Worried about the approaching autumn and its gales, Caesar accepted this, and he and his entire force returned to the ships and sailed back to Gaul.

The end result of these campaigns was that Rome gained a great deal more knowledge about Britain than it had previously, especially its wealth; they had created a readiness among some of the tribes to engage in trade with Rome, and to maintain diplomatic links. These advantages were to pave the way, nearly 100 years later, for Claudius' more successful attempt.

In facing the British in war, there were several aspects of conflict that were of particular note for the Romans. The first was the British use of chariots. Chariots had almost disappeared from continental warfare by this time, and Caesar's legions were unfamiliar with them, their tactics, and the ways to meet the threat. Caesar goes to some lengths to describe the noise and disruption caused by the chariots' rush at enemy lines and the way in which the warriors would then jump down to fight on foot. He notes their speed, ability to manoeuvre and role in providing means of rapid retreat for the warriors, as well as the great skill displayed by the drivers. The use of the chariots enabled a hit-and-run type of warfare, and allowed the speedy replenishment of troops as wounded or exhausted warriors were picked up and fresh ones brought in to the fighting.

It is estimated that Cassivellaunus had 2,000 chariots at his disposal; these were drawn by 4,000 trained horses and driven by trained charioteers, which suggests that inter-tribal warfare had occurred before the arrival of the Romans. Their use implies a knowledge of the landscape and its potential for ambush and attack, and prevented the Romans from fighting the sort of battle they preferred. Caesar was reacting to threats rather than being able to dictate the course of action, something which clearly frustrated him. There is a distinct peevishness in his accounts of these events.

Another point of some importance was the use of ambushes and prepared positions, something that contradicts earlier classical accounts of undisciplined and unorganised warriors who simply rushed pell-mell into battle. The attack on the foraging party in 55BC was well-prepared – the British lay in wait by a field that had not been harvested, knowing the Romans would be attracted to it. They waited until the legionaries had divested themselves of their weapons and begun to harvest the grain before attacking.

There was also a new type of settlement defence to deal with – the territorial *oppidum*. At the end of the Iron Age in Britain, in a few places, territorial *oppida* began to be developed. Unlike traditional European *oppida*, which were built as large enclosed settlements deriving from the earlier hillforts (although this type of settlement was also to be found in Britain), the territorial *oppidum* comprised a much larger area of the countryside, within discontinuous dykes – large earthworks, sometimes multiple, and utilising the natural topography. The *oppidum* of Camulodunum (Colchester) covered some 30 square kilometres *(Figure 4)*. Other territorial *oppida* include Calleva (Silchester), Verulamium (St Albans), and Noviomagus (Chichester).

Within the defences were a number of settlements separated by fields and woodland. In the case of Colchester, different types of activity were carried out at these settlements – apart from farming, there was a probable aristocratic centre, a ritual centre, and a production and market centre. These *oppida* were in effect an early manifestation of a garden city idea. Most of these sites are dated a little later in the first century BC, but Caesar's descriptions of British strongholds creates the possibility that some, at least, were under development in his era. The lines of dykes were well suited to defence by chariots – in the interior there was plenty of room for manoeuvre, and the gaps between the dykes allowed rapid sorties to be made. The dykes presented a confusing set of barriers to strangers, but the local warriors made good use of the opportunities for launching lightning strikes and then rapid withdrawals; Caesar was forced to alter the way in which he moved his infantry and cavalry, and could not deliver the decisive blows he desired against his foes.

Rebellion in Gaul

Caesar's return to Gaul was soon followed by rebellion amongst the Belgae. The harvest had been poor, and when Caesar's returning troops demanded more food from the local people, the Eburones, starvation threatened. Military posts were constructed near each village to collect the harvests to supply the legions spending the winter of 54BC in the area, and local resentment rose. One of the Eburones leaders, Ambiorix, found some Roman soldiers foraging for firewood, and killed some of them. The survivors fled back to their camp, which Ambiorix realised was too big for him to attack. Instead, he went to speak with the camp prefects, Sabinus and Cotta, and warned them that there was a much larger hostile force gathering, with the support of Germans from across the Rhine, and that this force intended to attack the camp. He suggested they would be well advised to abandon the camp and march to join another one so that they would not be as isolated as they were now. He would guarantee them safe passage.

After much debate and disagreement, the Romans decided to leave and head for the nearest camp that was within reach. They marched out in column, laden with all the supplies they could carry. As they crossed the intervening valley, Ambiorix and his warriors attacked and slaughtered nearly all of them – a whole legion and five cohorts. Only a few survivors made it back to the camp, where the majority committed suicide in shame at their defeat.

Ambiorix then attempted to instigate a more full-scale revolt; he tried the same strategy against a camp in the territory of the Nervii. The Eburones succeeded in setting fire to the camp, but the attack failed when Caesar, who had been to Rome, suddenly reappeared with fresh troops. Ambiorix disappeared, possibly across the Rhine. Further revolts began among the Treveri tribe (from Trier). Caesar was determined to crush the Belgae in retribution – four legions spent the winter destroying their fields, taking their herds and capturing many of the people. Five legions were sent against the Menapii, wreaking similar devastation; they eventually capitulated and Caesar placed his ally Commius in charge of them. The Roman punitive force then crossed the Rhine to devastate the German tribes who had supported the Treveri. After this period, the Eburones also disappear from history – the Roman reprisals amounted to genocide, and archaeology shows that their territory remained unoccupied for some time until resettled by a Germanic people, the Tungri, probably deliberately moved into the area by the Romans, with whom they were friendly.

Despite the recorded devastation in Caesar's account, archaeology has not been able to confirm many of the events he speaks of; indeed, there is remarkably little evidence for the conquest of Belgic Gaul at all in the archaeological record.

Vercingetorix

Caesar was now facing political opposition in Rome from Pompey, and the Gallic tribes realised that if his attention was taken by affairs at home, this was the perfect moment for a full-scale uprising. Tribes conquered in the early years of the Gallic campaigns decided to chance rebellion; a leader emerged from the Arverni tribe who was generally accepted by the others. His name was Vercingetorix.

The revolt started at Orléans in 52BC and spread rapidly. Caesar's legions were camped in the north; they became cut off from Rome and their commander. An attack on Narbonne caused Caesar to rush there first to deal with that problem; this done, he crossed the Cevennes in winter to attack the Arverni, which caught the Gauls by surprise. Vercingetorix was forced to turn from efforts to promote rebellion in the north to protecting his home territory, and Caesar marched at speed to meet him.

Much of the ensuing campaigns centred on attacks on *oppida*; Vercingetorix would attack an *oppidum* belonging to a pro-Roman tribe, forcing Caesar to come to its defence, and Caesar would attack an anti-Roman *oppidum* to seize supplies and force a reaction from Vercingetorix. The major problem for the Romans was supply. The Gauls instigated a scorched-earth policy. In the lands of the Bituriges tribe, twenty towns were burned to deny them to the Romans, leaving only the capital, Avericum, in which were 40,000 people, untouched because the inhabitants promised they could defend themselves. Caesar immediately began a siege of the town, effectively halting Vercingetorix's campaign.

Caesar's successes in this campaign were largely down to the speed at which he could move his troops, and their discipline in both attack and defence. The self-sufficiency of his army was enough to overcome, albeit with difficulty, the Gaulish raids on his supply trains, and to construct siege works and camps wherever needed.

The Gauls were not slow to learn, however. At Avericum, they were able to remove the grappling hooks the Romans had used to try to scale the walls, and used countermines to stop Roman attempts to tunnel underneath. The Romans built a ramp and a large mound and siege towers; the Gauls tunnelled underneath the mound, set fire to its wooden props and collapsed it. They used pitch to spread fire and confusion, accompanied by sally attacks from the gates, which were defeated with some difficulty. In the end, the town fell, and then Caesar used another of his winning strategies – he massacred almost every citizen inside – men, women and children. Of the 40,000 inhabitants, only 800 escaped.

Vercingetorix made every attempt to avoid all-out battle with the Romans. Instead, he pursued a strategy of mobility and concentrated on trying to destroy Caesar's resources – burning fields, isolating and picking off small detachments, which was largely successful. The engagement at Gergovia was a major success, combining this mobile scorched-earth and raiding strategy with multiple attacks, resulting in heavy Roman losses.

In 52BC Vercingetorix was eventually forced back to the hillfort of Alesia (modern Alise-Ste-Reine), where Caesar besieged him and his army *(Figure 29)*. There is a long history of debate about the exact site of the battle, but excavations in the 1990s have revealed the outlines of the Roman camps and siegeworks. The situation of Alesia, an isolated hill surrounded by a plain and then further hills, allowed the construction of massive siege structures – an inner ditch partially filled with water, a field of stake-filled foot traps,

Figure 29. Plan of Caesar's siegeworks at Alesia.

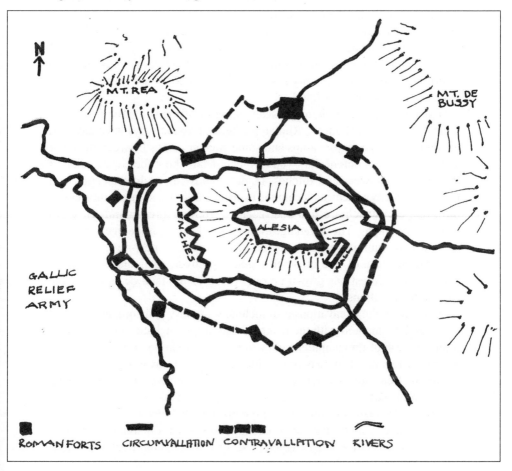

sharpened stakes and barbed iron spikes, two further ditches surmounted by cut branches and a breastwork, with frequent interval towers and redoubts, camps on the slopes of the surrounding hills, and an outer rampart 22km long – a total of 40km of earthwork constructed in less than a month by the legions *(Plate 14)*. There may have been as many as 50,000 men in Caesar's siege force.

As news of the siege spread, an extraordinary alliance of the Gauls was forged to come to Vercingetorix's aid – Caesar says they raised 8,000 cavalry and nearly a quarter of a million infantry, a force led by Caesar's one-time ally, Commius. This relief force occupied one of the nearby hills and mounted successive assaults, as did the besieged warriors within the hillfort. Eventually, these assaults failed and, with his people starving, Vercingetorix was forced to surrender. He was taken as a prisoner to Rome and held there until 46BC when he was executed at the time of Caesar's formal Triumph. Of the other Gauls, some 40,000 within the hillfort were enslaved, each given to one of Caesar's soldiers, and large numbers of skeletons have been found at the foot of Mount Réa, the site of the relief force's camp. Some of the Aedui and Arverni were set free, in order to return home to secure the loyalty of their tribes to Rome. Roman losses have been estimated at 12,800.

Excavations and modern landscape surveys of the site have revealed a great deal of detail about the Roman positions. Lidar surveys have unveiled the outlines of the major camps and some smaller camps between the outer and inner lines of defence, as well as much detail about the construction of the ramparts, towers and ditches. (Lidar stands for Light Detection and Ranging – a remote sensing technique using pulses of light (laser, ultra-violet, infra-red, etc) which are sent and received from an aircraft and related to ground topography. The advantage of this type of survey is that it can provide an image of bumps and dips in the ground surface despite them being invisible because of tree or other vegetation cover, particularly useful at Alesia where forest has grown up over much of the land occupied by the Roman fortifications).

Finds from the excavations also include weaponry and equipment – lead sling 'bullets' marked with the name of Caesar's lieutenant Titus Labienus, round stone shot for catapults, heavy iron bolts for shooting from a ballista, and iron arrow points with a long single barb. In an excavation on the slopes of Mount Réa, the total amount of weaponry recovered included fifteen swords and parts of forty more, all Gaulish, helmets, one of which was complete, also Gaulish, and 116 shield parts, mostly umbos – some Gaulish, some German, which must have belonged to Caesar's mercenary cavalry. There were parts of Roman daggers, 392 spearheads, both light and heavy,

Roman and Gaulish, 146 Gaulish arrowheads, eleven Roman ballista bolts, twenty-nine lead bullets, sixteen limestone shot, twelve 'stimuli' or caltrops, and other equipment.

Postholes also showed where fields of sharpened stakes, angled outwards, had been planted in the bottom of the ditches. Remains of horses show that most of those used in the battle were aged between five and ten years, and were all male. The tallest stood 150/160cm high at the withers, but this was unusual and the animal is thought to have been of Italian origin – the majority were around 130cm and were of local stock. There were also some animals averaging just 115/120cm high, and of a kind unknown in Gaul but found east of the Rhine – the horses of the German mercenary cavalry. A major new interpretation centre has recently opened at the site of Alesia.

Vercingetorix's ally Commius fought a number of further unsuccessful engagements, but then fled to Britain and established a kingdom around Chichester, beginning a dynasty which ended with Verica, who invited Claudius's conquest in AD43.

The last major battle of Caesar's conquest of Gaul was at Uxellodunum in 51BC, now identified as Puy d'Issolud on the River Lot. This is a high rocky hill within a bend of the river, with a natural spring. The position could not be approached, and so a siege commenced. Caesar was in central or northeast Gaul, but quickly came to oversee the affair. The besieged Gauls were relying on their spring for water, but also on being able to get water from the river. Caesar covered their route to the river with archers, slingers and siege engines to make this impossible. A siege tower was then erected that gave a field of fire towards the spring on the other side of the hill.

The Gauls responded by trying to burn down the siege tower, and rolled flaming barrels of pitch and dry wood down towards the Romans' positions. A feint by the Romans drew the Gauls off, allowing the Romans to put out the fires. The Romans then began tunnelling underground, in an attempt to find the source of the spring, which they eventually managed to do. The lack of water forced the surrender of the stronghold; the survivors were allowed to go free – after their hands had been cut off, a move Caesar regarded not as cruelty but as a necessary message to future would-be rebels.

The site, once the centre of debate as to its location, is now more securely identified, and recent excavations have discovered many details of the siege. Trenches near the spring have found areas of burned earth and weapons. There were 961 stone shots, weighing between 50g and 2.5kg, thirty-nine arrowheads, a ballista bolt, four Roman boot nails, and Roman and Gaulish pottery within an area of just 16 square metres. Earlier finds in the area include 700 more arrowheads, six spearheads, two lances, and another seventy-five ballista bolts.

Further modern archaeological trenches revealed the ferocity of the fire attacks, with red scorched earth lying deep over a wide area, and more than a thousand arrowheads scattered on the surface. Beneath the hill, the underground tunnels have been found and explored. The Roman works average one and a half metres wide and at least two metres high, and were driven into the hill with smaller tunnels branching off to the sides at intervals. At the far end, they meet with another tunnel, known as G4, which appears to be a counter-sap dug by the besieged Gauls in an attempt to disrupt the Roman efforts. At the earlier siege of Avericum, Caesar had noted the mining skills of the Gauls in constructing such siege counter-works, based on their experience gained from the extraction of minerals and ores. There are traces that suggest that a skirmish could have taken place underground.

The cost to France of the Roman Conquest was vast. A combination of deaths in battle, enslaved people, bad harvests (and the lack of able-bodied survivors to work the fields), and disease saw the population fall by at least 25 per cent during the next decade or so. The evidence for the early Roman occupation is hard to find, however. A few sites have possible military installations that date to the conquest, such as Liercourt-Hérondelle, but most Roman military sites in France date from the time of Augustus.

A possible exception is the Actiparc site near Arras, which was occupied before 40BC. Here, a fort was built within a banked and ditched enclosure, with barracks and granaries, in the territory of the Atrebates. A civilian settlement was planted close to the fort, also enclosed by palisades or fences. It seems to have been part of the formation of a militarised zone, dedicated to providing food and other supplies for the Roman military, using a population that was highly controlled and supervised.

The Germans
The next twenty or thirty years in France seem to have been fairly quiet, while the process of Romanisation gathered pace. Those rebellions which occurred were small and short-lived. It seems that the spirit had been taken out of the Gauls after Alesia. The same was not true of the yet undefeated Germans. Numerous German tribes are mentioned in the literature, although some appear to have been Celtic-speakers, while others were Teutonic. While some are mentioned as distinct local groups, there were also larger populations, such as the Suebi – Tacitus says they occupied more than half of Germany and comprised a number of distinct tribes with their own names, who are nevertheless known as Suebi in general. They are recorded as coming from Jutland, the Elbe, the Danube, the Vistula and the shores of the Baltic Sea, and Scandinavia as far north as Finland and Lapland. They wore their hair in a distinctive 'Swabian knot' to indicate their status. They appear to have

spoken a Germanic language, and their presence in Germany and later along the Rhine may have resulted from a southwards migration. They did not have a single leader, but elected war chiefs as necessary. Caesar came across them in the area between the Rhine and the Elbe rivers. They raided across the Rhine – the first occasion recorded being in 58BC under a leader called Ariovistus – and are also recorded as giving aid to the Sugambri. Dio Cassius equates them with Celts.

A group were defeated by Drusus in 9BC after they and two other tribes had captured and crucified twenty Roman centurions, but the Romans failed to pacify the tribe. Other mentions of them are imprecise and confusing. Most detail comes from Tacitus, who uses a very broad definition of these people, which nevertheless is full of exciting detail – their worship in sacred groves, bloodthirsty rites and their use of camouflage; one group, the Harii, we are told, dyed themselves black and fought at night. They are described as fierce and massively built with red hair and blue eyes, able to withstand cold and hunger, but not heat or thirst. They carried spears that were used both for throwing and for close combat, shields with little decoration, and only a few wore body armour, or a metal or leather helmet. They had small, sturdy horses.

Tacitus says they did not use battle formations, but operated as a single mass; they put their youngest men in the front of the line, a place of distinction. Another version suggests that this front line had light throwing spears, while the older warriors behind carried heavier spears for close-quarter fighting. They were prepared to give ground in a fight, as long as they then counter-attacked, and they took away the bodies of their fallen. Cowardice in battle was punished by execution. They arranged themselves in battle in family or clan groups, and kept their women and children close by in support for any wounded. The women were capable of rallying their menfolk on the field, baring their breasts and calling out, and otherwise were held in respect in society generally.

The men carried their arms at all times, and chiefs arose by means of their own prowess and the number of warriors they could attract into their bands. Chiefs were expected to lead by example in a battle, and their followers could not leave a fight before the chief did, on pain of infamy. They preferred warfare and the acquisition of booty to daily labour on the farm. They kept slaves, but were forbidden to use them with cruelty – in fact the description of their slaves is closer to medieval serfdom than the Roman model.

When not fighting, Tacitus tells us they liked to hunt, or else lie around idly, letting the women and old people do the work, and they lived in scattered communities rather than in large towns. They were monogamous and moral, and clean in their habits, with hospitable laws. They liked alcohol; Tacitus suggested that they could be overcome by plying them with drink so that they fell prey to their own vices. They turned weapons training into sports. These, then, were the warriors the Romans were to face.

Under Augustus, expansion began again, this time over the Alpine passes. Campaigns in 25BC and 15BC extended Roman control over the Eastern Alps, creating the possibility of opening up and infiltrating southern Germany. Trouble then erupted in northern Germany, with the Sugambri tribe in the area of the modern Netherlands, the ancestors of the Franks. In Caesar's time this tribe had aided people escaping across the Rhine from Roman attrition, but had also participated in looting the land of the Eburones following their destruction. They did not stop there, however; they went on to attack Roman units in retaliation for Caesar's earlier punitive raids against them.

In 16BC a raid by the Sugambri defeated a Roman army, and the emperor realised that attention had to be given to strengthening the eastern frontiers of Gaul and to attempt a penetration of Germany itself. To this end, legions stationed throughout Gaul were moved to the Rhine. By 12BC large-scale campaigns were under way. Augustus' stepson Drusus was given the task of subduing the Sugambri, and then proceeding by sea via a canal dug by the soldiers from the Ijssel Meer and the Rhine to the estuaries of the Weser and the Elbe. He conquered the Batavi and Frisii tribes of the Netherlands, and then several tribes in the northern Weser area. After defeating the Chatti (who were once again allied with the Sugambri, who refused to give in) he started actions against the large Marcomanni tribe, but he was forced back across the Rhine and died in 9 or 10BC as a result of a fall from his horse.

Drusus' successes enabled Rome to declare the existence of a province of Magna Germania, with its capital at Cologne, and to send troops into Germany to pacify the tribes. 40,000 of the Sugambri were forcibly relocated west of the Rhine. Forts and settlements were built east of the Rhine, such as those as Oberaden and Haltern. At Haltern, a tented encampment was replaced in about 5BC with a more permanent fortress, complete with ports on the River Lippe.

Waldgirmes is one settlement that has been excavated. It lies 100km east of the Rhine, and was founded in the first decade of the millennium. It might have been a trading town, or a colony for the resettlement of retired Roman soldiers, as no military structures have been found within it. It was intended as a permanent town – a gilded statue of a mounted emperor Augustus was erected in the courtyard of a monumental stone forum, many sections of which have been excavated. The town was sited close to a military camp and a native settlement, but despite its pretensions to permanence, it was rapidly evacuated in 9AD, for reasons that will become clear in the next chapter.

Chapter 8

Conclusions –
The End of Prehistory

*For over 400 years, the brutal invasions and conquests of the first
century BC and the first century AD allowed Rome to control much of
western and northern Europe. Their military power was supported by
political and commercial strength, so they could control trade and
production, and through the taking of hostages and the imposition of
forced loans on the one hand, and the offer of a measure of power in
the new provincial governments on the other, they brought the local
aristocracies into the Roman system. A casual reading of history seems
to suggest that all this was achieved with efficiency and speed – the
Romans march in and a new province is created. Of course, it was not
so easy. There was resistance, some of it very effective; none more so
than the campaign of Arminius (or Hermann) in 7AD, which more than
anything else helped Germania to stay largely free of the Roman
Empire. Even where the Conquest seemed more successful, there was
resistance. In Britain, a boundary had to be set along the line of
Hadrian's Wall in the second century, despite efforts to push further
north, and Ireland also remained free. Beyond the scope of this book,
there are strong hints of continuing resistance or rebellion in Gaul,
Gallia Belgica and Britannia throughout the period of Roman rule,
as well as pressure and raids from beyond the Roman frontiers, aided
and abetted in some cases by those inside. By the fifth century, Roman
control was finished in the northern and western provinces; the
peoples of France, Britain and Germany set up their own governments
and kingdoms. Only the small number of Christians clung on to the
vestiges of the Roman system, while around them the barbarian gods
re-emerged.*

The Varus disaster
Further campaigns against the Germans followed, including those of Lucius
Domitius Ahenobarbus, who penetrated as far as the Elbe and built a
causeway from the Rhine to the River Ems to facilitate troop movement in
northern Germany across the marshes. A war was planned against the

Marcomanni, but it was abandoned when a major uprising occurred in Illyricum in the area of Bosnia and Herzogovina in 6AD. In that year, Publius Quinctilius Varus became governor of Germania, having established a reputation for cruelty, harsh rule and excessive taxation in his previous posts in Africa and Syria.

He had at his disposal three legions – the Seventeenth, Eighteenth and Nineteenth. Varus embarked on a programme of bribery and corruption to gain influence over the German leaders, in order to establish profitable trading settlements in Germania, while practising his cruelty against defeated tribes. Among his trusted advisors was a German from the Cherusci tribe, Arminius.

Arminius had been given to the Romans as a hostage when he was a young man, and had served with the army. To all appearances, he had become thoroughly Romanised. In AD9 Varus and his legions left their summer camp near the River Weser to return to winter quarters on the Rhine. Now aged about twenty-five, Arminius, who had been promoted to lead Varus' own bodyguard, came to him and advised him that there was trouble among some of the local tribes and that Roman troops had been killed. Varus arrogantly decided to take immediate action and allowed Arminius to lead him and his forces towards the site of the purported rebellion, despite being warned by another Cherusci, Segestes, who was Arminius' father-in-law, not to trust Arminius. What Varus did not know was that Arminius had secretly organised an alliance between a number of free German tribes – the Cherusci, Chatti, Bructeri, Sugambri, Suebi confederation and others.

The three legions and their commander set out on a long march through the almost impenetrable German forests, a landscape with which many were unfamiliar as the soldiers were new to the region. The route down which Arminius led them had to be built as they went – trees chopped down, bridges built and paths strengthened to take the baggage wagons.

The Roman column numbered over 20,000 soldiers, as well as camp followers, civilian staff and servants. Dio Cassius reports that Varus did not send out advance parties, and that shortly after entering the gloom of the forest, a violent storm erupted. The soldiers were now slogging along muddy tracks, and the column stretched for several Roman miles – between 15 and 20km. Arminius had left the line of march, telling Varus that he intended to go to recruit some allies to assist them in the supposed confrontation with the rebels. In fact, he went to join the army of Germans that had been secretly assembled. As the Roman troops slogged through the dark, the wet and the mud, with thunder and lightning adding to the discomfort, not to mention their superstitious fear of the misty alien forests, the Germans began their attacks.

After a long day's march, the Romans struggled to set up a night camp, but found themselves surrounded, and the break-out they managed in the morning cost them many men. They marched on, with the Germans constantly harrying the rear of the column. By this time, the wagons and troops at the end were hours out of touch with the leaders at the front – they could not contact Varus to ask the column to halt in their defence. As groups fell behind, they were picked off, while the legionary commanders marched on, unaware of what was happening behind them. A trail of corpses stretched for miles. It is believed that the march and attrition went on for two or three days and nights, until at last the head of the column reached an open clearing of land at Kalkreise, a strip less than 100 metres wide between the forested slopes and a swamp.

Varus must have finally realised that he had walked into a trap. The path ahead was blocked by a trench across the road, and a 400-metre-long curving turf wall cut off any escape into the woods *(Figure 30)*. The ambush had clearly been prepared some time in advance. Varus was surrounded, and the German forces descended on the beleaguered Romans. The legions were slaughtered, and Varus and many of his officers are said to have committed suicide. Other soldiers were enslaved or sacrificed to their gods by the victorious Germans, while a very few were ransomed. Estimates suggest that 15–20,000 died. Three legions had been completely wiped out and their

Figure 30. The turf wall revealed by excavations at Kalkriese, North Germany.

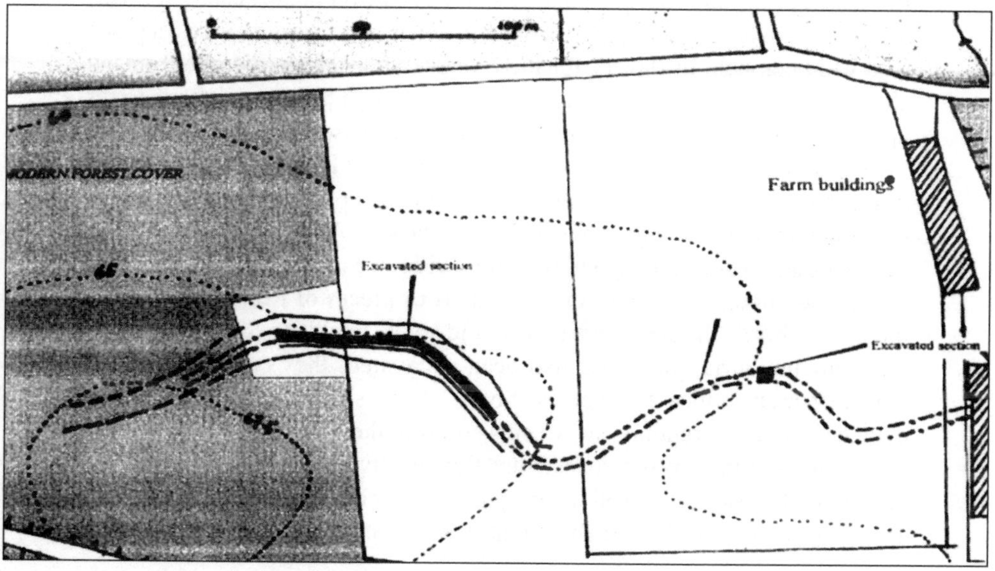

regimental numbers were never used again. Only a small contingent of cavalry managed to escape.

The emperor Augustus is said to have banged his head against a wall in despair, calling out *'Quintili Vare, legiones redde!'* (Quintilius Varus, give me back my legions!). An account written around 30AD by an old soldier called Velleius Paterculus, who may well have actually met both Varus and Arminius, gave his opinion:

> 'An army unexcelled in courage, the first of Roman armies in discipline, energy and experience in the field, through the negligence of its general, the perfidy of the enemy, and the unkindness of fortune ... was exterminated almost to a man by the very enemy whom it has always slaughtered like cattle...'

The victory at Kalkriese was followed by assaults on the other Roman forts and towns east of the Rhine – by the end of the year, Magna Germania was empty of Romans. Punitive expeditions were launched in the following years, until in 15AD Germanicus, nephew of the emperor Tiberius, succeeded in reaching the site of the Kalkriese massacre. He found heaps of bones, and skulls nailed to trees; there were 'barbarous altars' where Roman soldiers had been sacrificed. Gathering together as many as they could find, his troops interred these remains in mass graves.

Germanicus finally defeated Arminius at Idistaviso on the River Weser in 16AD. Actions against the Germans continued throughout the first half of the first century AD – and then in around 50AD a victory over raiding bands of Chatti resulted in the liberation of some Roman prisoners, survivors of Varus' legions who had been held in slavery for forty years. After this period, the Romans abandoned the idea of conquering Germany, although they made efforts to set up client kingdoms to ensure that the tribes would cease their attacks.

The actual site of the Varus disaster was lost for hundreds of years until an amateur archaeologist, a British army major, discovered the site while out metal-detecting in the region north of Osnabrück. In 1987 major excavations began along a 15-mile-long and one-mile wide stretch of land. The turf wall was found, along with coins and thousands of pieces of Roman equipment including horse harness, brooches and belt buckles. Some eight of Germanicus' burial pits have also been excavated; they contained mixed bones of men, mules and horses. Some of the skulls recovered showed evidence of battle trauma – sword cuts splitting the bone.

Among the finds was a spectacular Roman cavalry mask from a helmet, once plated in silver, as well as weaponry and lead catapult- or sling-shot. Traces of the turf wall itself show that there must have been fierce fighting over it, as parts had actually collapsed during the battle. It was three and a half metres wide at the base, although its height could not be determined with certainty. It has been suggested that it may have been over a metre at least. It was built in a zigzag form, allowing the Germans to attack from different angles as the Roman column passed. The ditch had been filled in very soon after the battle, probably to make the German progress onwards easier. It was only the poverty of the sandy soil that preserved the site – it was land that was unfit for ploughing and agriculture. Had it been fertile, all the evidence of the battle would have long since been dispersed and destroyed.

The Varus disaster demonstrates that the Germans were capable of co-operative advanced planning and preparation, and that they knew their enemy and his methods very well. Their abilities had been severely underestimated by the Romans: they were not mindless savages, but a dynamic, organised people with advanced military skills. It was in many ways a decisive action, discouraging further Roman conquest and ensuring the freedom of much of Germany from Roman domination.

The shock felt in Rome when news of the disaster reached the city was extreme – Suetonius says it nearly brought down the empire. Ten per cent of the imperial army had been destroyed in a single day. Settlements like Waldgirmes were quickly abandoned, Augustus threw all the Germans and Gauls living in Rome out, and expected Arminius to bring the Germans to march on Rome itself. By the Middle Ages, scholars had rediscovered the story of Arminius from ancient documents, and he became a national hero, his name now rendered as 'Hermann'. The effects were even longer lasting – the 400 years in which Rome maintained its barrier at the Rhine created a cultural and linguistic barrier between Germany and France that to some extent persists to the current day.

The conquest of Britain

In AD43 the Romans finally began the conquest of Britain under the emperor Claudius, utilising the stores and ships gathered earlier during Caligula's abortive attempt to cross the Channel. (Several previous campaigns had also been planned under Augustus, but were never carried out). There is some evidence that in the intervening years since Julius Caesar, a possible diplomatic Roman presence had been established near Chichester. Excavations at the Roman palace of Fishbourne have revealed a ditch that contained Gaulish pottery and a piece of a Roman sword scabbard dated to about 30AD.

There is still much controversy about where exactly the Romans landed – for a long time Richborough, on the Kent coast, was assumed to be the spot, because of the later triumphal arch erected there, but the record left by Dio Cassius is confusing, and it is possible that in fact there was more than one landing, with one section of the fleet making for Chichester and the friendly territory of the local tribe, the Regni, while another sailed towards the more hostile Cantiaci of Kent. Other possibilities include a landing in the Solent.

The British catalyst for the conquest was the expansionist policy of the Catuvellauni tribe, who, under their leader Cunobelinus (Shakespeare's *Cymbeline*), had taken over the lands of the Trinovantes of Essex and were pushing southwards into the territory of the Atrebates, a tribe based in Surrey, Sussex and Hampshire *(Figure 31)*. This was the tribe once ruled by Commius after the defeat of Vercingetorix at Alesia. He seems to have founded a dynasty of succeeding kings, the last of whom was Verica. Verica

Figure 31. British tribes at the time of the Roman Conquest in AD43.

was under pressure from the Catuvellauni, who had seized the Atrebatic *oppidum* of Calleva (Silchester) around AD25, and who, under the leadership of Caractacus, son of the king of the Catuvellauni, were taking over most of the northern lands of Verica's kingdom. His authority had shrunk to a small tribal group, the Regni, confined to southern Sussex.

Verica fled to Rome to ask for help in around AD40. This gave Claudius the perfect excuse to proceed with his invasion plans. (The Regni were rewarded after the Conquest with the construction of the palace at Fishbourne – a vast Mediterranean-style villa that probably employed imported Italian craftsmen to create a symbol of the new power in Britain).

Claudius had been more or less dragged to power following the unhappy reign of Caligula. He was elderly, weak and had more of a reputation as a scholar than as a man of action. A successful military campaign was a necessity if he was to avoid losing his position and power, and Britain had been a thorn in the Roman side for some time. It was rich, exporting all the things the Roman army in Gaul required – precious metals for paying the troops, wheat to feed them, iron to make their weapons, cattle for meat and their hides for tents, boots and a thousand other uses, and slaves; it was also said to be the source of support for the rebellions in Gaul that were believed to be manipulated by the druids. Previous attempts to invade had failed or been inconclusive, damaging the Romans' imperial morale, and they could stand on the coast of northern Gaul and *see* it, just beyond reach. Caligula had stockpiled ships and equipment that was sitting unused on the French beaches, so preparations for the invasion could be made quickly and without too much further cost.

A force of four legions (around 20,000 men) embarked, probably near Boulogne, under the command of Aulus Plautius. One of the legions, the Legio II Augusta, was commanded by the future emperor Vespasian. The other legions involved were Legio IX Hispana, Legio XIV Gemina and Legio XX Valeria. After establishing a beach-head, Aulus Plautius moved inland. The first major engagement of the invasion took place at a river crossing (possibly on the Medway, but various Sussex rivers have also been suggested). The British, we are told, were led by the sons of Cunobelinus – Caractacus and Togodumnus. Whether this means that the tribes had formed an alliance (probably an unusual occurrence) or whether the Catuvellauni had decided to take on the Romans alone, we do not know.

After two days of sporadic fighting, the British were pushed back to the Thames, and then into the Essex marshes. The Romans used Batavian auxiliaries from the Rhine delta in the Netherlands, who at one point swam across the river to create a bridgehead. During the opposition to the Thames crossing, Togodumnus was injured and soon died. At the Thames, Aulus

Plautius awaited the arrival of Claudius himself before continuing to harry the British. Claudius arrived, possibly at Chichester, with supplies for the legions and with war elephants, a truly amazing sight for the conquered British tribes. Claudius accompanied the army to Camulodunum, the Catuvellaunian capital, where the Romans founded their own first capital in Britain, and then returned home after just a couple of weeks.

Caractacus was not captured, and retreated westwards to continue fighting. Aulus Plautius sent one legion north towards Lincoln and the Humber estuary, a second into the south Midlands and another westwards towards Exeter. Archaeological evidence of Vespasian's campaign in the West Country has been found. He is said to have captured Vectis – the Isle of Wight – and met fierce resistance from the Durotriges of Dorset. A body with an iron Roman ballista bolt embedded in the spine was found at Maiden Castle, and at Alchester in Oxfordshire, a fort with timber gateposts dated to AD44/45 and a tombstone of a soldier of the II Augusta have been excavated. The use of artillery *(Plate 13)* is also indicated at the hillfort of Hod Hill where iron ballista bolts were found clustered near one of the major buildings, perhaps the residence of the local chief, and a legionary camp that remained in use until around AD50 was subsequently built within the ramparts.

The conquest of Britain was a long-drawn-out affair. Caractacus had retreated into first south and later north Wales and he began a guerrilla campaign against the Romans which lasted until his defeat in around 50BC, betrayed by the queen of the Brigantes tribe, Cartimandua. Roman efforts concentrated on the Iceni in Norfolk and in Wales and the Brigantes of northwest England. North Wales in particular proved a difficult target; the Romans could not move easily in the mountains and valleys, and the conquest proceeded slowly. It was not complete in 60AD when Boudica of the Iceni led her people in rebellion. Suetonius Paulinus, the new Roman commander, had taken his troops to Anglesey, to seize the island which was the headquarters of the druids, who had been receiving refugees from the fighting.

The druids represented the intelligentsia of Iron Age society, and were probably instrumental in organising and supporting the resistance movement. Druids could be both male and female, and, drawn from the most able sons and daughters of the aristocracy, served the tribes as judges, bards, priests, doctors and advisers. They were likely to have excellent networks between themselves and the tribes (a sort of old boys' club) for the passing of information, and clearly became a thorn in the sides of the Romans.

Paulinus created a bridge of boats for the infantry to cross over the Menai Strait to Mona, the isle of Anglesey, while his cavalry swam alongside their horses. They were met by a horde of armed defenders on the beach, men and women dressed in black, screaming and waving lit torches, and more druids stood in a circle praying to the gods. Overcoming their initial superstitious horror, the Romans charged and eventually destroyed the resistance, cutting down and burning the sacred groves of the island.

News of the Boudican revolt then reached Paulinus, who had to turn back immediately to deal with this new threat. The final conquest of Wales did not take place until the governorship of Agricola in about AD78 or 79, over three decades after the initial invasion.

Most Roman accounts suggest that the defeat of the British was due not to any lack of courage, but to the disorganised way in which they fought. Once the Romans advanced in their formations, they were unstoppable, and the heart went out of their enemies. The Romans were also, however, guilty of over-confidence from time to time. They had assumed that, once defeated, the Iceni and other southern tribes would stay peaceful, and had therefore not fortified the new settlements at Colchester (Camulodunum), St Albans, London and elsewhere. These settlements were populated by veteran soldiers, who had completed their term of service, or by merchants and speculators who had come to see what profits they could make out of the newly conquered land. It was the Roman custom to give veterans grants of land in new provinces, where they would settle, perhaps marry local women, and form the nucleus of a Romanised way of life as an example to and a source of control over the local people. In this way, Roman culture and customs were spread across the empire.

Boudica's husband Prasutagus had been a client king under Roman rule, but when he died around AD60, his desire to leave part of his land to his wife and daughters rather than to the emperor Nero was ignored by the Roman procurator, Catus Decianus. Roman law did not allow women to inherit property. When she protested at the seizure of her lands and wealth, Boudica was flogged and her daughters were raped. Roman descriptions of Boudica tell us she was 'possessed of greater intelligence than often belongs to women'; she was a tall woman with very long red hair and a harsh voice, her eyes had a piercing glare, and she wore a gold torc around her neck, a many-coloured dress and a thick cloak fastened by a brooch – very unlike the submissive portrait of a woman preferred by Roman society.

She gathered together her people and marched on Camulodunum, probably picking up on the way other disaffected Britons, who were angry about being forced to surrender their weapons, which diminished them in their own eyes and the eyes of others. To carry arms was a mark of status, and they were also suffering under the imposition of swingeing interest claims on the loans they had been forced to accept by Roman entrepreneurs in order to pay off the taxes and tributes imposed during the Conquest.

Claudius had apparently granted sums of money to friendly tribal leaders to gain their allegiance. Decianus now decided these had to be paid back immediately.

Seneca, Nero's tutor, was one of the speculators – he had reportedly forced the British to accept loans of 40 million sesterces that they did not want in the hope of a juicy profit, but then decided to call the loans back in without warning, sending heavy-handed agents to enforce the collection.

Camulodunum had been designated as the capital of the new Roman province but, according to Tacitus, the Romans there treated the local people brutally and taxed them heavily in order to build a great temple to Claudius in the town. Decianus failed to send sufficient troops to protect the citizens, and Boudica's forces destroyed them and their settlement in two days of slaughter. It is said that many of the citizens took refuge in the newly-built temple to Claudius, but died when the British burned it down. The foundations of this structure still survive and can be visited – the Normans used them to build a castle keep on top, which is now the home of Colchester Museum. The IX Hispania legion attempted to come to the help of the city, but was roundly defeated, the infantry being wiped out and only the commander and a small force of cavalry escaping.

Boudica's forces (70,000 strong according to Tacitus) moved on, and now threatened London, which at the time was an unofficial mercantile settlement less than twenty years old. The citizens sent to Paulinus, who was rushing back from Anglesey, for aid, but he decided that the town must be sacrificed while he better prepared his troops for battle. Decianus Catus ran away to Gaul. London was set ablaze – a 25cm-thick layer of ash and burned debris is found all over the area of the pre-60AD settlement, and even the graves were desecrated. Boudica then moved on St Albans (Verulamium) and that too was destroyed. This was an army of angry and desperate people – they were in no mood for the niceties of war, and Tacitus recounts acts of extreme violence and cruelty. The Romans claimed that 70–80,000 people were massacred in these three towns.

By now Paulinus had gathered sufficient troops from the Fourteenth and Twentieth legions, perhaps 10,000 men, and chosen a battle site somewhere along Watling Street. Dio Cassius claims Boudica's forces had swelled to 230,000 people, although this is probably an exaggeration, and the number of armed warriors must have been far smaller. Paulinus had chosen his spot well – it was a restricted area, a narrow valley backed by a forest, which denied the British room to manoeuvre their chariots, and negated the effect of their numerical superiority. The field was further restricted by the carts and other vehicles that held the families of the warriors, drawn up behind the battle lines.

First launching a spear attack at the Britons, the Romans then charged in a wedge formation, and slaughtered the warriors. Tacitus claims that 80,000 Britons died, but only 400 Romans. This is unlikely to be true – large numbers of new troops and especially warrant officers were quickly sent from the Rhine forts after this battle, presumably to replace those lost in the fighting. Boudica's fate is unknown – Roman reports have her committing suicide, or falling ill and dying. Punitive campaigns were instigated, but these were soon halted by the new procurator, Classicianus, who feared that they simply created more hostility and could result in the loss of the whole province. Classicianus managed to hold the province together – he eventually died in London, which became the new capital, where his tombstone has been unearthed.

The conquest continued to move slowly northwards. Roads were built to facilitate troop movements and forts were constructed. Trouble broke out among the Brigantes, or to be precise between Cartimandua and her husband Venutius. Venutius led his tribe in armed opposition to the Romans, and Cartimandua asked the Romans to rescue her, which they did in about AD70. It took three years of heavy fighting to subdue Venutius and his warriors, and once they had been conquered, it was necessary to build a network of forts and roads to hold northwest England, although the Romans had not managed to extend control further, at least on any permanent basis, by the time Agricola arrived in 78AD, and the process of conquest was far from complete. At this time we have good historical material to enable us to follow events, as Tacitus, Agricola's son-in-law, wrote a biography of the general, presumably using his own first-hand account *(Figure 32)*.

Previously conquered tribes had rebelled and were no longer under Roman control in Wales, and Agricola was forced to invade Anglesey for a second time. Only then was he able to try to push the domination of Rome northwards; he moved up into Scotland in 79AD, where he built a military road on the line between the Tyne and Solway, with a fort at either end, and then campaigned as far as the Firth of Tay until 81AD. Here another line of road and forts was constructed. Between 82 and 84AD he moved along the eastern and northern coasts, using naval forces as well as the land troops, against stiff opposition. Agricola began to gain some success, winning a major battle at Mons Graupius against a large army of Caledonians supported by many chariots. At this battle, Agricola's troops included Batavian and Tungrian cohorts, manned by Belgae recruited from Gaul, and it seems that the Roman legions themselves took little part in the fight. Despite heavy losses, said to number 10,000 dead, the Caledonians were able to withdraw and disappear into the forests.

Agricola secured his successes with new roads and forts, and the strengthening of existing installations. He built a ring of forts around the

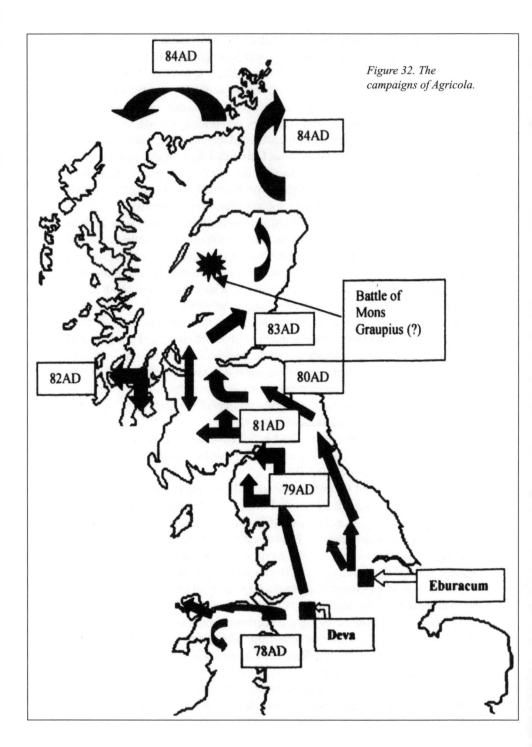

84AD

84AD

Figure 32. The
campaigns of Agricola.

Battle of
Mons
Graupius (?)

83AD

82AD

80AD

81AD

79AD

Eburacum

Deva

78AD

access points to the Highland region, and set up a strong presence in the Lowlands. The line between the Forth and Clyde became the limit of Agricola's expansion, not least because his successes had encouraged his political masters back in Rome to decide that he did not need so large an army, and the British garrison was reduced by the strength of a whole legion. Legio II Adiutrix was sent to Dacia (modern Romania), and Legio XX had to be sent south to hold the garrison. This sounds like an organised withdrawal due to outside pressures, but the truth may have been less calm and collected.

A fort built at Inchtuthil in Perthshire has been excavated, and because the site has not been disturbed in later centuries, a wealth of material has been found there. It included a large hospital, workshop and barracks, all built of timber. There was a headquarters building in the centre of the fort. The fort was only occupied for a short time – from 82 or 83AD to 86 or 87AD, and the site earmarked for the commandant's residence was never built upon.

A remarkable find during the excavations was a deeply buried hoard of over 800,000 iron nails, from small to massive spikes 372mm long, weighing a total of nearly ten tons. The fort had been deliberately slighted when it was abandoned, to deny its use to the British, and the burial of these nails must have been a priority. The sheer amount of iron represented would have been of great use to the Caledonians had they been able to seize them, and they must also have represented a considerable expense for the Romans. The fact that they were not carried away suggests that the withdrawal may have been rather hurried, an impression borne out by the rather incomplete attempts at burning the remaining timber structures. It is possible, therefore, that the Caledonians were proving themselves to be far from accepting defeat.

One of Agricola's feats was to send ships around the whole coast of Britain, confirming to the Romans for the first time that it was an island. Eventually, the limit of Roman occupation was defined along the line of Hadrian's Wall, built in the early second century AD, although a short-lived attempt to occupy Scotland, with a new line of defences known as the Antonine Wall in 142AD, was abandoned after only twenty or so years, at a time when another revolt broke out in the lands of the Brigantes. The troops from Scotland had to be reinforced with further soldiers from Germany to deal with this rebellion.

Later, forays were made into Scotland from time to time, notably in 209AD under Septimius Severus, when an attempt was made to wipe out the belligerent tribes of the north. Severus lost 50,000 of his own men, according to Dio Cassius, because despite their losses, the tribes maintained an effective guerrilla campaign that forced Severus back to Hadrian's Wall.

In the end, the Romans never managed to subdue Britain totally, and did not even make a start on Ireland. For the remainder of the Roman occupation, rebellions broke out with some regularity, and of all the Roman provinces, only Britannia required a standing army for its whole existence. We lack much historical detail, but what survives suggests that armed resistance, raids and civil trouble occurred several times in each century of the occupation. A further problem was that the Roman forces in Britain themselves had a tendency to mutiny. In the end, it is probable that the province of Britannia cost the Romans far more than they gained.

The British themselves gained much from the Romans – roads, towns, international trade connections – but they also lost a great deal. The Roman empire saw a period of stagnation in many areas of social and industrial life, with few innovations in the fields of technology or art. Once the Romans left, and with the arrival of people from the northern European littoral who shared similar culture, religion and histories with the British, the country reverted in many ways to its Iron Age roots, and the great flowering of Anglo-Saxon culture could begin.

Aftermath and reflections

With the conquest of Britain, Roman expansion in northern Europe more or less came to a halt. The process of Romanisation commenced, turning the tribal people of Gaul, Britain and Gallia Belgica into citizens of the empire. Towns were built, with their fora, temples, baths, amphitheatres, aqueducts, shops and taverns – all the accoutrements of Mediterranean civilisation transported into the northern bogs and forests. Rebellions occurred periodically, and new campaigns began from time to time, but the focus of Roman military might had changed, and apart from Trajan's campaign in Dacia (modern Romania), the role of the Roman army in northern Europe became more that of a peacekeeping force for some time.

The emperor Claudius fixed the Rhine as the frontier between the provinces of Gaul and free Germany. There were still problems – the Batavians of the Netherlands rebelled in 69AD, joined by the Frisii and other neighbouring tribes, and a large number of defecting Roman troops, and had a series of successes until defeated by Vespasian at Trier. The Rhine frontier was strengthened with legionary fortresses and towns, and seems to have remained relatively quiet until around 166AD when German tribes pushed south into Italy and Greece, reaching Athens before a Roman force was gathered to defeat them.

By the third century AD the threat from Germany became far more serious, with frequent incursions across the Rhine and Danube. In 268 there was a major invasion of migrating tribes into Gaul as groups such as the Alamanni were pushed westwards by Goths and others migrating from western Asia. The Franks were raiding in the North Sea and the English Channel, and the situation was highly unstable. Numerous attempts to seize power in Rome by military commanders during the third and fourth century led to fights between units of the Roman forces themselves, rather than against the barbarian tribes, who quickly seized the opportunity to raid and loot.

By the start of the fifth century, the situation in northern Europe had become untenable for the Romans. The influx of tribes from across the Rhine effectively cut off most of the north from Roman control, and, importantly, cut off the money supply, leading to mutinies among the remaining Roman troops. The influence of the Germanic tribes was increasingly strong, as can be seen in changes in style of glassware and pottery, and even military buckles and other equipment worn by Roman soldiers.

Gaul was completely overrun in 406AD by Vandals, Alans, Suevi and Burgundians, and Britain had ceased to be a province by 410AD. Whether the Romans simply abandoned Britain, or whether the British abandoned the Romans we do not know. There is a small amount of evidence to suggest that the British more or less threw the Roman administration out and set up their own forms of government, according to some texts from Gaul which record a similar expulsion and the creation of civil control 'in the manner of the British'. Northern Gaul itself was probably abandoned at the same time, and southern Gaul was effectively lost within the next two decades.

The late Roman army was a very different beast from the armies of Julius Caesar. By the fourth century, troops were actively recruited from native settlements granted land in return for military service. Barbarian names are recorded for units across the Empire, and generals with barbarian backgrounds emerged. It seems likely that local militias were recruited to defend the more distant provinces towards the end, officered by warleaders or client chiefs from among the population, and how far these troops behaved or fought like Romans or like their Iron Age predecessors is in question.

The uniform of the soldiers became more Germanic in its form and style – trousers, light chainmail, mounted troops, long hair and moustaches were all adopted. Warmer clothing had become essential – apart from the trousers, they wore long-sleeved woollen tunics, socks and laced boots. Decoration was added – coloured woven or embroidered bands were sewn on to cloaks and tunics, and warmer round caps were also favoured. Officers wore bronze or iron cuirasses, but for other ranks the chain mail was more comfortable, reinforced for mounted troops with protective metal plates. Cavalry helmets had wide cheek-pieces, and these were also adopted by the infantry. In fact, by the end of the period, the cavalry were wearing helmets reminiscent of medieval helms. Some helmets were fitted with nose guards, and some became almost entirely enclosed.

Shields were now oval, made of longitudinal planks of wood covered with leather, apparently often painted. A longer sword, the *spatha*, replaced the *gladius* and a heavier thrusting spear was in general use. A heavier *pilum* for throwing was joined by lead-weighted darts, carried clipped to the reverse of the shield. Bows were still carried by specialist troops.

Fortifications became more like later castles – deeper ditches and higher walls, with crenellations along the tops, projecting corner and interval towers, and projecting gate towers. Newer forts were designed using the contours of the site, rather than the formal 'playing-card' shape of earlier sites. The towns of northern Gaul contracted into a form called a *castellum* – walls surrounded a much smaller urban area, often using building material and tombstones from destroyed houses and cemeteries that were left outside the walls. In form and size, they anticipated the Norman castles that were to rise 500 years later, often using the Roman walls as their foundations.

Tactically, late Roman forces avoided the kinds of large-scale battles of generals like Caesar, instead adopting ambushes and guerrilla tactics wherever possible. Battle strategies became more defensive, utilising the shield wall and allowing the enemy to expend their energies against an immovable barrier, in the way that King Harold drew up his forces on Senlac Hill in 1066. This formation is very strong – unless the enemy succeeded in drawing forces away from the shield wall, as William the Conqueror's troops did.

The Romans had learned lessons from the north Europeans; by the end of their dominance in the region, they were to a large extent adopting the very same types of weapons, armour and tactics that had been used against them in the first century BC.

The Anglo-Saxons and other tribes who rose in the fifth century AD in northern Europe had much in common with the late Roman army when it came to warfare. Helmets and chainmail were very similar – the famous Sutton Hoo helmet has clear origins in the late Roman cavalry form. The shield wall was a central part of battle tactics, and they used similar spears and long swords, although there were many variations and changes over time. They fought not in legions but in warbands, led by chiefs distinguished by the finery of their armour and jewellery – pieces like those found in the Staffordshire hoard that came to light recently. In this, they resemble their Iron Age forebears. Three or four hundred years of Roman occupation had failed to turn the northerners into true Romans – and when the Romans left, the old preferences and habits resurfaced.

Reasons for winning and losing

The northern tribes had their successes and their failures against the Romans; the Romans were not universally victorious. The advantage of the Roman way of war was primarily based on organisation and resources. Theirs was a state system, ranged against smaller tribal organisations. The state could continue to supply men and materiel for long periods, to sustain campaigns, until the enemy was worn down. They deliberately targeted the crops and animals of a region, and were willing to kill or take as slaves entire populations, whereas the 'barbarian' tribes did not usually attempt to involve non-combatant populations in warfare. Tacitus, in his *Annals*, says of the campaigns of Germanicus against the Germans: 'The country was wasted by fire and sword fifty miles round; nor sex nor age found mercy; places sacred and profane had the equal lot of destruction, all razed to the ground.' Roman war was total war.

The Romans also proved adaptable, copying weapons, armour and tactics that they learned from their enemies. They had weapons factories, could build military roads, and had an extensive resupply network, on land and at sea. They had logistical capabilities that the tribes lacked completely. Their ability to build forts or fortified camps gave them the opportunity to rest during campaigns, and provided defensive strongholds wherever they were.

They also had access to more manpower and were less encumbered by local and tribal emotional ties. They were professional soldiers fighting for pay, not local warriors fighting to protect their homeland and families, and so they could absorb losses better, both materially and emotionally. They were a united force with a single government and culture, while the tribes were divided by their histories, localities and even their languages, and were disunited.

The Romans were also consummate politicians. They deliberately avoided destroying the elites of conquered populations, instead co-opting them into the structures and management of the occupation through bribery, offers of citizenship, and preferential trade deals. They encouraged the local aristocracy to quell rebellion amongst their own people in return for special status amongst the new Roman governmental organisations.

The tribespeople certainly did not lack courage. Even the Romans acknowledged their martial prowess; it is also certain that they could learn as quickly as the Romans did. Opposition was most successful when it came in the form of guerrilla warfare – this was a tactic that the Roman army was slow to learn how to respond to effectively. Tribal strength was often to be found in their cavalry, attacking with speed and ferocity against the less mobile legions. But they could sustain neither their campaigns, nor their attacks. There was no reserve, either of men or supplies, in place. If they could win in the first full-on assault, they did so effectively, but when it came to a slogging match, they lacked endurance. When an effective leader rose, such as Arminius or Vercingetorix, who could bring the tribes together, the Romans suffered heavy losses, but there was no permanent central government, and tribal rivalries and histories often interfered with their actions against the invaders.

Conclusion

While most people are familiar with the development of warfare in the classical world – Greeks and Persians, Egyptians and Hittites, Romans and Carthaginians – the history of war in northern Europe before the end of the first millennium BC has tended to be something of a specialised topic for an informed few archaeologists. It is hoped that this book will have redressed this balance a little. Leaving aside the thorny question of what counts as war, and at what level of social development war occurs, it is clear that our species has always had a tendency to pursue its aims through violent encounters between ourselves. In most cases, this violence will have had its origins in fear and the need to protect families and communities from aggression, actual or threatened.

Early violence was mostly personal, but as communities grew in size and complexity, larger-scale attacks occurred. We started to see *them* as being opposed to *us*. This may have begun with our reactions to the Neanderthalers – did we see them as human beings, albeit of a different species? When farmers moved into the north of Europe, did people start to view them as a different sort of being from those already present – the Mesolithic hunters and gatherers? There are numerous examples of apparent attack against incomers and migrating groups – *they* were moving in and threatening the land and resources we perceived as *ours*.

Raids against early settlements could have begun as a fear reaction too – unless we take what they have got, we might starve. But alongside this come the motivations of greed and jealousy, and the realisation that by using violence, resources and the security they provide could be acquired more easily and with less effort. Criminal acts might not be wars, but they can start them.

Over time, and with the rise of more complex political organisation, these reactions become more formalised – specialist warriors and war leaders with specific equipment and weapons emerged, whose main responsibility was to protect *us* from *them*, but who also realised that *we* could be stronger and more successful if we took what we needed from other groups by force. Such changes occurred across the planet in early societies. We tend to imagine that prehistoric societies were isolated, that they knew little of other lands and people, but the truth appears to be that, albeit at second hand, information and technology travelled a very long way, even from continent to continent, long before the written word appeared. Similar forms of weapons and armour developed in societies thousands of miles apart, and surely not all by coincidence.

The ability to organise for war, to build defences and fortifications, and to develop strategic and tactical approaches to defence and aggression, grew alongside other aspects of society. The use of horses, vehicles and boats for trade and warfare enabled the peoples of the north to expand their interests and increase their wealth and power over much wider areas.

The notion of the arms race is not new. As societies grew in size and entered into ever greater competition with each other, new weapons and armour forms were developed, sometimes with great speed. The various forms of sword, spear and shield found in the Bronze Age suggest a process of rapid experimentation in their design, trying to find the most effective forms of protection and attack. The role of leaders developed too – it became necessary not only to acquire status as a war leader, but to demonstrate it with elaborate decoration and costly equipment, not only on the battlefield itself, but on other social and political occasions; 'parade' armour, swords that had never been sharpened, bizarre helmets: all added to the status and visibility of those in power, a status that could be passed on by inheritance within dynasties.

Development of power and status then required development of power bases – visible constructions in the landscape that announced to locals and visitors alike that here was a group that was not to be messed with. Often, these probably had multiple purposes – not only as a statement of strength, but as central places for the payment of tax or tribute, as production centres, as market places, as places to collect and store produce for trade, as religious centres and as settlements for a greater population. Most such strongholds in western Europe were either abandoned or altered under Roman occupation, when newly-created settlements followed the Mediterranean model of an urban centre.

It is intriguing to consider how these sites might have developed if the Romans had not arrived, especially the territorial *oppida* of late Iron Age Britain, with their groups of different hamlets and villages connected and at the same time separated by their own landscapes. Such urban design did not resurface until the twentieth century – at Milton Keynes, for example.

As we have seen, the peoples of northern Europe were by no means primitive, in their political and social organisation and in their technological innovations and skills. In fact, the Romans learned a great deal from them and adopted many of their inventions. But the Roman Conquest tended to

185

halt innovation – it is, after all, preferable not to have to deal with too many new ideas when trying to control a vast empire. It is much easier to police a status quo than to encourage development. In some ways the Roman Conquest had lasting effects – the roads, the towns – but in others, it was ephemeral, more so the farther north one looks. Once the Romans left, the Germanic influence and indigenous preferences resurfaced strongly, and the world of the so-called Dark Ages was once again a period of brilliant artistic and technological change, much of which was a direct successor to the inventions and ideas of the Iron Age. The legacy of the Roman world was only kept alive by the efforts of the Christian church.

In warfare, the tribal organisation of warbands and war leaders was resurgent; it would be a very long time before professional trained armies reappeared in the north. During the troubled years of the early medieval period, hillforts were sometimes refurbished and used again, as well as the by-now decaying Roman fortresses. Kings rose to power through strength of arms, and government depended on military strength and local agreement rather than state control. Until the introduction of gunpowder from the east, little changed in either the forms of weapons and armour, or in the applications of strategies in battle until, in Britain at least, the tactical brilliance of Alfred the Great in Wessex created the defence-in-depth system of the burhs.

Warfare in the prehistory of Northern Europe was no more 'primitive' than in any other period of history until recent times, and no less devastating for those involved. The weapons, armour and defensive strategies developed before the coming of the Romans continued to form the basis for all future developments – the plate armour and chainmail, the various forms of lance and spear, the bow and arrow, the hillfort – and were instrumental in the history of the forming of the modern world. The medieval knights in their helmets, plate and mail and the archers of Agincourt and Poitiers owed much to their prehistoric forebears; sites given defences in prehistory continued to be used into the twentieth century (at Dover and Carisbrooke in England, for example, and the use of promontory forts as sites for anti-aircraft batteries and heavy artillery emplacements along the Atlantic Wall). The changes to warfare after the coming of the Romans took a very long time to make themselves felt to any major degree – not really until the arrival of gunpowder as far as weaponry is concerned, and even later in terms of training and manoeuvring armies. The use of covert and guerrilla techniques developed in the prehistoric period continues today.

Further Reading

This list is by no means exhaustive, but indicates some of the sources for the material contained within this book that may be accessible for the general reader.

Jacques Briard (1979) *The Bronze Age in Barbarian Europe – From the Megaliths to the Celts*, London, Book Club Associates

John Carman and Anthony Harding (eds) (1999) *Ancient Warfare*, Stroud, Sutton

Julius Caesar *The Gallic Wars*

Jean Guilaine and Jean Zammit (2005) *The Origins of War: Violence in Prehistory*, Oxford, Blackwell Publishing

Julian Heath (2009) *Warfare in Prehistoric Britain*, Stroud, Amberley

Paul Hill and Julie Wileman (2002) *Landscapes of War: The Archaeology of Aggression and Defence*, Stroud, Tempus

Richard Osgood et al (2000) *Bronze Age Warfare*, Stroud, Sutton

Richard Osgood (1998) *Warfare in the Late Bronze Age of North Europe*, British Archaeological Report International Series 694, Oxford, Archaeopress

T. Otto, H. Thrane & H. Vandkilde (eds) (2006) *Warfare and Society: Archaeological and Social Anthropological Perspectives*, Aarhus, Aarhus University Press

K. Randsborg (1995) *Hjortspring – Warfare and Sacrifice in Early Europe*, Aarhus, Aarhus University Press

Stuart Piggott et al (eds) (1974) *France Before the Romans*, London, Thames & Hudson

A. Whittle (1996) *Europe in the Neolithic*, Cambridge, Cambridge University Press

Julie Wileman (2009) *War and Rumours of War: The Evidential Base for the Recognition of Warfare in Prehistory*, British Archaeological Report International Series 1984, Oxford, Archaeopress

Index

189